FEB 0 9 2007

W9-ANB-068

Publishing for Profit

Chicago Public Library
Bucktown-Wicker Park Branch
1701 N. Milwaukee Ave.
Chicago, IL 60647

Publishing for Profit

SUCCESSFUL BOTTOM-LINE MANAGEMENT FOR BOOK PUBLISHERS

Revised and Expanded Third Edition

Thomas Woll

Foreword by Jan Nathan
Executive Director, Publishers Marketing
Association

CHICAGO
REVIEW
PRESS

Library of Congress Cataloging-in-Publication Data

Woll, Thomas, 1948–
    Publishing for profit: successful bottom-line management for book publishers /
    Thomas Woll; foreword by Jan Nathan.
        p.   cm.
    Includes index.
    ISBN 1-55652-617-2
    1. Publishers and publishing—United States—Management.
I. Title.
Z471.W58   1998   98-23962
070.5'068—dc21   CIP

Notice: The information in this book is true and complete to the best of our knowledge. It is offered without guarantee on the part of the author or Chicago Review Press. The author and Chicago Review Press disclaim all liability in connection with the use of this book.

Cover design: Monica Baziuk

© 1998, 2002, 2006 Cross River Publishing Consultants, Inc.
3 Holly Hill Lane, Katonah, New York 10536
Telephone (914)232-6708   Fax (914)232-6393
e-mail: twoll@aol.com   www.pubconsultants.com

Published by Chicago Review Press, Incorporated
814 North Franklin Street
Chicago, Illinois 60610
ISBN-13: 978-1-55652-617-6
ISBN-10: 1-55652-617-2

All rights reserved. No part of this book may be reproduced or transmitted in any form or by any means, electronic or mechanical, including photocopy, recording, or any information storage and retrieval system, without prior permission from the publisher, except by a reviewer who may quote brief passages in a review.

Printed in the United States of America

Third edition

10 9 8 7 6 5 4 3 2 1

R0409193171

To my mother,
Bernice Woll,
still the best editor I've ever known;

and

to my aunt,
Evelyn Shrifte,
who taught me more about this business
than she ever realized.

Contents

Tables and Forms

Foreword

Working in the world of book publishing since the early 1980s as Executive Director of Publishers Marketing Association, I have been afforded the opportunity of observing change and growth in this industry, all in an incrementally more rapid fashion than in the previous 10 to 15 years.

Technology has been both a boon and a challenge to publishing, allowing many to decide, literally overnight, to publish. And many have! Publishing and being a publisher, however, are not necessarily the same. Over the years, I have seen some excellent books brought into print, but not "published." Some survived on their merit, while others disappeared, many times due to the inability of the company, individual, or individuals to complete the process that takes one from *publishing* to *publisher*.

In many instances, word of mouth; networked bits and pieces of information; books that would help growth in specific areas of publishing but not the whole; and/or mentors were the only sources of information for those who chose to enter this competitive, yet compatible, community.

While reading *Publishing for Profit*, I found myself smiling many times as I encountered phrases that I seem to use daily in describing both this industry and the workings therein—including, "It depends." I guess it is this indefinable quality that tends to attract so many into sharing a bit of themselves and their ideas by placing into print (or onto tape) something that each and every publisher deems to be unique.

Initially, I pondered, "Is *Publishing for Profit* really a book for all publishers?" There are so many parts that a start-up one- or two-person operation may not think relevant. But, the more I read, the more I felt that it is one of the best references available today on how to become a book publisher. It provides a solid foundation and answers every question that is asked of me daily. For the company ready to take the first, second, or third steps toward growth, there are solid guidelines, definitions, forms and templates, suggestions, and possibilities to explore and develop. For the more experienced publisher, who many times gets immersed in day-to-day survival and may forget some of the basics, *Publishing for Profit* serves as a great refresher course, ensuring that during the course of growth some key concepts are not forgotten.

The definitions of each person's function within an established company should be read by everyone. Whether you have a staff of one or 1,000, these are functions that must be performed to complete the publishing process. The instructions on pricing, production considerations, and profitability of each title will help many to understand that sometimes, though your heart wants to publish, your spreadsheet says, "No," or at least, "Not in the current way you are going about this project."

Over the years, I have observed Tom Woll gathering a variety of experience from, among others, Rodale Press, one of the best direct marketing organizations in the United States; to Storey Communications/ Garden Way Publishing, a midsize, niche-oriented successful publishing house recognized throughout the world for its fine craft and gardening books; to John Wiley & Sons, as Vice President and General Manager of its Professional & Trade Division. His accumulation of diverse experience has been large; his ability to absorb and share what he has learned along the way is even larger.

This book should really be entitled *Publisher: The Successful Career Guide*. Reading and then referring to this book will definitely help many to move from merely publishing one, two, or three books, or even a small list of books, to the fine art of being a publisher.

JAN NATHAN
Executive Director
Publishers Marketing Association

Acknowledgments

This book is the result of a career spent in the creative, stimulating, enjoyable world of book publishing. The knowledge gained over the course of these years is the direct result of interaction with people far too numerous to count. To all of them, my heartfelt thanks for sharing their wisdom with me.

A few people deserve special mention and special thanks:

My wife, Elizabeth, and our children, Rebecca and Hannah, for putting up with my constant disappearances while working on this book.

Terri Lonier, Don Tubesing, and Kae Tienstra for reading the manuscript and providing superb comments, and Suzanne Lawlor for her knowledge and help with the portion of chapter 13 on merchant accounts.

Jan Nathan, for many years of friendship and for her excellent work on behalf of smaller publishers everywhere.

Howard, Bill, and Helen Fisher for their encouragement and help.

And finally, every coworker and client I've ever worked with, who, through each job and each consulting assignment, has given me invaluable insight and perspective on the business of publishing.

Introduction

In the era of the Internet, when electronic data exchange can take place in a millisecond, why would anyone in his or her right mind think of starting a traditional publishing company?

This question is not only appropriate to ask, but also essential to both ask and answer if the company is to succeed and thrive in the digital age.

A publishing company is a relatively easy business to start: barriers to entry are few. If you have

- a new idea or concept
- a different slant on an old idea
- a modest amount of money to produce your product
- some means of selling and distributing your product, whether from your own car or through a full-blown sales and distribution organization, and
- a place to store your product, whether your basement or a leased warehouse or a digital archive, you can become a publisher.

How much capital and space you need depends upon your publishing plans. In many cases, if you are publishing one or two books, relatively little of either resource is needed.

This minimal investment requirement is alluring to many who don't understand the complexities and implications of all that publishing requires. Just as Moby Dick carried Ahab to his death, the captain's arm beckoning his mates to follow, the surface can be eerily calm and reflective. From afar, it's easy to miss the fact that a rope holds Ahab hostage to the great white whale, and to forget that the beast is just as facile below the surface, submerged, as it is above.

Publishing is an extremely tough business. Average profits are, at best, small unless one happens to have the luxury of a major bestseller in a particular year. Unlike most other industries, publishing allows unlimited returns from its retail and wholesale customers. In essence, every book sold is *on consignment*—and, depending on the book and the year, publishers' bottom lines can be dramatically affected. What looks like a profitable sale today can turn into a disaster tomorrow.

In addition, publishing has a very small account base that is getting smaller by the day. Two major book chains control more than half of the retail marketplace; one major wholesaler supplies about 35 percent of books sold to retailers. This means a limited amount of the overall bookselling market is "wide open" to other sales efforts. At the same time, the two major chains are virtually impossible for smaller publishers to access on their own unless they publish five or more new titles per category per season. Without this consistent commitment to an ongoing publishing program, smaller publishers must work through vendor-of-record programs or through select distributors. In short, the business, though easy to enter, is very tough to sustain.

Publishers generally start companies because of a compelling idea or concept that they have; an idea they feel has not yet been adequately addressed and, therefore, that should find ready acceptance in the marketplace. Many leap in without complete knowledge of basic publishing structures, norms, and policies. Many have no business experience of any kind. Some of these companies survive—some even thrive. But many more struggle, blinded by ambition and the hunt for success just as Ahab did, and many, like him, succumb.

Unfortunately, as much as we'd like to think the contrary, ideas alone do not sustain publishing ventures or any other business. Ideas within a firm organizational structure, capitalized adequately, transformed into a tangible (or today, a digital) product, properly planned, do survive and can flourish. The purpose of this book is to provide a framework and structure to those who are new to the norms of book publishing or to those who want to broaden their experience.

One of the great strides that took place within the publishing industry occurred during the early 1970s, when the "gentlemanly profession" began to realize that its survival required more attention be paid to the mathematics and business of publishing. Its survival required more than just the editorial acquisition and output of books that might or might not have a market. If companies were to be profitable and continue to carry out, and even expand, their mission to disseminate ideas and promote literacy, then the only way to do that was to sell books profitably and stay in business. Huge advances could be paid, but only after the proper analysis was done to ensure that enough books could be sold to make a profit or at least break even. A bankrupt company didn't do anyone any good, least of all the employees, the stockholders, or the private owner. Realpolitik met publishing head-on.

The purpose of this book is to provide a framework and structure to those who are new to the norms of book publishing or to those who want to broaden their experience.

Since then, modern management techniques have invaded and pervaded the publishing industry. Whether they are all for the good is open to dispute, but one result is that there are now industry standards for most of the financial parameters necessary to run one's business successfully. Publishers can now benchmark their performances against others to determine if they are on the right track. Figures are available from the Association of American Publishers (AAP), the Book Industry Study Group (BISG), the Association of University Presses (AAUP), the Huenefeld-PubWest survey, and the Publishers Marketing Association.

In addition, the market in which books are sold has changed dramatically over the past few years. Gone are many of the best-known independent booksellers who supported larger and smaller publishers. In many cases they were victims of poor management; in other cases of having the great misfortune of being in a location prime for a competing superstore. It's hard to compete when these megastores can buy at greater discounts, stock an enormous depth and breadth of inventory, special-order as well as the independents, sponsor events and coffee bars, and stay open 14 hours a day, seven days a week. As a result, the bookselling community is, from the standpoint of the number of owners, shrinking.

With fewer accounts in which to sell books, the smaller publisher has a greater challenge than ever. How can any company be profitable if it can't get its books into the hands of buyers—whether wholesale buyers or retail account buyers, or consumers? How does the publisher reach these markets, sell its books into the market, and promote the books in such a way that the books will sell through into the consumer's hands? These are not easy questions to address, or simple issues to resolve. If, however, a publisher is to survive, then these questions must be asked. More than that, they must surely be answered.

This book is the result of many years of hands-on publishing experience, both as participant and observer, working with a range of organizations, from a small family company with revenues of about $500,000, to a start-up that eventually did about $4 million in sales, and with book divisions of very large companies with revenues up to $80 million. It is also the result of years of consulting for a variety of clients of different size, each facing its own unique challenge, each responding in a different manner.

Every one of these roles required that I learn a variety of lessons, among them the need

- to integrate all aspects of a publishing company
- for internal structures that permit logical, controlled growth, and open communication within the company and between individuals
- for adequate financing and budgetary parameters
- for regular financial reporting
- to review and fully understand the financial reports one gets.

These lessons also relate to the dynamic nature of the publishing business, and to the inevitable challenges and questions that arise every day and the need for excellent staff to review and resolve these issues quickly and definitively.

Over time, it has become clear to me that smaller publishers' needs and problems differ in degree from those of larger companies, but do not differ much in kind. Financing, internal organizational structures, editorial procurement and scheduling, pricing, sales and marketing, productivity, fulfillment and distribution, production and manufacturing, accounting and royalties, and other such issues apply to both large and small publishers. The difference is in the *degree* of complexity, not the *kind* of problem or issue.

There is much that smaller publishers can learn from their larger cousins' systems and organizational structures. On the other hand, there is much that larger companies can learn from the focus, entrepreneurial spirit, creativity, and flair of smaller firms.

This book will help publishers, whether new or established, recognize and face the realities of a rapidly changing publishing environment. It concentrates on the basic publishing functions and then expands upon those concepts, progressing to a more advanced level. The book also provides names and addresses of resources that will aid publishers and allow them to access more easily the larger publishing and general business community.

This book is not meant to be an explanation of various day-to-day publishing functions or marketing concepts or methods. Other books cover these subjects admirably. Rather, this book will provide practical information to help you manage and control the various publishing activities that are performed on a daily basis. It will tell you what the current publishing norms are and why current practices are the way they are. It will help you understand the absolute necessity of planning and organization if your company is to achieve profitability. Ultimately, I hope this book will stimulate you to begin or to expand this critical effort in your own company.

A word about the charts and illustrations: these are not meant to be definitive. Every publisher has its own way of doing things. The charts and illustrations will give you an idea of how to think about various functions and how to work through the profitability of certain situations. Think of them as sample templates and adapt them to your own needs, whether as hard copy or as digital forms on your computer. The point of all of them is to illuminate the need to have templates that you can easily and simply use to facilitate your work. Use them accordingly.

In the many years I've worked in the publishing industry, one of the things I've learned to appreciate most is that people within the industry willingly share information with others. Because there is little job training in the industry, much of the knowledge that one ultimately possesses is gained through the mentoring process. I'd say that one serves an apprenticeship in the industry, except that term implies a lengthy period of tutelage under the guidance of an expert. In our industry, length of service is a relative term!

It is in the spirit of mentoring that this book is written.

PART I

The World of Publishing

CHAPTER 1

C^3
Commitment
Consistency
Credibility

Before a publishing company can begin, three critical tenets must be accepted. If you adhere to all three, you will be well on your way to success. Without any one, your publishing efforts will most likely fail. These three critical factors are what I call C^3—*cubed* because credibility, which results from merging the attributes of commitment with those of consistency, is significantly more meaningful and important to a publisher than simply being a product of the first two. When a publisher is credible it can do and achieve infinitely more than if it is just consistent in its activities or committed to a goal. Yet without consistency or commitment, credibility is impossible.

Let's look at these tenets individually.

Commitment

Before beginning any publishing venture, you must be committed to seeing it through some very rough times, from start-up through continual daily crises. You must initially be committed to

- funding the enterprise yourself or through loans
- developing your editorial concept and niche
- progressing on a regular schedule
- producing quality products that your target audience wants at a price it can afford

3

- marketing your product and getting the word out about it
- excellent fulfillment and customer service.

Commitment applies to many factors you will be faced with. And many will probably think you should be committed as well!

Consistency

Whether you plan on being a trade, professional, direct response, academic, or religious publisher, consistency is critical. Each type of publishing runs on a seasonal basis, which you as a publisher must recognize and adhere to if you want to be a successful member of that community. It does no good to try to bring out books at a time when they are not needed or when they are least likely to succeed. This is true whether you are a trade publisher getting books out in time for Christmas or an academic publishing house getting books out in time for the coming school year.

Whatever your market, you must make sure your program runs on a consistent schedule so everyone involved knows what is coming and when it is coming. Your company must acquire books consistently, and they must be produced on a regular schedule that meets the needs of your vendors and your customers. There must be a consistency to the commitment, especially on the part of management, who is responsible for funding the program. Without consistency, chaos results too easily.

Many publishers ask how many books are necessary to ensure their success in the marketplace. They wonder, "Is there a critical mass of books that must be published to ensure their recognition and sale within the market?" The answer to this question is simple. It's not the number of new books you publish that's important, but the quality and consistency with which they are published. That's the key! If your budget limits you to only two books per year, that's fine, as long as you continue to publish that number each year. That way your reps, distributors, wholesale buyers, and retail buyers begin to know you—and begin to understand your publishing program. If you can publish two books a year well, and do so on time, providing all the support needed to make each book visi-

Without consistency, chaos results too easily.

ble and achieve solid sell-through at the retail level, then you will, through consistency, become credible.

Credibility

This trait is the result of successfully coalescing the first two factors. Credibility is the necessary ingredient large and small publishers strive for, but it is highly elusive. It can be defined concisely as doing what you say you're going to do, when you say you're going to do it. It implies being honest, open, and just in your dealings with people.

It's not the number of new books you publish that's important, but the quality and consistency with which they are published.

One reason credibility is so elusive in the publishing process is because events always seem to conspire to prevent completing projects on time. You may, if you are under-capitalized (i.e., if you haven't made a great enough financial commitment), be unable to produce your book because the printer wants money up front. You may find your authors don't deliver their manuscripts on time, jeopardizing your entire program. You may well find that your printer puts you on press last, because you are a new account, and a small one at that. You may have an interview or autographing party set up and the author's plane may be delayed. These are only a few of the reasons that your credibility can be hurt, and over which you have little or no control.

Credibility is a fragile trait that is built over time but it is one you ultimately must have to be successful. To be credible, you must focus on commitment and consistency. With these two under your belt, credibility will be achieved.

CHAPTER 2

The Publishing Environment

To see just how interrelated commitment, consistency, and credibility are, you need to understand the publishing environment in which every publisher functions.

Graphically, the progression of any book flows from

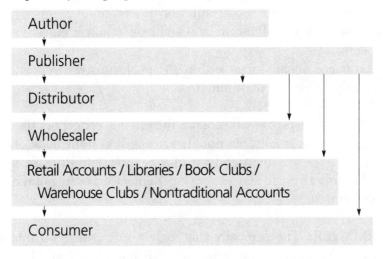

Author
↓
Publisher
↓
Distributor
↓
Wholesaler
↓
Retail Accounts / Libraries / Book Clubs /
  Warehouse Clubs / Nontraditional Accounts
↓
Consumer

In its simplest definition, the essence of the book publishing process is to create a profit by disseminating information. The idea is to create books that will flow smoothly from the author through the publisher, through each of a number of intermediary organizations, and ultimately into the hands of the consumer. The flow may be direct or it may get highly circuitous:

- directly from the publisher to the consumer via direct response means
- from the publisher to the retailer and then to the consumer
- or from the publisher through the distributor, to the wholesaler, to the retail account, and then on to the consumer

There are many other routes as well, and many that are in operation at the same time.

Each of the organizations in the delivery chain has its own needs and its own timing demands. Thus, you as the publisher may want to publish a particular book as quickly as you can to minimize the time your cash is being tied up. You may think that the quicker you can edit and produce a book, the quicker you will generate cash and profitability. Unfortunately, this is not true most of the time. Why? Because each of the other organizations in the route to the consumer has its own time constraints and organizational needs that you must adhere to if your book is to make its way down the road in an orderly fashion.

Because of the sheer volume of books published each year, every organization has to impose order on the flow of books to make sure it can handle the volume successfully and at a profit.

Let's see how this all interrelates and look at how it impacts you as the publisher.

The major organizations within the publishing environment are commonly defined by their functions:

AUTHOR: The person who creates the original concept of the book and whose name usually, but not always, appears on the book. It may, for instance, be ghostwritten or it may be a work-for-hire, in which case the author's name may not appear. Remember: every norm has an exception to it.

PUBLISHER: The company that acquires or creates an informational product (book, audiotape, video, digital output, etc.) from the author or creator and sells that product through a variety of means (direct response, sales representatives, distributor, wholesaler, or some other way) to a customer (whether wholesaler, retailer, or consumer). The publisher can add value to the author's work by editing, designing, producing, and selling the work. Or it may buy the completed work from an outside packager or another publisher and simply sell the work.

DISTRIBUTOR: An organization that takes books from a publisher, warehouses those books, and sells them to wholesalers, retailers, libraries, and consumers. Distributors also accept and process returns from their accounts and forward those returns back to the responsible publisher. Distributors can and do perform other tasks for publishers (e.g., publicity, telemarketing, special sales), but their primary function is warehousing, selling, and order fulfillment. Distributors contract with publishers and charge them a fee for providing services to the publisher. Distributors are different from wholesalers in that distributors don't purchase inventory from their publishers but hold it on consignment or as an agent of the publisher.

Many smaller publishers store their books at the distributor and use distributors to help sell their books. These publishers find that the distributor's ability to consolidate a number of publishers within one sales catalog and presentation, and to have their books be part of shipments containing a variety of books that help the retail and wholesale accounts achieve higher discounts, ultimately aids their sales efforts. In addition, most publishers find the regular payment schedules from distributors to be an excellent way to maintain cash flow while avoiding the risk of bad debt and the difficulties of trying to collect accounts receivable money from a significant number of accounts. Many smaller publishers find the distributor's fees, usually totaling around 30 to 35% of net sales, prohibitive.

Among the major distributors today are Publisher's Group West, National Book Network, Independent Publishers Group, and Consortium Book Sales & Distribution.

WHOLESALERS: These accounts purchase books from both publishers and distributors for sale to other accounts, primarily retailers, libraries, businesses, internet bookstores, and others. Wholesalers provide a service to publishers and distributors because the wholesaler actually buys books and fulfills its own orders. For many retail accounts, the wholesaler provides a "one-stop shop" from which the retailer can buy the books of many publishers at once.

Often, an account can purchase books from a wholesaler at

more favorable discounts than it might if it bought directly from the publisher or distributor because orders for many books from many publishers can be consolidated by using a wholesaler. Ingram Book Company is the largest book wholesaler in the country, followed by Baker & Taylor.

RETAIL ACCOUNTS: These stores purchase books from publishers, distributors, and wholesalers. Their ultimate purpose is to sell books to the general public. Retail accounts can be very small independent bookstores, huge superstore chains, or something in the middle. Recently, the larger superstores have predominated within this segment of the bookselling marketplace (See **Book Sales by Channel** on page 11).

LIBRARIES: Publicly and privately funded organizations that provide books free or for a fee to the public or their members. Books are loaned or rented for specific periods of time and returned to the library for subsequent loan or rental. Libraries purchase both directly from publishers and indirectly through wholesalers and/or distributors.

BOOK CLUBS: Direct response membership organizations that buy books directly from the publisher at deep discounts, or that print their own editions of a publisher's book for sale to their members, usually at a discount to the suggested retail price. Book clubs provide a "one-stop shop" for books of similar interest. For a publisher, book club sales almost always supplement wholesale, retail, and library sales.

WAREHOUSE CLUBS: "Membership" organizations that sell to "members" at significant discounts. Warehouse clubs make their money by selling vast quantities of merchandise, including books. Clubs are relatively new in the world of bookselling, yet they have made a major impact since their inception in the 1980s. They purchase from a variety of sources, including directly from the publisher. The major supplier, or wholesaler, to the warehouse clubs is Advanced Marketing Services. Warehouse clubs are high-volume and high-risk because publishers can be hit with enormous returns very quickly.

DISCOUNTERS and MASS MERCHANTS: Traditional retail stores that sell to the public at a discount, such as Wal-Mart,

Target, and others. These accounts are serviced primarily by independent distributors (IDs). Among the major distributors are Levy Home Entertainment, Anderson Merchandising, Aramark, and others.

Discounters and mass merchants sell a limited number of books, primarily bestsellers, usually at some discount to the retail price. Again, they make their money by selling books in volume. Like warehouse clubs, there can be returns problems here as well.

NONTRADITIONAL ACCOUNTS: All "non-trade" retail accounts that are not one of the above. These include gift stores, toy stores, educational supply stores, catalogers, direct sales companies and more.

The *1996 Consumer Research Study on Book Publishing,* commissioned by the American Booksellers Association and the Book Industry Study Group, gives a good idea of where adult books are currently selling. Of the total adult books sold in that year, the following channels of distribution accounted for the shares noted (percentages have been rounded):

Book Sales by Channel

Retail Bookstores	45%
Larger chains	26%
Smaller independents	19%
Discount Stores	9%
Warehouse Clubs	6%
Food/Drug Stores	5%
Book Clubs	18%
Mail Order (other than book clubs)	4%
Used Bookstores	4%
Other	9%

An even more dramatic reflection of the chains' predominance comes from "The American Book Buyers Study" commissioned by *Publishers Weekly* for its 125th anniversary. This study shows that fully one-half of all U.S. readers now buy their books in chain bookstores and only 15% from independents.

Whatever statistical base you choose to look at, today's bookselling environment is undergoing rapid change—change that you, as a publisher, must understand; change to which you must respond.

Like most other industries, bookstores, book clubs, and other organizations that cater to the needs of the consuming public exist in a seasonal environment. Seasons directly impact the public's buying patterns. The Thanksgiving to Christmas holiday period is, for most retailers, the busiest time of the year. It accounts in some cases for two-thirds of the year's revenue. Other holidays and seasonal events throughout the year also generate sales, especially Valentine's Day, Mother's Day, Father's Day, and Back to School promotions.

Today's bookselling environment is undergoing rapid change—change that you, as a publisher, must understand; change to which you must respond.

Thus, retail accounts and other accounts selling to the public typically promote their products to take advantage of these strong selling seasons. Book publishing is no different. Bookstores are constantly looking for ways to tie books to various promotional events and sell more books because of their marketing efforts.

If publishers are going to ensure that sales efforts reach their greatest potential, then publishers must fully understand, and work within, the retail cycle. This means that to get books to wholesalers and retailers on time, the publisher must work far enough in advance to be certain that a book's publication coincides with the needs of the marketplace, whether wholesale or retail—hopefully both.

How do publishers do this? How far in advance is it necessary to start?

Publishers achieve synergy with their market needs through careful planning. The publisher has to know how many books—and what books—are to be published in each season, coinciding primarily with the two book retailing seasons, fall/winter and spring/summer. Sometimes, if the publisher's list is large, it will create a third selling season by breaking out winter as a separate season. For our purposes, two seasons are sufficient.

It is self-evident that if a store is planning a promotion in one month, it needs the merchandise for that promotion beforehand. The publisher must complete its editorial-production-sale-fulfillment cycle in advance of the wholesaler's or retailer's promotional date.

And this means the publisher should optimally start the initial planning process three years in advance:

- The first 12 months of this 36-month lead time should be taken up with the earliest planning for the list.
- The second 12 months should be spent having the book written and ensuring its timely delivery to you the publisher.
- The final 12 months of this cycle should be spent editing the book, pre-selling subsidiary rights, selling to the final market, producing, warehousing, and shipping the completed book.

Given this optimal time frame, the publisher should be able to easily integrate the title into whatever promotional or selling season is best for the book and the market.

Why does it take twelve months to put out a book once it's in-house? Because you must allow enough time for

- editing
- transmitting the book's key information and specifications to the major databases
- editorial development and responses from your author
- production and design
- manufacturing
- getting out advance review copies and normal publicity and marketing materials
- pre-selling and then selling to the direct market
- shipment from the manufacturer to your warehouse
- entering the inventory into your inventory system
- invoicing
- picking, packing, and shipping from your warehouse to the wholesale or retail account
- the account to unpack those books and enter them into its system
- the account to put those books onto the shelves from which they'll hopefully be sold

And all this has to happen within the advanced time frame required by the wholesale or retail accounts that are putting together promotions and catalogs.

Publishing Time Line

YEAR 1 Month	1	2	3	4	5
Editorial/ Design & Manufacturing Track	Title Proposal/ Proposal Considered	Proposal goes to Editorial Comm., Title P&L Run, Proposal Accepted	Contract Signed	Author Writes Ms.	
Sales/ Marketing Track		Sales Provides Numbers for P&L			

YEAR 2 Month	13	14	15	16	17
Editorial/ Design & Manufacturing Track	Ms. Read & Reviewed for Acceptability	Ms. Editing & Development Begins		Editing Completed	Fully Edited Ms. to Publisher for Final OK
Sales/ Marketing Track	Launch Mtg. to Inform Staff re: Ms.			Marketing & Promo Plans for New Season	

YEAR 3 Month	25	26	27	28	29
Editorial/ Design & Manufacturing Track	Proofs Reviewed by Editorial/ Author		Blues & Color Proofs Generated	Corrections/ Revisions Made	
Sales/ Marketing Track				Pre-Sales Meeting	Sales Manager Holds Sales Meeting

Publishing Time Line *continued*

6	7	8	9	10	11	12
						Ms. Delivered

18	19	20	21	22	23	24
	Final Ms. Transmitted to Production		Ms. Design Begins Incl. Jacket/ Cover Prelims	Design Completed Proofs Done Cover Final		
		Ms. to Rights Staff for Sub-Rights Work		Marketing Plans for New Season Final		

30	31	32	33	34	35	36
Printing & Binding Begin		Books Delivered	Invoicing Begins Books Shipped to Accounts			Publication Date
Selling Season for New Titles Begins	Publicity Sends Out Bound Galleys		Publicity Sends Out Regular Review Copies			Marketing & Publicity Efforts Enacted

You might typically expect to see a schedule, from the publisher's perspective, as shown in the preceding **Publishing Time Line**.

Can a book be published faster than this optimal schedule? Absolutely. Sometimes it's important to get to the market as quickly as possible, especially if the information in the book is timely. Smaller publishers are excellent at doing this because their systems are flexible and their organizational hierarchies are small.

At the same time, the moment you start to compress the publication schedule, the more you begin to pressure those responsible for doing the work. All too often, this results in mistakes or poor performance. Smaller publishers are notorious for rushing books through the publishing process, hell-bent on getting books out quickly without regard to the market's normal needs or structure. All too frequently, the result is books sitting in the publisher's warehouse, unable to be shipped because there's no distributor for the book; subsidiary rights sales that don't occur because there's not enough lead time to have the book properly considered; and lost sales because the marketing effort hasn't been adequately addressed and carried out.

With proper planning and lead time, you will be able to take advantage of the market's seasonality and promotional efforts. You'll be able to work with the accounts to generate the greatest possible sales for your book. And in the process, you'll generate something that will accrue to your company's benefit throughout its life: *credibility*— that crucial attribute that takes so long to attain.

However early or late you begin the process, the ultimate goal must be to establish credibility, so you must be certain to deliver your book on time. When is that? Whenever you say you will do it.

Looking at somewhat different needs, you might concentrate on special sales outlets such as book clubs. If these accounts select your book, they can add significant sales and some contribution to profit. Because clubs operate almost exclusively through direct-response catalogs, they usually need nine months lead time to put the catalog together and allow enough time for mailing (or e-mailing) and customer response. Thus, if you want to work with a club, you must submit material to it at least that far in advance for alternates—and usually further in advance for main selections (more about this later). If you don't adhere to the schedules needed by clubs or others using your books, these clubs and other special sale accounts won't buy from you. The marketplace is too competitive to bother with publishers who don't cooperate, don't understand, or choose to ignore the systems and schedules of these accounts.

The point in relation to all of these outlets for your books is that the outlet responds to the needs of its customers. If you, as a publisher, want to sell books through that outlet, then you too must respond to the need of that outlet. And that means you must make a commitment to do so. You must be consistent in your orientation and approach to these outlets. If you do both of those, you will gain credibility that will ultimately result in greater sales of your books through those outlets.

COMMITMENT, CONSISTENCY, and CREDIBILITY should be the goal of every publisher. They are tenets that are absolutely crucial to ensure growth in today's highly competitive publishing environment.

PART II

Managerial Organization: Strategy and Techniques

CHAPTER 3

Define Your Niche

With more than 80,000 publishers publishing over 195,000 new titles every year (according to R.R. Bowker's 2005 statistics), it's amazing that any book can find its way onto the bookstore shelves, let alone be considered successful. Yet the expectation for success, not just in one book, but in every book launched, is every publisher's goal.

The Author's Guild some years ago defined a successful book of fiction as selling 5,000 copies; of non-fiction as selling 7,500 copies or more. That definition probably still holds today. The difficulty with these respectable figures is that from the standpoint of market share and visibility, such numbers will most likely consign a book to quick obscurity. If the publisher or the author make money on a book at this level, it will be minimal.

To avoid this situation, larger publishers are turning more and more to authors with celebrity status. Publishers can print hundreds of thousands of copies of a celebrity's books. They gain visibility in the marketplace and realize economies of scale in the manufacturing process. By publishing such books, margins increase and the revenues and profits derived from selling such books support much of the company's remaining publishing ventures, including the publication of books by new writers. (And just like smaller publishers, many of these other non-celebrity publishing ventures result in net sales for larger publishers of between 2,500 and 7,500 copies.)

Smaller publishers can't afford this luxury. They can't pay the high advances the larger companies do for the bestsellers or well-known authors. Smaller publishers don't have extensive capitalization or cash flow to support such advances or to pay for the large manufacturing and marketing expenses. Few smaller publishers have the successful sales record necessary to entice such well-known authors to join them. In some cases, there has been a strategic decision on management's part not to publish at this bestseller level, because the risk of failure is so high. In many more cases, smaller publishers base such publishing decisions simply on the realistic recognition of the limited resources available to them.

Can smaller and independent publishers compete in today's publishing arena? Can they get their books into retail stores and break out a book to achieve success and profitability?

The answer to these questions is, of course, yes. In fact, the ability of smaller publishers to penetrate the major chains is perhaps greater today than it has been in the past. Barnes & Noble, in a revealing quarterly report published relatively soon after the company embarked on its superstore concept, reported that its purchases from the top ten American publishers had declined from 74% of all Barnes & Noble purchases in 1994 to 46% in 1997—a staggering 38% decline for the larger publishers, or a corresponding gain for all other publishers of 108%! These figures should encourage smaller publishers everywhere; they mean that their share of the market is increasing substantially and that opportunity abounds for those who understand the needs and requirements of the publishing and retailing environments.

For publishers, this process of positioning and understanding begins with the earliest concept of the publishing plan: the editorial thrust of the house. Does the creation of such a plan differ for publishers of different sizes? Quite simply, no.

Research, Research, Research— Look Before You Leap

Every publisher intuitively believes that the books it wants to publish are those it should publish and are those the public wants. Yet time and again, this hypothesis is proven wrong when books published with the highest expectations receive tepid reviews, sell in very low quantities, and are subject to high return rates.

The only way to avoid this fateful end is to be sure you don't delude yourself in the first place. Like good businesspeople everywhere, you must assess the market for your potential product and the potential profitability that may result if you can launch the product successfully.

How do you go about this task of market research? There are a number of ways, including having a consultant do it for you. I recommend that you spend your own time researching this essential assignment. The reasons are twofold: First, by doing the research yourself you can learn a tremendous amount about the market, its parameters, your competition, and the retail environment in which your books must exist—all of which are vital for you to understand. Second, you're more likely to accept the results of your research if you get them firsthand.

In short, if you're going to invest a vast amount of your future time, effort, and money in your business then you should certainly spend a little of each to ensure that there really is gold at the end of the rainbow!

What Do You Want to Be?
The first key to establishing and running a successful publishing company is to define your editorial niche. Ask yourself the following questions—and be sure to answer them truthfully:

- In what subjects will your company specialize?
- Why?
- What makes your books unique within the market?
- Do you have particular expertise within this market?
- Do you know who the expert authors are? Can you reach them?
- Who are your competitors within this subject category?
- What stores carry the kind(s) of books you'll publish?
- Where in the store is the category placed?
- What are the attributes of competitive books?
    Size
    Price points
    Hardcover or paperback
    Number of pages
    Use of color
- What is the average number of copies sold within this category?

- If you sell this many, will your profitability goals be met?
- If not, what variables must change to achieve profitability?
- If not, how many new books will you have to sell to be profitable?
- How many new titles within the category are published seasonally?
- Are sales in the category expanding or are they contracting?
- How will you distinguish those titles you plan to publish?
  Editorial content
  Size or format
  Price
  Color
  Author

If you can't answer most of these questions clearly and completely, then you should think about them again. As the executive of your company, you must be clear about the kind of book you want to publish, and the manner in which you want to sell that book. If you're not clear about the kind of book, you will be unable to determine if the book you're considering fulfills your goals. And if you aren't clear about how to sell the book, you'll undoubtedly go astray in the complex marketing process (more about that later).

Furthermore, if you can't state clearly and concisely what your niche is, how will your staff be able to do so when acquiring new books and talking with your buyers? You must be able to articulate your niche clearly with a short sentence or two.

As I began to write this book, I happened to have a meeting with the executive editor of a large New York publishing company. We were discussing a series of books the company wanted to publish, when the editor commented: "We aren't trying to be all things to all people. This series is meant to fill a niche in the marketplace, a niche we are known for publishing well. The series should add to that niche recognition and expand it if possible." It was a concise statement of purpose and strategy that publishers of all size would be wise to recognize and emulate.

You must be able to articulate your niche clearly with a short sentence or two.

Every publisher goes into business to create books for the reading public—most to sell those books profitably to that audience. Each publisher, because of the subjectivity of the editorial process, defines that audience in a different way and therefore creates books for the audience with a somewhat unique strategy or focus. And it is this individuality of program that ultimately creates an image of the publisher in the mind of fellow publishers and retailers.

If the program is distinctive enough, an image may be created in the mind of the public at large. Before someone says that in the vast majority of book purchases this is not the case, that the public doesn't buy books due to publisher's brand recognition, let me say at once that I would agree. In the majority of cases the publisher's imprint means nothing to the consuming public. However, if a publisher can truly break out its imprint and have it recognized by the public in a meaningful way, identified with a specific editorial or market position, then that publisher will have achieved the ultimate success in niche publishing. As an example, one can consider the wonderfully distinctive Modern Library, and the equally distinctive books of the small publisher Black Sparrow Press, each of which made its mark directly with the reading public.

Publishing differs to some extent from other consumer products because the products created are for the most part not brand-sensitive. If you go into a bookstore and browse the shelves, most books stand out as individual titles, not as a part of a series that's identified by a particular image or brand name. The greatest brand identification—whether by publisher's brand name or by product brand name—exists in two categories: travel books, where many series are identified by the publisher's name (Frommer, Michelin, Baedecker, Passport, etc.) and in the children's book area, where many series are identified by the author's name, which itself has become a brand name (Dr. Seuss, Beverly Cleary, etc.).

Certainly there are many more throughout the store, but the point is that most books on the shelves stand by themselves. The publisher's image, as strong as might be a Random House, Simon & Schuster, or Workman book, has nowhere near the consumer identification or strength of a Coca-Cola, Nabisco, Ford, Procter & Gamble, or other significant consumer brand.

According to the Gallup Organization, the primary reason consumers buy a book is the subject. Because of this, and the fact that consumers don't, for the most part, buy books by brand name, smaller publishers can compete with larger publishers and can build a brand name for themselves by publishing in relatively narrow, defined editorial areas and choosing great book subjects. By focusing on an editorial niche and strategically and consistently building that niche with every new book published, the list becomes identified with that category in the mind of buyers at all levels, from the wholesale buyer to the retail bookstore buyer to the consumer. At this point, success will become easier, because buyers will seek out your products and agents will begin to send new material to your publishing house.

Who Is Your Market and Who Is the Competition?

Once you've defined your own editorial niche and determined what you think it should be, or what you'd like it to be, take nothing for granted. Research your market and your competitors completely.

How does one begin the research that will prove or disprove the hypothesis that you have a product the public wants?

First, talk to those already established in the publishing business: publishers, editors, sales managers of publishing companies. Talk to retail book buyers, librarians (your local library is an excellent place to get firsthand information), and others. Now is not the time to be shy. Ask them

- What books sell best or are asked for most?
- What books do they find sell the best over long periods of time?
- What books and subjects do customers continually request?
- What categories are over-published, and which could use additional support?
- Who are the dominant publishers within the category?
- What makes their products so appealing?
- What terms are competitive?
    Invoice terms
    Returns
    Discounts

Second, research book trends: Is one category of books declining in popularity and another ascending? Are some books too seasonal to support a year-round program? For instance, can books relating to Christmas crafts and holiday cooking be sold year-round and provide enough margin for your program? Or, if they are highly seasonal, what can you publish to compensate in the other times of the year?

Look at demographic trends: What are people doing with their time? What activities do they participate in? Gardening, for instance, is the country's number one leisure-time activity and thus accounts for the surge in publishing in this category. What do demographics tell us about future publishing potential in various categories? For example, health should rise as the population ages; children's books sales may fall.

In short, take nothing for granted. Read the material that's available. There are numerous resources to help you define both current and future trends. Some of the best sources of information on past and projected trends include

- Association of American Publishers Statistics
- Book Industry Study Group projections
- Bookscan sales data
- Veronis, Suhler's publishing forecasts
- NPD-IPSOS Surveys
- Publishers Marketing Association Surveys
- American Booksellers Association surveys with Gallup
- *The U.S. Department of Commerce Census of Retail Trade*
- The U.S. Department of Commerce, Census Bureau demographic statistics
- Trade magazines including
    Publishers Weekly
    Library Journal
    American Bookseller
    Booklist
- Other publishers' catalogs
- Various bestseller lists
- Ingram Book Company's i-page.

As you do your research, don't wear blinders. The research you do should lay the groundwork and influence your publishing decisions. If the research shows there are too many dominant players, or terms are such that you can't publish profitably, recognize that fact. Either move on to review another niche, or bow out gracefully now. Don't spend your time, effort, and money in a fruitless pursuit. There are definitely other niches you can occupy with success—you just have to find them.

TIP: If you're online, a vast amount of information is waiting for you directly through many government-sponsored websites. Not only is the information easily accessible, but it will provide you with numerous additional resources. Here are a few popular—and valuable—sites:

- the IRS, for tax information and forms: www.irs.gov
- the Small Business Administration, for a variety of material: www.sba.gov
- and even the Library of Congress, for copyright information and forms: www.lcweb.loc.gov

In addition, most large publishers have established their own websites. These can provide a wealth of competitive information, especially in relation to subjects, price points, and titles. In effect, the entire publishing world is literally at your fingertips. Also, check out "the Earth's largest bookstore" at www.amazon.com, Barnes and Noble at www.barnesandnoble.com, and R.R Bowker's Bookwire at www.bookwire.com. At these sites, you can conduct searches by topic, author, and other criteria. They offer a vast amount of excellent source material and information. You'll be amazed at how much research information you can glean in a very short time.

Develop a Clear Vision: The Mission Statement

Once you've researched your hypothesis and determined that it's sound and worth pursuing, the next step is to summarize your concept in a mission statement to guide you and your staff (if you have staff) in your everyday decision-making process.

While many smaller publishers feel it is not worth the time or effort to create a mission statement, I strongly urge them to take the time to do so. Why? Simply because the mission statement is the first tangible, concrete step in precisely defining and articulating your publishing niche and your goals.

The mission statement consists of at least four parts:

- a clear statement of your company's editorial goals
- a definition of your niche within the competitive marketplace

- your definition of the market
- a commitment to your goals

You may want to include more than four parts. For instance, you might want to define the kind of product you are creating fully and completely; you might want to articulate what is driving the company, that is, whether you will be editorially, market, or service driven; and other such specific items. This is fine, so long as you keep in mind that the mission statement's function is to be actionable. That is, people should be able to look at it when questions arise, and actually use it to formulate and reinforce their daily management decisions and actions.

One of my clients, a new trade publisher, approached the question of its editorial niche by formulating a short mission statement that is available to its staff and that helps them position the company to authors, buyers and others. The statement reads, in part:

> Our mission is to publish authoritative, visually stimulating materials of the highest quality based on sound scientific knowledge and medical facts. Consistent themes throughout our publications include cultural diversity, ethnicity, and the legal, ethical and financial concerns of older adults. Our publications are for people in their 50s and older . . . Our books depict aging as a normal, positive process and contain information such as assessment guides, how-to tips, helpful checklists, and very practical examples. Our authors are nationally known providers of care for older adults. Each book is reviewed by experts in their fields to ensure that we have included the most current, accurate, applicable information. Most books are 4-color and are designed to provide easy access to information as well as to serve as a quick reference.

This statement was written before the company had published its first book—which is the right time to take your niche seriously. With the mission set forth, anyone in or out of the company can be made aware of—on a daily basis—exactly how this publisher envisions its mission, and the format in which it expects to deliver its message.

Other examples of mission statements follow:

> Pierpoint-Martin Publishing is dedicated to serving three con-

stituencies: Our customers, our employees and our shareholders. To our customers, we are dedicated to providing exciting, informative, high-quality fitness-related books and other information products. To our employees, we are dedicated to providing a challenging and rewarding work environment that offers the opportunity to succeed. And to our shareholders, we are dedicated to maximizing the value of their investment in the Company.

We at Interweave Press produce genuinely useful, informative, and aesthetically pleasing literature and related products that nurture and extend the special interests of our communities of readers.

We recognize that our success as a business depends on serving our customers well; we pledge to do so while seeking personal satisfaction in doing good work.

We believe in a supportive and caring workplace where the needs of individuals are kept in balance with the goals of the organization as we mutually grow and prosper.

We are going to live our work-lives by these principles:

Balance: Between the needs of the individual and the organization.

Commitment: To each other and to Interweave Press.

Respect: Recognition, acceptance, and celebration of differences between individuals and jobs.

Optimism: It will be okay!

Once in hand, the mission statement begins to focus everyone's concept of the company in numerous ways.

1. Given a defined editorial niche, you then can focus attention on the skills and knowledge of those you want to hire.

   • Do they have the kind of academic and work experience that will make them experts in the field?

   • How focused is this experience in the areas in which you wish to publish?

   • What additional strength does each person hired bring to the company? In other words, if you are a health publisher, what qualities does your editor need? Does she know and have access to health agents and authors? Does she have the expertise to read a manuscript and make editorial judgments herself? Or must you incur added expense by sending it out to expert readers, developmental editors, or peer reviewers? Does your marketing director have a wealth of experience in the health market or does his background stem from more general experience?

2. Once you've defined your niche, you can gain a firm understanding of your competitors' products, which, in circular fashion, allows you to find gaps in the market where books are needed and where opportunity lies. This, in turn, solidifies your niche positioning even more. Ultimately, as you grow, your position will become clearer to others in the industry, and to authors and agents as well, who will begin to submit material to you. Many publishers, either through lack of experience, fear of having to pay high advances, or simply because they publish only one or two books a year, don't solicit books from agents. What many find is that as they grow and their niche becomes clearly defined, agents in fact find them, exactly because they have positioned their companies strongly vis-à-vis the competition. Because agents need to sell their clients' books to stay in business, they eagerly look for publishers of any size who can sell these books, keep them in print, and treat their authors well. If a publisher defines its niche well, then it can find additional outlets into which to sell books that may be unknown to—or simply ignored by—others. This, in turn, means both frontlist and backlist titles can have longer lives and greater ultimate sales.

3. Another key reason for defining your editorial niche well is that such positioning allows your company to plan its marketing strategy in a much more targeted, coherent and cost-effective way.

If you're trying to sell a varied array of disparate books to a broad audience, you must spend your advertising and promotional dollars in a scattered effort that has little focus and continuity. On the other hand, if you have a very defined, focused editorial list of books, then you can spend your money in a narrowly targeted promotional effort in which the impact of promoting one book accrues to the benefit of others in the list.

If, for instance, you are selling health books, you can target your marketing to health bookstores; health-related television and radio talk shows; health magazines; health book clubs; HMOs; doctors; associations; and others who have an interest in the subject. You can promote one book to this audience or your entire list, with costs being allocated over more than one title.

If you have a very defined, focused editorial list of books, then you can spend your money in a narrowly targeted promotional effort in which the impact of promoting one book accrues to the benefit of others in the list.

The repetitive nature of your promotional efforts will help establish your line as authoritative in the eyes and minds of those to whom you are promoting your list. This, in turn, leads them to you as the source of additional promotional material that they can use. Obviously, this is not the case if your list is a melange of different kinds of books on various subjects.

One publisher who has done an excellent job of defining its niche is Storey Publishing. This company, now owned by Workman Publishing, has focused almost all of its publishing attention on the gardening, cooking, and craft areas. As a result, it has become a highly regarded force within these trade categories.

Storey is but one of many success stories that show, again and again, that *focus is essential in book publishing.*

If you try to be all things to all people, you will be nothing to most.

Organization Chart

Now that you know what you're supposed to be doing, you must know who will perform each task and who is responsible to whom. It's time to formalize your organizational structure. If you're a one-person operation, you probably don't need an organization chart because you're the one doing *everything.* (If this is the case, the following material will help you clarify the many roles you must perform to be successful.) But if you have more than one person in your company, and you have a variety of functions going on, it makes life easier for your entire staff if a clear organization chart is created that specifies exactly what everyone does and who reports to whom.

In many cases, the reporting structure is simple and can be answered by one question: Who writes the checks? Usually the person in charge. But as companies grow, even the check-writing function may be delegated to a bookkeeper, an accountant, or in larger companies, to a chief financial officer. And as each layer is added, the reporting structure becomes more and more complex.

To alleviate confusion, a simple **Organization Chart,** as on page 35, should be created and provided to anyone interested in seeing it.

The organization chart should start at the top with the role or position title of that person ultimately responsible for all decisions and the success or failure of the company as a whole, usually the President, Chief Executive Officer, or Owner. Because you're trying to clarify the decision-making structure, it is the role or function that's important, not the name of the individual.

Most publishing houses have several key functional areas: editorial; production and manufacturing; sales and marketing; and back-office (including accounting and fulfillment). In most cases, each of these functional areas provides a primary organizational heading for the chart. The appropriate roles are placed under each heading.

Thus, under the editorial and sales functions one might find a structure consisting of:

Editorial	Sales
Publisher	Sales & Marketing Manager
Editor-in-Chief	Trade Sales Manager
Senior Editor	National Accounts Manager
Editor	Regional Sales Manager
Associate Editor	Sales Representative
Editorial Assistant	Sales Assistant

The point is not to specify and chart a lot of jobs just because they may be needed one day. The point is to chart your own company realistically for the sake of clarifying its present structure. In this way, everyone in any particular role can know who reports to whom and who must approve the decisions that have to be made.

Understand, too, that an organization chart reflects a company's structure at a particular moment in time. It can and must change to reflect the results of events that continually impact the company's structure throughout that company's growth. As each person is added to staff, the chart should reflect that change so everyone is kept up-to-date.

Many people feel that organization charts, once created, can't be changed. They try to fit every new employee or function within the original version. This usually creates an unwieldy structure. The fact is, if your organization needs to change to improve work flow or if you grow to a point at which new roles are added, don't be captive to your organization chart—change the chart to reflect your new reality. The organization chart is first and foremost a tool to help you view your company as a whole. If it hinders that perception in any way, it should be modified to suit your needs.

Job Descriptions

Now that you've determined the organizational structure of your company, those people performing the various functions have to know

- for what they're responsible
- to whom they are responsible
- what the basis of their job performance will be.

Good job descriptions indicate all of these functions in a compact manner. Additionally, a good job description will allow a person who is unfamiliar with a function to understand it because the description will accurately reflect both the day-to-day and long-term responsibilities of that function.

Many smaller publishers feel that job descriptions only apply to larger companies and not to them. A real-life example from one of my clients should put that notion to rest quickly.

A client's husband had started a successful small professional publishing company with only two employees. After working hard at the business for some time, and getting it successfully off the ground, the founder abruptly died. His wife, who had significant business experience but no publishing experience, decided to continue the business. Unfortunately, her husband had never specified who did what within the company and what the detailed responsibilities of each function were. Despite the wife's good business skills, without knowledge of publishing and without job descriptions to guide her, she was forced to start almost from the beginning—relearning the everyday functions of a publishing company. The fact that she ultimately succeeded is a testament to her skills and learning ability. As she readily admits, job descriptions certainly would have made things easier.

Organization Chart

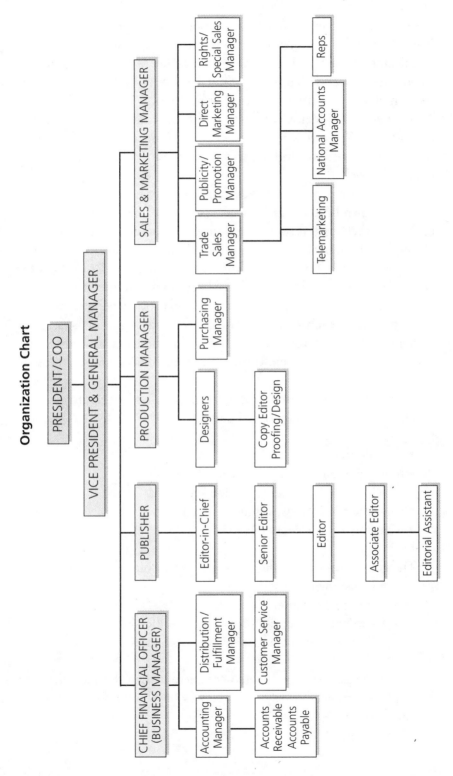

While this example may be extreme, everyday staff turnover also demands job descriptions. If someone on staff decides to leave, or if you decide she should leave, then it's incumbent upon the company to provide an accurate, up-to-date job description so a new staff member can be quickly introduced to that position.

Though we all feel we're irreplaceable to some extent, the fact is few of us are. You owe it to your staff and your successors to document the jobs that are done and the way they are done. This includes your own job as well.

The easiest way to write job descriptions is to have each staff member write down his daily tasks over a period of time, say a month. As each task is recorded it should be arranged in order of importance. At the end of the month, the descriptions should be collected and commonly formatted. They should then be passed around to others for comment. Once the comments have been discussed, the forms should be revised and completed. Each staff member should get a set relative to his needs and each should update the forms annually or as tasks are added or subtracted from the roles. If this is done consistently, you'll find that it takes a very small amount of time to accomplish an essential task.

How should a job description be written? The best approach is to break it down into its functional parts:

- the job title
- to whom the person holding the job reports
- whom the person holding the job supervises
- what the budget responsibility of the job is
- what the job is accountable for

The general responsibilities of the job can be broken down by
- budgeting/financial
- staffing/personnel
- particular responsibilities of the specific job
- departmental management responsibilities

If all of these steps are covered completely, then the incumbent or any replacement will have a better idea of what the expectations for the job are.

The illustrations that follow show what job descriptions might look like for the Vice President and General Manager, the Publisher, and the Sales and Marketing Manager. Note that these job descriptions are not meant to be definitive but are meant only as examples of format and detail. Your own job descriptions can—and should— reflect your own company's organizational needs and tasks. Because these tend to be fairly dry reading, you might want to skip to the next chapter and come back to read these when you begin your own job description process.

On the other hand, you may want to see how job descriptions can provide direction to the individual and to the people who work with that individual. Job descriptions also provide direction to the company as a whole, and they help integrate various company and functional areas. At some point, you will want to spend a good deal of time with these descriptions and become completely familiar with their structure and role.

VICE PRESIDENT & GENERAL MANAGER

Reports to:	Chief Operating Officer or Owner
Directly Supervises:	Chief Financial Officer
	Publisher
	Production Manager
	Sales & Marketing Manager
Budget Responsibility:	Yearly sales budget
	Expense budget
	Production and manufacturing budget
Accountability:	Editorial title acquisition
	Net sales and growth
	Cost of goods
	Operating contribution to profit
	Inventory management

General Responsibilities:

The Vice President and General Manager is responsible for all aspects of the publishing company, including new product development, staff hiring, and performance. The Vice President and General Manager is responsible for the overall profitability of the company's publishing program, including inventory management, for all departments within the company.

Specific Operating Responsibilities:
Budgeting/Financial

1. Direct, establish, and implement, in association with corporate staff and finance office, approved annual operating and capital budgets and cash flows for all functions.
2. Direct, establish, and implement, in association with corporate staff and finance office, 3- to 5-year estimated budgets and cash flows for all functions.
3. Review individual editorial and total corporate budgets with COO and finance department and get final approval of them.
4. Monitor financial performance for conformance to approved budget; assure that corrective actions are taken when necessary; keep COO advised of financial condition including monthly profit and loss statements.

5. Oversee and approve the selection, negotiation, and management of contracted services in relation to corporate commitments, including the financial aspects of manuscript acquisition, use of freelance staff, etc.

Staffing/Personnel

1. Hire, instruct, and supervise all staff.
2. Monitor personnel-related activities, including salary determination, performance reviews, merit increases, training programs, and disciplinary actions; assure that actions are taken that support the goals of the company, are fair to employees, and are in accord with policy; keep COO appropriately advised of personnel-related issues.
3. Evaluate, with input from the managers and others.
4. Establish, in association with the COO and others, an evaluation process based upon the accomplishment of objective goals agreed upon by staff members and their supervisors at the beginning of the fiscal year.
5. Lead staff in developing long-range goals, direction, and plans in support of mission, vision, and long-range goals.
6. Delegate responsibility to staff for developing plans and for recommending methods for implementation of plans regarding editorial development and new forms of publishing media, automation, equipment, and new policies and procedures.
7. Review staff recommendations ensuring that the fundamental course of direction is consistent with goals and can be translated into practical, actionable procedures.
8. Lead development of the management team through regular meetings to communicate information, respond to various issues raised, give direction to activities and recommendations, and integrate resources and activities appropriately.

Operational Procedures

1. Participate in the corporate strategic planning process.
2. Initiate and coordinate the corporate strategic planning process with the needs of the strategic plan.
3. Regularly participate in planning sessions with the COO to develop long-range goals and plans, including making recommendations for such goals and plans.

4. Work closely with the COO and managers to explore and develop ideas to the point at which they can be assigned to others for development.
5. Provide leadership to achieve linkage between long-range goals and plans and current operational activities of the company.
6. Keep abreast of publishing industry trends and their possible impact on corporate activities.
7. Oversee projects assigned by the COO.
8. Ensure that the fundamental course of activity is consistent with goals and is actionable.
9. Provide leadership and direction for the implementation of approved recommendations, evaluate their results, and provide guidance as appropriate.
10. As major challenges require, address the needs of customers and service companies.
11. Report all performance issues, including problems and opportunities, to the COO accurately and in a timely manner.

Departmental Management

1. In association with the Sales and Marketing Manager, direct the publication of *The Author's Newsletter,* the principal means of disseminating corporate and divisional news to the company's authors.
2. Maintain close working relationships with the rest of the company and encourage staff to do the same.

PUBLISHER

Reports to:	Vice President & General Manager
Directly Supervises:	Editor-in-Chief
Budget Responsibility:	Acquisition budget
	Developmental editing budget
	Royalty advances
Accountability:	New Title Sales, Acquisition, and Contribution
	Backlist Sales Contribution
	Manuscript Delivery Dates
	Manuscript Transmittal Date to Production
	Publication Date (with Production)

General Responsibilities:
1. Establish the long- and short-term goals and objectives of the editorial department.
2. Ensure those goals and objectives meet the goals, objectives, and mission of the company.
3. Manage the acquisition, development, and publication of manuscripts and other products that may be agreed upon.
4. Achieve budgeted financial goals.

Specific Operating Responsibilities:
Budgeting/Financial
1. Create and maintain a strategic 3-year schedule of new products by product line and year.
2. Create and manage yearly editorial budgets in consultation with the Vice President and General Manager and the financial department that will fulfill the 3-year strategic plan.
3. Responsibly manage and allocate financial resources in relation to all acquisitions and all editorial personnel.
4. Develop budgets for each new title, including completing Title P&Ls for pre-contract title review.
5. Manage and approve with the Vice President and General Manager all negotiations in relation to the acquisition of manuscripts and other products including author advances and royalties.
6. Be responsible for the sales contribution of both frontlist and backlist titles as per yearly budgets and goals.

Staffing/Personnel

1. Hire, instruct, and supervise Editor-in-Chief; editorial assistants; and other editorial or administrative personnel assigned to the acquisition function as may be needed within the bounds of yearly and long-term budgets and plans.
2. Ensure job descriptions for all editorial functions are completed and up-to-date.
3. Assign projects to editors.
4. Motivate staff and provide ongoing training.
5. Evaluate staff in cooperation with the Vice President and General Manager.

Title Development/Acquisitions

1. Acquire manuscripts and other products to fulfill the objectives determined in the strategic 3-year plan and in yearly budgets.
2. Work with the Vice President and General Manager to create a formal approval process acceptable to all parties.
3. Work with the Vice President and General Manager to facilitate all necessary approvals in a timely way.
4. Maintain a database of potential authors and agents.
5. Maintain the file of all contracts between the publishing house and its authors.
6. Establish and lead in-house editorial meetings.
7. Identify new areas of strategic publication.

Departmental Management

1. Work with the Vice President and General Manager to ensure that the editorial goals and financial targets are met and are coordinated with the goals and targets of other functions within the corporation.
2. Maintain a calendar of editorial due dates for all manuscripts currently under contract and share that calendar with others throughout the editorial department.
3. Work with the Production Manager to ensure that all dates are met and that books are produced on time and to specifications.
4. File for copyrights and oversee the protection of the publishing house's copyrights.
5. Represent concerns of the acquisition function and staff at meetings.

SALES & MARKETING MANAGER

Reports to:	Vice President & General Manager
Directly Supervises:	Trade Sales Manager
	Website Content Coordinator
	Publicity/Promotion Manager
	Direct Marketing Manager
	Rights/Special Sales Manager
Budget Responsibility:	Net Sales Budget
	Marketing Budget
	Co-op
	Advertising and Promotion
	Publicity
	Subsidiary Rights Budget
	Sales Travel and Entertainment Budget
	Complimentary Copy Budget
Accountability:	New Title Sales Contribution
	Backlist Sales Contribution
	Monthly/Yearly Sales Growth as Budgeted
	Marketing Budget as % of Sales
	Books Reviewed
	Sub-Rights Sales Dollars

General Responsibilities:

Plan and oversee all activities necessary to achieve and expand the sales, marketing, publicity, and subsidiary rights functions within the division or company for all products that may be sold through the division, including books, audiotapes, and other merchandise that may be agreed upon.

Specific Operating Responsibilities:

Budgeting/Financial

1. Create and maintain strategic 3-year sales, marketing, and subsidiary-rights plans.

2. Create and manage yearly sales, promotion, and subsidiary rights budgets in consultation with the Vice President and General Manager and financial department that will fulfill the 3-year strategic plan.

3. Establish, in conjunction with the Vice President and General

Manager and the financial department, sales terms applicable to all accounts sold consistent with industry policy and legal boundaries.

4. Develop budgets for each new title, including provision of sales estimates for new Title P&Ls for pre-contract title review.
5. Be responsible for the sales contribution of both frontlist and backlist titles as per yearly budgets and goals.
6. Manage and approve all negotiations in relation to use of marketing funds.

Staffing/Personnel

1. In association with the Vice President and General Manager, hire, instruct, and supervise all sales, marketing, publicity, and subsidiary-rights personnel assigned to the company as may be needed within the bounds of yearly and long-term budgets and plans.
2. Ensure job descriptions for all sales and marketing functions are completed and up-to-date.
3. Assign projects as appropriate to sales, marketing, publicity, and subsidiary rights staff.
4. Motivate staff and provide ongoing training.
5. Evaluate staff in cooperation with the Vice President and General Manager.

Sales, Marketing, Publicity, and Subsidiary Rights Development

1. Understand and become expert in all sales venues, including retail and wholesale accounts, libraries, book clubs, audio clubs, internet, and other markets in which company products are currently sold or may potentially be sold.
2. Personally sell some of the top accounts.
3. Establish orderly, consistent review and publicity procedures.
4. Oversee the creation and implementation of all promotional and marketing material and campaigns including copy, image, ad placement, and more.
5. Plan and establish regular internet, telemarketing and direct-response campaigns and train staff in up-selling, cross-selling, and other sales techniques.
6. Determine, with the Editor and Trade Sales Manager, the best "handles" for each book or product.
7. Maintain a database of current accounts and future potential accounts.

8. Establish and lead in-house sales and marketing meetings.
9. Identify new areas of strategic expansion.
10. Ensure, with the Operations Manager, that accounts are serviced in a manner that emphasizes customer satisfaction at every opportunity.
11. Ensure that all sales leads and requests are fulfilled in a timely way.
12. Coordinate with the marketing and subsidiary rights staff so that all sales materials are provided in a timely, professional manner.

Departmental Management
1. Work with the Vice President and General Manager to ensure that the sales goals and financial targets are met and are coordinated with the goals and targets of other functions within the company.
2. Maintain a calendar of critical sales and marketing dates for all books and share that calendar with others throughout the company.
3. Represent the concerns of the sales, marketing, and subsidiary rights functions and staff at meetings of the core management group.
4. Determine, with the Vice President and General Manager and Sales and Marketing Associates, appropriate goals and objectives for each year.

CHAPTER 4

Make Planning Primary

Almost all of us, toward the end of the year, inaugurate the coming New Year when we buy the forthcoming year's calendar. Whether a wall calendar, the desk variety, or a Blackberry version, we are trying to organize ourselves. A calendar is merely a tool that allows us to look at the year, the month, the day of the week and what we are supposed to be doing on a particular day. Some people record their activities within large blocks of space; others within half-hour time blocks. The important issue is to record the activity so we don't forget it. How we record it is secondary so long as we remember the appointment.

Our business lives are no different than our personal lives. If we don't set down our future plans and the dates on which those plans and appointments are to take place, we are likely to miss the appointment. Too many misses, and we begin to get bad reputations and people don't take us seriously. Too many misses, and we find our goals unmet. Too many misses, and our credibility with clients, accounts, financiers, and others is shot.

To run your business effectively and efficiently, you must bring order to it. How you do this varies from person to person and company to company, but the key point is to *commit* to doing it. I encourage clients to plan using a step-by-step approach:

1. Define your corporate goals and objectives for the year.
2. Communicate those goals and objectives to each functional department.

3. Based on those objectives and goals, have each department create its goals and objectives.
4. Based on those goals and objectives, create budgets and action plans.
5. Review the budgets and plans with your staff for feedback and share the results with them.
6. Finalize budgets and plans.

Setting Goals and Objectives

Goals and objectives are relatively common planning tools for larger publishers who often go through elaborate yearly strategic planning sessions to define these key elements for the next year and, optimally, for three to five years into the future.

For smaller publishers, the planning process to determine goals and objectives is much less formal, usually done in the owner's head and expounded upon only when he or she talks to agents, potential authors, loan officers, and others. Unfortunately, because the results of this planning process are not concretely written down but are frequently kept in the owner's head, other members of the staff may not have a clue as to what today's objectives should be, let alone the ultimate goals of the company.

For both you and your staff to have a clear idea of where you think the company should be going in the short term and the long term, you need to give everyone involved specific notice of

- **what should be done**—what are the overall corporate and divisional goals?
- **how should it be done?**
- **who should do it**—who is responsible for completing each step toward the goal?
- **when should it be accomplished**—what date do you need the goal fulfilled?

Let's look at each of these pieces one at a time.

What should be done? Before you and your staff begin the process of publishing, you must be clear about what it is you want to do. You must have a corporate goal from which all other sub-goals and objectives emanate. A good start in this direction is to complete the mission statement described in chapter 3. This will provide a base upon which other details can be added.

You must generate satisfaction and get your staff to accept the goals if you are to reach them successfully.

Once you've delineated your mission, you and your staff can set goals that will support that mission. I want to emphasize the need to make this a *team effort*. If you simply impose goals on people and tell them they must meet those goals by doing things in one way, you will simply breed discontent. In fact, you must generate satisfaction and get your staff to accept the goals if you are to reach them successfully.

Some of the goals that you may set include

- the level of profitability necessary for your business to succeed
- obtaining a certain number of new authors and manuscripts
- restructuring your company and your staff
- the kind and number of titles you want to publish
- the time for fulfillment turnaround.

Of course there are many other goals to determine, but these are good ones to start with. All should be quantifiable, realistic, and consistent with other goals set within the company. As a manager, you must

- monitor the accomplishment of goals and objectives
- teach your staff how to solve problems when they occur
- demonstrate how to avoid problems by proactively identifying them in the first place.

This doesn't mean you have to do everything yourself—in fact, the opposite is the case.

Your best means of accomplishing the most on a daily basis is to hire talent that has knowledge derived from prior experience or from your direction of what should be done. In my experience, one of the most overlooked aspects of any personnel decision is to hire someone with common sense and drive. These two attributes can make up for a lot of inexperience—and are very hard to find together. If you delegate decision-making authority, you will have more time to accomplish what you need to get done.

Once you have specified your goals, you should prioritize them. Not all things can be done at once. Which are the most important? Which can wait?

How should it be done? Often, we assume that goals are accomplished by default on our way through the publishing process. In fact, this rarely happens. A key responsibility of management is to ensure that what should be done actually gets done in a timely way. Objectives allow you to translate the specific goals into concrete tasks that define the steps or processes necessary to accomplish the goal.

Once your staff members commit to doing something, then you have a criterion for measurement, one that they themselves agreed to.

For instance, if one goal of the Editor-in-Chief is to ensure that manuscripts are considered in a timely manner, then one of the objectives to get to that goal is to hold editorial meetings once a week. This is a quantifiable objective (he did or didn't hold meetings once a week), there is responsibility for the action (the Editor-in-Chief), and there is a time period attached to it (once a week).

Who should do it? Decisions and actions are made by people who are encouraged and empowered by management to think and act with the company's best interests at hand (remember the mission statement?).

The best way to make sure that this happens is to enlist your staff into the process by letting them set objectives that they feel they can actually attain, and that they will be comfortable accomplishing. Once your staff members commit to doing something, then you have a criterion for measurement, one that they themselves agreed to.

When should it be accomplished? To run your company effectively, you need schedules of various kinds (see chapter 2). These can relate to

- publication dates
- production dates
- manuscript acquisition dates

- sales conference dates
- fiscal year dates
- and more.

When you assign a task to someone, you must also assign a date for completing that task.

When you assign a task to someone, you must also assign a date for completing that task. It is up to you, as the manager, to make sure tasks are completed on time. If you become slack in your expectations, you will receive slack responses. The firmer you are in your requirements, the more likely your staff will be to respond on time.

As the executive, you must be able to make informed, timely decisions based upon information obtained from others involved in the process. If they are late getting information to you that you need to make effective decisions, you'll either be late making your own decisions or those decisions will be based on incomplete information.

In either case, your ultimate credibility will suffer. This is especially true in relation to goals and objectives. For your company to run smoothly, goals and objectives must be set. And each must take into account the four key variables noted above.

Some examples of goals and objectives that would apply to most publishing houses are:

Goal:	**To achieve a 25% return on investment on all reprints**
Objective:	Bid all reprints to three manufacturers within 1 week of job request (Janet, Production Assistant)
Task:	Identify the most appropriate reprint vendors (Janet)
Task:	Fill out estimating forms and submit to manufacturer (Janet)
Objective:	Check with sub-rights accounts using book at time of reprint decision to determine if they need additional stock that can be run-on (Frank, Sub-Rights Associate)
Task:	Check sub-rights accounts to see if they purchased title (Frank)
Task:	Call sub-rights accounts to see if any need stock (Frank)
Task:	Report results to Janet (Frank)

Goal:	**To reduce out-of-stocks to 5% or below this year**
Objective:	Build inventory reporting systems to identify inventory levels
Task:	Information Technology (IT) will review current software for adaptability or deficiencies regarding inventory reporting within 30 days (Sharon, IT Director)
Task:	IT will adapt software if possible within 3 months. If not possible, it will investigate new software that will allow flexibility and meet needs, within 30 days (Sharon)
Task:	IT will work with Sales to ensure new software meets sales needs (Sharon and Jim, Sales Manager)
Goal:	**To increase flow of manuscripts to editorial department by 50% in next 6 months**
Objective:	Establish program of greater outreach to agents and authors
Task:	Call 2 agents per day for next two weeks (Jill, Editor-in-Chief)
Task:	Visit 3 college campuses each year (Sarah, Senior Editor)
Task:	Attend Frankfurt Book Fair and meet with 15 publishers (Jill and Sarah)

Every person in your organization, from the president (or owner) on down, should have goals and objectives that translate into tasks to be completed on an everyday basis. If each completes those for which he is responsible, they should coalesce into the successful achievement of each person's goals as well as divisional and corporate goals.

One final piece of advice. Don't make every goal a *financial* goal. While these should be priority goals, it is equally important to make some goals *educational*, so your staff can learn more and attain more as they develop greater expertise and take on more responsibility. Goals and objectives are important qualitative and quantitative benchmarks. Use them well, use them wisely, and your company will be better off for the effort.

Budgeting

If you can add, subtract, multiply, and divide—or if you can push the buttons on a calculator or computer that can do those functions for you—then there's no excuse for not budgeting.

What is budgeting? It's simply the act of putting your publishing estimates and plans in numerical form. Whether it's a budget for one title or 100, the process is the same. And it's simple. Many publishers, who tend to be from the liberal arts side of the educational fence, feel that numbers are foreign beings. I am perhaps the classic example, having taken four years of college Russian to avoid one semester of introductory calculus. (And yes, the calculus caught up with me in graduate school, when it was the first prerequisite for graduation!) So I can sympathize with all of you liberal arts–oriented editors and publishers.

But the fact is, budgeting does not necessitate taking calculus, and it's not rocket science. If you graduated from the sixth grade, with a comprehension of the four basic math skills, you can complete a budget. So don't be intimidated. Take a minute to see how easy a budget really is.

Realize, as well, that there are many different kinds of budgets, from sales budgets to production budgets to complete income statement budgets. You should be using budgets for all your financial needs. As one publisher said: "We just paid $4,000 in taxes and thought we had a great quarter. In fact, we lost money!" If the publisher had a budget in place, and monitored it on a regular basis, this kind of surprise wouldn't happen. The loss may well have occurred, but it wouldn't have come as a surprise.

Let's understand why a budget is important. As we've discovered, planning is a key to successful publishing. Through proper planning, you can know what corporate resources will be needed and when. You can then begin to allocate these resources properly. Whether these resources are the number of people on your staff; the amount of money that will be needed to run your company for a *Planning and budgeting are keys to successful publishing.* period of time; or the time it takes to move a book from acquisition of manuscript through bound book, you must have a firm understanding of how much of each resource you'll need; when you'll need it; and what the expected return is from each.

At the same time you are working on managerial goals, objectives, tasks, and budgets, you are simultaneously working on functional goals, objectives, and tasks that tie in to those at the managerial level. You are also developing budgets functionally, from the ground up. So be sure to read Part III, Functional Organization, before starting your budgeting process.

As you will see in Part III, at the editorial level you are creating two items that will tie directly into your overall budgets:

1. A *3-Year Editorial Plan* tells you approximately how many titles you expect to publish each year and when during the year they'll be published.
2. *Title P&Ls* completed for every title you purchase tell you how many books you estimate you'll sell as well as the net revenue, the cost of goods, including the royalties due to be paid, and more per book.

Because I'm discussing managerial functions here, let's assume for the moment that your functional areas have completed their 3-Year Editorial Plan and their Title P&Ls. All of the relevant projected number of titles per season, per category are estimated, as are your sales projections, cost of goods, and more. Now let's take the next step, slowly and logically, and begin to build a corporate or overall sales and revenue budget.

Building Your Budget
The first step in building a budget is to set up the **Budget Template**. To do this

1. Put the months across the top of your template, starting with the month you'll invoice your first book and running 12 months from that date. Put one month per column.
2. In the last column, after the 12th month, put a total column.
3. Put the titles down the left side—one title per row.

This template works for building a budget that will provide both unit and sales summaries, which you will need. You can run two separate templates for each summary respectively, or you can use one template showing both units and sales. It's your choice.

Budget Template

Title	Price	Advance (Total)	Jan	Feb	Mar	Apr	May	Jun	Jul	Aug	Sep	Oct	Nov	Dec	Total
Units															
Frontlist															
Title 1	$24.95	6,500	2,600	1,950	1,300	650	300	250	200	150	100	80	50	50	7,680
Title 2	$19.95	4,250			1,700	1,275	850	425	125	75	50	50	375	250	4,650
Title 3	$12.95	1,250										500	375	250	1,125
Title 4	$16.95	3,500						1,400	1,050	700	350	200	100	50	3,850
Title 5	$22.95	2,500									1,000	750	500	250	2,500
Frontlist Units			2,600	1,950	3,000	1,925	1,150	2,075	1,375	925	1,500	1,580	1,075	650	19,805
Backlist Units			1,500	1,500	1,500	1,500	1,500	1,500	1,500	1,500	1,500	1,500	1,500	1,500	18,000
Total Units			4,100	3,450	4,500	3,425	2,650	3,575	2,875	2,425	3,000	3,080	2,575	2,150	37,805
Sales $															
Frontlist															
Title 1	$24.95	$84,331	$33,732	$25,299	$16,866	$8,433	$3,892	$3,244	$2,595	$1,946	$1,297	$1,038	$649	$649	$99,640
Title 2	$19.95	$44,090			$17,636	$13,227	$8,818	$4,409	$1,297	$778	$519	$519	$519	$519	$48,239
Title 3	$12.95	$8,418										$3,367	$2,525	$1,684	$7,576
Title 4	$16.95	$30,849						$12,340	$9,255	$6,170	$3,085	$1,763	$881	$441	$33,934
Title 5	$22.95	$29,835									$11,934	$8,951	$5,967	$2,984	$29,835
Frontlist $			$33,732	$25,299	$34,502	$21,660	$12,710	$19,992	$13,146	$8,894	$16,835	$15,637	$10,541	$6,275	$219,224
Backlist $	Avg. $16.95		$13,221	$13,221	$13,221	$13,221	$13,221	$13,221	$13,221	$13,221	$13,221	$13,221	$13,221	$13,221	$158,652
Total Sales			$46,953	$38,520	$47,723	$34,881	$25,931	$33,213	$26,367	$22,115	$30,056	$28,858	$23,762	$19,496	$377,876

Now that you've put the template together (not very tough is it?), all you have to do is fill in the blanks. To begin with, let's work with units.

Take out your Title P&Ls (see Part III) and look at the number of copies per title you estimated you'd sell. If this quantity still makes sense (occasionally it may not, but nine times out of ten it should) then you have a starting point. All you have to do now is spread the sales quantity over the estimated months of sale, beginning in the month in which the title will be invoiced. Before you can do this effectively, you have to understand the pattern of sales within the markets for your products.

For trade publishers, the usual method of sale is to establish a date on which your book will be invoiced. In most cases, your sales representatives will sell your book to the wholesale and retail bookstore buyers six months in advance of this date. Thus, you will have a number of advance orders for your book at the time you ship that book. *Advance orders* are those orders that are in-house prior to the initial date on which you ship your book. They will all be invoiced at once, when the book is in the warehouse, entered into your inventory and billing systems, and released, or approved, by the person responsible for ensuring that everything related to that book is now in order and the book can be put into the marketplace.

Because there is a build up of advance orders—received between the time the sales reps begin selling and the release of the book—these advance orders cause an initial surge in the order pattern of trade books. Once this initial surge has been completed, new orders and reorders tend to follow a more level pattern.

Over the past few years almost all publishers have seen the accumulation of advance orders decline and the surge of orders upon release diminish. This is because of the increased role of "just in time" (JIT) inventory management by most wholesalers and retailers due to

- increasing predominance of the superstores, which carry a broader assortment of titles but smaller quantities of each
- greatly reduced numbers of independent trade booksellers (membership in the American Booksellers Association has dropped from 4,496 in 1995 to 1,703 in 2005 according to *Publishers Weekly*)
- increased role of wholesalers, who can supply the retailers effectively and swiftly.

In the past, one might have seen a percentage of sales over the first four months in a pattern of 65%—20%—10%—5%. That is, new orders for new books would be filled in the ratio of 65% of the new orders being invoiced upon *release* or shipment of the new book, 20% the next month, 10% the month after that, etc.

In today's trade marketplace, this initial surge has been greatly reduced. Now, smaller and most midsized publishers tend to see a pattern that approaches 40%—30%—20%—10%, with the first month's sales closer to 40% of the total advance.

Taking a hypothetical sale of 1,000 advance orders for your new book, we can see that in the past you may have sold 650 copies the first month; 200 the second; 100 the third; and 50 the fourth. Now, however, you more likely will sell 400 the first month; 300 the second; 200 the third; and 100 the fourth. So what, you might say? As long as you sell what you estimated, what's the difference? In some respects you're right. From a units standpoint, if you estimated 1,000 copies and sold 1,000, you printed the right quantity and you can go back to press. It's a great start!

But hold on a minute; let's look at the effect from a dollar standpoint. Where once you would have invoiced sales for 650 copies in month one, you now will only invoice sales for 400 copies—a change of almost 40%! Think of the impact on your cash flow. In a business already stretched tight, this new order pattern forces even greater demand for capital infusion prior to collecting your accounts receivable. Thus, independent booksellers aren't the only ones under stress today—so are you as a publisher!

To build your budget, use a pattern that fits the sales pattern for your books. If you don't have a pattern established yet, use a conservative one, like the second noted above. Start each title in the month it will be invoiced. When you have entered all of your titles, total the columns at the bottom, and in the total column. The two should crossfoot, or be equal whether added down the total column or across on the total row. If they don't, check for errors. Once done, you will have your first budget—in units—in place. This will allow you to view your unit sales by title, by month, and in total.

If you have any backlist titles, estimate the number of books you sell in a year and then divide that total by 12, evenly spreading the resulting number over the 12 months. This works fine unless you are planning a special promotion for one or more books in any particular month or if you find a seasonal sales pattern. If this is the case, then spread sales according to that pattern.

To see how sales for the year will occur, and how much cash you can expect to receive in a particular month, you need to convert the unit budget to dollars. Again, this will vary by marketplace, but in the trade arena we can use certain legitimate estimates.

When you sell a book in the trade market, you almost always provide a discount—usually 40 to 50% off of the retail price. In most cases, the wholesalers and those with larger central warehouse locations (read chains and superstores) as well as those who order larger quantities of books receive a higher discount than accounts with multiple "ship to" locations and those who order smaller quantities. In actuality, because most of a publisher's sales go to the wholesalers and major retailers who buy in bulk, the average publisher discount is somewhere around 47 to 48% off of the retail price.

Using this figure, you can now determine your estimated sales revenue. First, take the retail price and multiply by the converse of the discount. Let's assume a $20.00 book. Therefore $20.00 x (1.00 − .48). This will give you the discounted dollar amount received, in this case $20.00 x .52 or $10.40. If you've run your Title P&Ls, you can simply plug in your figures from those sheets. It's certainly faster to do it in spreadsheet form, however. Check yourself by making sure the numbers you derive this way tie into those you calculated when doing the Title P&Ls.

Now, multiply this per unit revenue by the number of monthly units you projected will be sold. Again, using our second example above, we would have dollar revenues in month one (assuming a $20.00 retail price) of 400 x $10.40, or $4,160. To get the other figures, you simply use the same procedure.

As you can see, there's absolutely nothing difficult about this process. In fact, with a computer spreadsheet program, you can complete a budget incredibly fast. The key is to make the budget as accurate as possible, so you can begin to use it both for cash-flow reasons, and as a benchmark against your actual sales. In other words, if your actual sales come in less than you've projected, you should ask why. Similarly, if sales come in high, you should determine the reason for that as well.

Once you have your sales budget, in both units and dollars, you can begin to construct your complete corporate budget, which I will discuss shortly.

A budget is extremely important because it allows you to see how many units you project will be sold, the revenues associated with the sale of those units, and the costs and expenses that ultimately will be deducted against the revenues. The benefit of the budget is that it allows you to see your projected profit—or loss—*before* it happens and provides a benchmark against which you can review any variance, whether positive or negative.

Cash Flow

A cash-flow projection is similar to a budget, in that it allows you to see the ebb and flow of your cash. It differs because the cash-flow projection is structured not around your invoice date or revenue, but around the date at which the revenue is actually received and spent. In other words, because the book industry *reality* is 90 to 120 day payment terms, your cash projections for revenue should reflect that delay and "budget" receipt of cash at that time. Expenses, however, are usually paid by your company immediately upon purchase or within 30 to 60 days.

You may be selling books, but you'll have to pay for them before you receive any cash for the sale of those books.

As you can immediately see, in the book business there is an imbalance between expenses and revenues—by as much as 60 to 90 days. In other words, you may be selling books, but you'll have to pay for them *before* you receive any cash for the sale of those books. While this is not unusual in book publishing, it's not a pretty picture. If you don't have the capital to support this kind of negative cash flow, you'll soon find your company in deep trouble. And this is exactly why cash-flow projections are critical to ensuring not just the success, but the *survival* of your company.

In addition, at the end of the year you will have large fourth-quarter sales that have created (hopefully!) profits. You'll have to pay taxes on these in April, probably before you have received the returns or even payment for the books. This is a good reason for U.S. publishers to consider a corporate form of business with a fiscal year that ends other than on December 31.

How do you create a cash-flow projection? It's actually easier than you might think.

Using a template similar to that of the unit and dollar projections, set up a monthly framework for 12 months. One of the best templates

Cash-flow projections are critical to ensuring not just the success, but the survival of your company.

I've seen (see **Cash Flow–Without Backlist** and **Cash Flow–With Backlist**, following) comes from Eric and Steven C. Brandt, of Archipelago Press, in Friday Harbor, Washington (from the book *Entrepreneuring: The 10 Commandments for Building a Growth Company*, Third Edition, © 1997 by Steven C. Brandt).

Down the left side of the template, note all revenue and expense categories similar to your budget, only this time start with net revenue; that is, gross revenue *minus* returns. The categories for outflow proceed down through printing and binding; plant or development costs; royalty; and so on, through rent, telephone, etc.

If you start at the beginning with revenue, you now want to simply record your revenues when you receive them, not when they are invoiced. If you aren't going to get paid for 90 days, then you record your cash flow beginning 90 days after the date of invoice. If your invoice date is January, your cash-flow revenue stream begins in April.

If you pay the printer 30 days from delivery of bound books, and bound books are delivered in November, then slot your printing expense into late December or early January. You can easily see why book publishing is a cash-poor business. You've now got a negative cash flow because you've paid for books for which you haven't yet received any income—and won't get any income for another 90 days! Then, just when you think you should receive payment, don't be surprised if your accounts send you returns instead—and deduct the credit for the return immediately. In effect, your company has become the bank for the account—financing its cash flow but receiving little in return. And you thought this was a "gentleman's business"!

Most publishers pay royalties twice a year. Be sure to plan carefully for these, because they are usually one of the largest expenses of any publishing company.

After cost of goods, spread your fixed costs evenly over each of the 12 months. Spread your variable costs to the months in which these costs will have to be paid.

Working down the columns, add all the inflows and subtract all the outflows. The net result is either cash-positive or cash-negative.

Then add these monthly positives and negatives across the bottom to get a monthly cumulative cash flow total, as well as a yearly total.

Book publishing is a cash-poor business.

Study these numbers closely, looking for any seasonal patterns to the cash stream. If you are cash-positive, you are in good shape. Are there any months when you'll need cash? Where will it come from?

Are you cash-negative? If so, what can you do to get back to a positive position? Can you increase prices? Cut expenses? Decrease royalty and/or cost of goods? In what month are you most negative? How much will you have to borrow at that point? Do you have a line of credit that will cover that amount? If not, you should begin to figure out how to get the line of credit or how you'll cover those negative months.

Many business owners and managers don't really understand the intricacies of the cash-flow projection. One of the best uses you can make of yours is to track your expenditures to determine just where your cash is coming from and where it's going. If you consistently do this, you will get a firm grip on your business needs and cycles. You will begin to understand

- where your money is going
- how much will be required
- when it will be required.

This information is essential for you to manage your company skillfully and successfully.

It's not uncommon to find companies that are profitable on their income statements that also run a negative cash flow. And while larger companies might survive this situation for some time, smaller companies can't do so for long. A negative cash-flow position can be maintained only by borrowing or by not paying bills in a timely way. In either case, for the smaller publisher, this can lead to disaster because your credibility (there's that term again) is only as good as your last paid invoice.

The only way around a negative cash flow is to plan for it well in

Cash Flow–Without Backlist

	Jan	Feb	Mar	Apr	May	Jun	Jul	Aug	Sep	Oct	Nov	Dec	TOTAL
Projected Cash Inflow													
Book Sales													
Frontlist Units Sold	0	3,500	2,275	550	500	900	400	3,300	400	350	200	200	12,575
Distributor Payment 35%/120 days						$14,651	$9,523	$2,302	$2,093	$3,767	$1,674	$13,814	$47,825
Direct Sales	$450	$1,100	$500	$1,800	$1,300	$1,300	$1,300	$1,300	$1,300	$1,300	$1,300	$1,300	$14,250
Sub-rights/ Other Income			$5,000		$14,000	$15,500			$1,000				$35,500
Gross Cash Inflow	$450	$1,100	$5,500	$1,800	$15,300	$31,451	$10,823	$3,602	$4,393	$5,067	$2,974	$15,114	$97,575
Projected Cash Outflow													
Book Production													
Printing/ Binding					$350			$5,500					$5,850
Development Costs				$1,000	$1,500	$500							$3,000
Royalties			$2,500						$16,500				$19,000
Payroll													
Salaries/ Wages	$4,000	$4,000	$4,000	$4,000	$4,000	$4,000	$4,000	$4,000	$4,000	$4,000	$4,000	$4,000	$48,000
12% Benefits	$480	$480	$480	$480	$480	$480	$480	$480	$480	$480	$480	$480	$5,760
Accounting													
Bank Service Charges	$100	$100	$100	$400	$100	$100	$100	$100	$100	$100	$100	$100	$1,500
Professional Fees	$40	$40	$40	$40	$40	$40	$40	$40	$40	$40	$40	$40	$480
Advertising/ Promo													
Brochure/ Catalog Design					$250								$250
Printing		$300		$300	$800								$1,400
Supplies- Mailing	$200	$300		$500									$1,000
Mailing List Rental	$500												$500
Consultants' Services													$0
Coop Mailings/ Shows			$500						$1,000				"$1,500
Print/ Classified Ads													$0
Computer													
Online Service	$35	$35	$35	$35	$35	$35	$35	$35	$35	$35	$35	$35	$420
Software				$100		$50							$150
Hardware		$125		$100									$225
Other Expenses													
Insurance	$500												$500
Memberships/ Fees	$100					$200	$165						$465
Miscellaneous	$300	$300	$300	$300	$300	$300	$300	$300	$300	$300	$300	$300	$3,600
Office Supplies	$25	$25	$25	$25	$25	$25	$25	$25	$25	$25	$25	$25	$300
Federal Express		$50	$50	$50	$50								$200
Postage & Shipping	$1,500	$300	$800	$1,200	$100	$100	$100	$500	$100	$100	$100	$100	$5,000
Rent-Office	$500	$500	$500	$500	$500	$500	$500	$500	$500	$500	$500	$500	$6,000
Research													$0
Taxes	$750	$750	$750	$750	$750	$750	$750	$750	$750	$750	$750	$750	$9,000
Telephone	$150	$150	$150	$150	$150	$150	$150	$150	$150	$150	$150	$150	$1,800
Travel			$200		$2,000				$750				$2,950
Video													$0
Website/ Internet				$1,500					$1,500				$3,000
Total Cash Outflow	$9,180	$7,455	$10,430	$11,430	$11,430	$7,230	$6,645	$12,380	$26,230	$6,480	$6,480	$6,480	$121,850
Monthly Net Cash	($8,730)	($6,355)	($4,930)	($9,630)	$3,870	$24,221	$4,178	($8,778)	($21,837)	($1,413)	($3,506)	$8,634	($24,275)
Balance Forward	$3,000	($5,730)	($12,085)	($17,015)	($26,645)	($22,775)	$1,446	$5,624	($3,154)	($24,991)	($26,403)	($29,909)	
Net Cumulative Cash Flow	($5,730)	($12,085)	($17,015)	($26,645)	($22,775)	$1,446	$5,624	($3,154)	($24,991)	($26,403)	($29,909)	($21,275)	

Cash Flow–With Backlist

Item	Jan	Feb	Mar	Apr	May	Jun	Jul	Aug	Sep	Oct	Nov	Dec	TOTAL
Projected Cash Inflow													
Book Sales													
Frontlist Units Sold		3,500	2,275	550	500	900	400	3,300	400	350	200	200	12,575
Backlist Units Sold	1,250	1,250	1,250	1,250	1,250	1,250	1,250	1,250	1,250	1,250	1,250	1,250	15,000
Distributor Payment 35%/120 days					$5,233	$19,884	$14,756	$7,535	$7,326	$9,000	$6,907	$19,046	$89,685
Direct Sales	$450	$1,100	$500	$1,800	$1,300	$1,300	$1,300	$1,300	$1,300	$1,300	$1,300	$1,300	$14,250
Sub-rights/Other income			$5,000		$14,000	$15,500			$1,000				$35,500
Gross Cash Inflow	$450	$1,100	$5,500	$1,800	$20,533	$36,684	$16,056	$8,835	$9,626	$10,300	$8,207	$20,346	$139,435
Projected Cash Outflow													
Book Production													
Printing/Binding					$350			$5,500					$5,850
Development Costs				$1,000	$1,500	$500							$3,000
Royalties			$2,750						$16,800				$19,550
Payroll													
Salaries/Wages	$4,000	$4,000	$4,000	$4,000	$4,000	$4,000	$4,000	$4,000	$4,000	$4,000	$4,000	$4,000	$48,000
12% Benefits	$480	$480	$480	$480	$480	$480	$480	$480	$480	$480	$480	$480	$5,760
Accounting													
Bank Service Charges	$100	$100	$100	$400	$100	$100	$100	$100	$100	$100	$100	$100	$1,500
Professional Fees	$40	$40	$40	$40	$40	$40	$40	$40	$40	$40	$40	$40	$480
Advertising/Promo													
Brochure/Catalog Design					$250								$250
Printing		$300		$300	$800								$1,400
Supplies-Mailing	$200	$300		$500									$1,000
Mailing List Rental	$500												$500
Consultants' Services			$500						$1,000				$1,500
Coop Mailings/Shows													$0
Print/Classified Ads													$0
Computer													
Online Service	$35	$35	$35	$35	$35	$35	$35	$35	$35	$35	$35	$35	$420
Software				$100		$50							$150
Hardware		$125		$100									$225
Other Expenses													
Insurance	$500												$500
Memberships/Fees	$100					$200	$165						$465
Miscellaneous	$300	$300	$300	$300	$300	$300	$300	$300	$300	$300	$300	$300	$3,600
Office Supplies	$25	$25	$25	$25	$25	$25	$25	$25	$25	$25	$25	$25	$300
Federal Express			$50	$50	$50	$50							$200
Postage & Shipping	$1,500	$350	$800	$1,200	$100	$50	$100	$500	$100	$100	$100	$100	$5,000
Rent-Office	$500	$500	$500	$500	$500	$500	$500	$500	$500	$500	$500	$500	$6,000
Research													$0
Taxes	$750	$750	$750	$750	$750	$750	$750	$750	$750	$750	$750	$750	$9,000
Telephone	$150	$150	$150	$150	$150	$150	$150	$150	$150	$150	$150	$150	$1,800
Travel			$200		$2,000				$750				$2,950
Video													$0
Website/Internet				$1,500					$1,500				$3,000
Total Cash Outflow	$9,180	$7,455	$10,680	$11,430	$11,430	$7,230	$6,645	$12,380	$26,530	$6,480	$6,480	$6,480	$122,400
Monthly Net Cash	($8,730)	($6,355)	($5,180)	($9,630)	$9,103	$29,454	$9,411	($3,545)	($16,905)	$3,820	$1,727	$13,866	$17,035
Balance Forward	$3,000	($5,730)	($12,085)	($17,265)	($26,895)	($17,793)	$11,661	$21,072	$17,526	$622	$4,442	$6,169	
Net Cumulative Cash Flow	($5,730)	($12,085)	($17,265)	($26,895)	($17,793)	$11,661	$21,072	$17,526	$622	$4,442	$6,169	$20,035	$20,035

advance and to ensure that your company is capitalized properly with high enough lines of credit from the bank or other sources to allow you to work through these cash peaks and valleys. It's actually common for every business to have such cycles; remember our discussion of seasonality earlier, which almost always results in these difficult positions. Unfortunately, your creditors don't want to hear about this. They want to be paid what they're owed, when it's due—without excuses.

Don Tubesing, the former owner of Pfeiffer-Hamilton and Whole Person Associates, a superb small publisher in Minnesota that recently sold parts of itself to Scholastic and University of Minnesota Press, makes some very cogent points when he talks about cash flow. The reason many publishers have difficulty funding their growth with internally generated profits is that these publishers don't take into account the dramatic implications of taxes, inventory, and accounts receivable on their cash flow until it's too late. As publishers grow, they hesitate to borrow, because they don't want to incur the interest costs on those loans. Most correctly prefer to finance themselves using internal cash flow. While this may work well for a while, Don's excellent point is that in a growth mode, the company's need for cash grows faster than the availability of cash thrown off from profitability.

In other words, the more successful a company is, the greater its profits. But the greater the profits, the greater the federal and state taxes the company must pay. As taxes increase, that "free cash" available to put back into the business is decreased. But this isn't all. If the company is growing, it will also increase inventory (your cash in boxes of product) and accounts receivable (your cash loaned to your customers). This, in turn, creates an even greater need for cash and therefore pressure on the business—pressure that can only be relieved by borrowing. Don's chart of this situation, **Relationship Between Growth Rate and Profit Required to Fund It**, shows this clearly.

Don uses the example of a company with net sales of $200,000. If that company earns a 10% net profit, it nets $20,000. Subtracting taxes at about a 30% tax rate, leaves $14,000 to fund both inventory (that is, the product they are making and selling) and accounts receivable. The reason we have to fund accounts receivable (see also chapter 12) is that in the publishing business we normally don't get paid before shipping our products or immediately upon shipping. We almost always have a lag between the time books are shipped and the

Relationship Between Growth Rate and Profit Required to Fund It

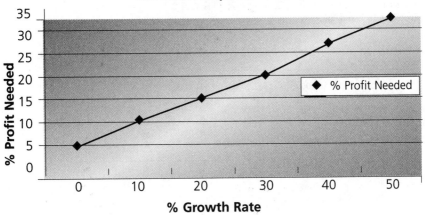

time we collect our money for the sale. Thus, we are actually lending our money to the buyer in the form of inventory that is not paid for.

If, as we grow, the owners and managers understand that our growth comes from selling more books than we did before, or selling the same number of books at higher prices, or reducing our expenses, or a combination of these, then growth demands more of our resources be put into inventory and receivables. This doesn't mean proportionately more, but more in dollar terms. In other words, if the dollar amount of inventory sitting in our warehouse, or, as Don says, sitting in boxes, is about 12% of our net sales at any time and the cost of our receivables is 18% of net sales (and these figures will vary from seasonal lows to seasonal highs), then if we keep these percentages steady (totalling 30% of our net sales), the increase in this amount in dollar terms, when deducted from the net profit, is what we will need to fund future growth.

Using this as a paradigm, you can see what happens as you increase your sales and your growth rate. As the growth rate increases, taxes also go up. So too do inventory and accounts receivable. Thus, the profit needed to fund this growth increases as well. The more you grow, the less able you are to fund this growth from internal funds unless your profit margin increases along with your sales growth. From a time perspective, we must generate profit now to fund next year's future growth. (See *Sales Growth and Cash Flow* following.)

Sales Growth and Cash Flow

Sales Growth at 10% Year 1; 20% Year 2; 30% Year 3
Profit of 10% per Year

Year	Net Sales Dollars	Profit at 10%	Tax Dollars at 30%	Net Profit	Inventory at 12%	Receivables at 18%	Total Combined $ Invested in Growth Assets
0	$200,000	$20,000	$6,000	$14,000	$24,000	$36,000	$60,000
1	220,000	22,000	6,600	15,400	26,400	39,600	66,000
2	264,000	26,400	7,920	18,480	31,680	47,520	79,200
3	343,200	34,320	10,296	24,024	41,184	61,776	102,960

Year	Net Profit from Above	Less Additional Inventory $	Less Additional Receivable $	Equals Net Cash Available
0	Baseline Year			
1	$15,400	$2,400	$3,600	$9,400
2	18,480	5,280	7,920	5,280
3	24,024	9,504	14,256	264

Sales Growth at 10% Year 1; 20% Year 2; 30% Year 3
Profit of 10% Year 1; 20% Year 2; 30% Year 3

Year	Net Sales Dollars	Profit at 10/20/30%	Tax Dollars at 30%	Net Profit	Inventory at 12%	Receivables at 18%	Total Combined $ Invested in Growth Assets
0	$200,000	$20,000	$6,000	$14,000	$24,000	$36,000	$60,000
1	220,000	22,000	6,600	15,400	26,400	39,600	66,000
2	264,000	52,800	15,840	36,960	31,680	47,520	79,200
3	343,200	102,960	30,888	72,072	41,184	61,776	102,960

Year	Net Profit from Above	Less Additional Inventory $	Less Additional Receivable $	Equals Net Cash Available
0	Baseline Year			
1	$15,400	$2,400	$3,600	$9,400
2	36,960	5,280	7,920	23,760
3	72,072	9,504	14,256	48,312

Let's take Don's $200,000 company and see what happens to it. In the first instance we'll assume a 10% sales growth rate in year 1, 20% in year 2, 30% in year 3, a 30% corporate tax rate, and a constant 10% profitability.

What happens through the years? If we use year 0 as a baseline, we can see the changes:

Inventory: We tied up an additional $2,400 dollars in year 1, an additional $17,184 by year 3.

Receivables: We grew these by $3,600 in year 1, and $25,776 by year 3.

Total of the two: We have grown the combined amounts by $6,000 at year 1, by $19,200 at year 2, by $42,960 at year 3. Net cash available shrinks every year.

In short, we are growing our business. These amounts aren't necessarily losses. In fact both inventory and accounts receivable are both assets. But the result of our growth is that both are tying up our cash and therefore must be funded.

As you can clearly see, if you consistently increase your growth rate while keeping profitability at a flat rate, you will need a greater amount of cash—even though you're technically *profitable*.

Thus, to break even, cash-wise, you must increase your profitability level along with your growth to fund this growth internally.

Looking at the same chart, in the second instance, if we increase profit dollars from 10% to 20% to 30% each year, maintaining all other factors as they were, we can see the results.

The net cash available is significantly better than before. But don't forget, as your profit before taxes increases, so too will your tax rate up to a point. And you may still have negative cash flow even though you are showing a profit on your P&L.

Robert Follett, in his excellent book *How to Keep Score in Business: Accounting and Financial Analysis for the Non-Accountant* (Follet Publishing Co., now out-of-print), makes a point similar to Don's when he discusses working capital, which is the difference between current assets and current liabilities. As Follet says,

> . . . theoretically, working capital is the capital in the business that is working on a day-by-day basis to produce profits . . . As a business grows it needs more working capital. As sales expand, customers owe the business more money. Accounts receivable grow. Inventory usually must grow, too, to accommodate a growth in sales. The growth of accounts receivable and inventory expands current assets. Where does the money come from for this?
>
> The company is likely to owe its suppliers more as it buys more inventory. So the suppliers help to finance some of the asset growth. The company may accrue larger payrolls and other expenses. Current liabilities grow. Often short-term loans are borrowed from the bank to help meet the need for expanded working capital.
>
> Current liabilities can almost never grow as fast as current assets

grow when a company is expanding sales. So the growth in working capital needed to support sales must be financed from some other source . . .

Sometimes none of these sources are available. Money may be tight and banks or other lenders reluctant to lend. The stock market may be depressed and no stock can be sold. Profits may be inadequate to finance working capital needs. When these situations occur a company can literally expand into bankruptcy.

The key to maintaining your profitability and your cash flow is to plan well in advance so you'll know what you'll need when. This way, you can minimize the time you'll have to borrow and pay interest and know when you'll be in the best position to plan for heavy expenditures. With your cash flow under control, you have a much better chance of getting a loan to tide you over during these tight times.

One common question that arises from this analysis is how any publisher can make a profit and have positive cash flow throughout the process. The fact is, it's very difficult.

One way is to think of, and plan for, the progression of your business as a series of steps, rather than as a continuous upward 45-degree-angle line. As we've seen, growth necessitates added investment in inventory and receivables—which can't be immediately recovered. If, however, one decides to slow the growth, or maintain it, then there is time to sell the inventory and collect the receivables, which can then be used to fund future growth internally. Thus, the cycle systematically progresses in step fashion from expansion to plateau, expansion to plateau, rather than from expansion to expansion.

When running your own business, it's not difficult to position your company in this way. In fact, it's one of the benefits of being a private company. In today's world, public companies may have the theoretical comfort of long-term planning, but in reality find that quarterly earnings targets all too often become that which investors—and boards of directors—look at to determine success or failure. And focusing on short-term earnings often can and does lead to long-term problems.

Another way to have positive cash flow is to maintain your internal expenses as you grow your sales. If you're selling more books, for instance, and maintaining your sales and marketing expenses at the same level as before, it will throw more dollars to the bottom line. Similarly, if you have a very successful book, your second printing should show significantly greater margin because you probably won't have development costs to worry about.

And don't forget that as you build your editorial niche and gain critical mass in different categories, your marketing costs will have greater impact on sales, because they can promote not just one book, but an entire

Most companies do need to borrow to cover seasonal cash fluctuations.

category or line of books. All of these efficiencies mean more money to the bottom line, which should increase your overall margin and your ability to cover your own cash needs.

The fact is, though, that most companies do need to borrow to cover seasonal cash fluctuations. This is normal and is what keeps banks in business. It's a reason for you to establish a relationship with your banker and to make sure that you know exactly what your banker requires to grant your loan request or your credit line. A critical ingredient of this will be a cash-flow analysis.

So don't make excuses and don't rely on chance. Do your cash-flow planning early—and do it well.

Income Statements and Balance Sheets

John Tracy, in his book *How to Read a Financial Report* (John Wiley & Sons), has an excellent description of the various tasks of managers as they relate to the income statement, balance sheet, and cash-flow statements. As Tracy states,

> The Income Statement reports the profit performance of the business. The ability of managers to make sales and to control expenses, and thereby to earn profit, is measured in the Income Statement. Clearly, earning an adequate profit is the key for survival and the manager's most important imperative. But the bottom line is not the end of the manager's task.
>
> Managers must also control the financial condition of the business. This means keeping the assets and liabilities within proper limits and proportions relative to each other and relative to the sales and expense levels of the company. And, managers must prevent cash shortages that would cause the business to default on its liabilities or to miss its payroll.
>
> The business manager really has a threefold task: earning profit,

controlling the company's financial condition and preventing 'cashouts'. Profit performance alone does not guarantee survival. In other words, you can't manage profits without also managing the changes in financial condition caused by the sales and expenses that produce your profit. . . .

In a smaller company you, as manager, must assume oversight of all of these three functions. If you don't do them yourself, you must know what to look for. And to do this well, you must understand the income statement and balance sheet in addition to the cash-flow statement.

At the end of the day, when all of your books have been sold, when returns have come back, when bills have been paid and receivables collected, you want to have a record of exactly what kind of month, quarter, and year you've had, and what shape your company is in. The income statement and balance sheet provide you with the answers to these questions.

The income statement is simply a picture of your business over time, usually done monthly, quarterly, and yearly. It shows what has happened to each revenue and expense item over the course of the period being looked at. In other words, how many dollars worth of books have you sold in the first three months of the year, or over the course of the entire year? How much money do you have left over (the gross profit) after you've reduced your sales by the actual cost of goods and royalties? How much do you pay in salaries relative to your net revenues? The result of subtracting expenses and taxes from revenues is the company's *net profit*.

Profit performance alone does not guarantee survival.

The balance sheet, on the other hand, looks at your business at a very specific moment in time. It tells you how your company is doing on that particular day. And rather than provide detail about each revenue and expense item, it summarizes its components under the headings ASSETS and LIABILITIES. Within those two headings one finds CURRENT ASSETS and CURRENT LIABILITIES (those that will be recognized within one year) and LONG-TERM ASSETS and LONG-TERM LIABILITIES. The net result of subtracting liabilities from assets tells you how much *owner's equity* you have in your company at the moment in question.

Looking at your income statement enables you to benchmark it against the publishing industry averages from sources such as the AAP, Huenefeld-PubWest Survey of Financial Operations, as well as the American Association of University Presses. The income statement items on page 130 are from the AAP's 1994 statistics (the last year for which trade publishers' data is available). The Huenefeld figures are from the 2004 survey that reports data for 2003. Ask yourself how your company compares with these industry averages. If your line items and total are under the average, great. If they're over the average, ask why and how you might improve performance in that area to match or better that of the rest of the industry.

The Income Statement

For most publishers, the income statement is the foremost management tool at their disposal. Because it reflects what's happening over time, it allows you to view and monitor progress of the business throughout the year by comparing the actual dynamics and results of the company or division with those you've projected in the budgets. You should compare literally every line item on the income statement with those you projected in your initial budgets and determine why things are happening. Why are revenues lower or higher than projected? Why is cost of goods higher or lower? Why are costs in various areas off the mark?

It is just as important, when comparing these figures, to understand why some line items are more favorable than you budgeted as it is to understand why some are less favorable. If you understand the dynamics of your business, you'll manage it better.

What does the income statement cover and why is it important? It covers every aspect of your business:

- Sales
- Expenses
- Taxes
- Profits

As noted, the formula is simple: sales minus expenses and taxes equals profit.

$$\text{Sales} - (\text{Expenses} + \text{Taxes}) = \text{Profit}$$

I won't go into the formal double-entry accounting mechanics that ultimately result in the ability to create the income statement here, because almost every accounting package, or your CPA, can do this for you. But I will spend some time with the actual statement itself.

How is the initial income statement used as a budget? As I've already said, you want to project as early as possible those revenues and costs you will incur throughout your year, whether it's your first year in business or your twenty-fifth. You want to know where you're going throughout the year. What are your financial goals? You don't want any negative surprises. Furthermore, you don't want your investors to be surprised, or you'll put the investment at risk. Financial lenders— whether banks, credit companies, or individuals—want to know their investments are on safe ground. They want to be assured that you know what you are doing and where your business is going.

These lenders base their continued loans on your ability to meet their guidelines and benchmarks. And to manage your business with understanding, you must realistically estimate what you'd like to have happen, and what is actually happening. That's what the income statement does. It should be used as both *budget* and *benchmark*.

At the beginning of the year, therefore, you should have a budgeted income statement in place. As the year progresses, preferably on a monthly and quarterly basis, you should compare the actual results you've achieved with those budgeted. Set up three columns, the first of which shows your budgeted results, the second your actual results, and the third the variance of the two.

Let's now set up the **Budgeted Income Statement** (sample on page 73). See also the discussion about Title P&Ls in chapter 7.

Begin with revenues. You've already estimated revenues in your sales budgets, so these should be in good shape. Don't forget that for income statement purposes, we'll have at least three summary lines of revenue:

- Gross Sales
- Returns
- Net Sales

In publishing, gross sales is derived by adding the returns amount to net sales. In other words, net sales plus the returns amount equals the gross sales.

Budgeted Income Statement

	Jan	Feb	Mar	Apr	May	Jun	Jul	Aug	Sep	Oct	Nov	Dec	Budget	Actual	Variance
Gross Sales	$46,953	$38,520	$47,723	$34,881	$25,931	$33,213	$26,367	$22,115	$30,056	$28,858	$23,762	$19,496	$377,875	$350,000	($27,875)
Returns	$9,391	$7,704	$9,545	$6,976	$5,186	$6,643	$5,273	$4,423	$6,011	$5,772	$4,752	$3,899	$75,575	$70,000	($5,575)
Net Sales	$37,562	$30,816	$38,178	$27,905	$20,745	$26,570	$21,094	$17,692	$24,045	$23,086	$19,010	$15,597	$302,300	$280,000	($22,300)
Other Publishing Income		$500		$4,500			$200			$7,500			$12,700	$5,000	($7,700)
Total Sales (with OPI)	$37,562	$31,316	$38,178	$32,405	$20,745	$26,570	$21,294	$17,692	$24,045	$30,586	$19,010	$15,597	$315,000	$285,000	($30,000)
Cost of Goods															
Development Costs	$2,500	$2,500	$2,500	$2,500	$2,500	$2,500	$2,500	$2,500	$2,500	$2,500	$2,500	$2,500	$30,000	$30,000	$0
PPB	$7,982	$6,548	$8,113	$5,930	$4,408	$5,646	$4,482	$3,760	$5,110	$4,906	$4,040	$3,314	$64,239	$50,000	($14,239)
Royalty	$3,756	$3,332	$3,818	$5,040	$2,074	$2,657	$2,209	$1,769	$2,404	$6,059	$1,901	$1,560	$36,580	$28,000	($8,580)
Total Cost of Goods	$14,238	$12,380	$14,431	$13,470	$8,983	$10,803	$9,192	$8,029	$10,014	$13,465	$8,441	$7,374	$130,819	$108,000	($22,819)
Gross Margin	$23,324	$18,936	$23,748	$18,935	$11,762	$15,767	$12,102	$9,663	$14,031	$17,122	$10,569	$8,223	$184,181	$177,000	($7,181)
Direct Provisions															
Inventory write-off	$1,127	$924	$1,145	$837	$622	$797	$633	$531	$721	$693	$570	$468	$9,069	$8,400	($669)
Author advance write-off	$376	$308	$382	$279	$207	$266	$211	$177	$240	$231	$190	$156	$3,023	$2,800	($223)
Bad Debt write-off	$563	$462	$573	$419	$311	$399	$316	$265	$361	$346	$285	$234	$4,535	$4,200	($335)
Total Provisions	$2,066	$1,695	$2,100	$1,535	$1,141	$1,461	$1,160	$973	$1,322	$1,270	$1,046	$858	$16,627	$15,400	($1,227)
Gross Profit	$21,258	$17,241	$21,648	$17,400	$10,621	$14,306	$10,942	$8,690	$12,708	$15,852	$9,524	$7,365	$167,555	$161,600	($5,955)
Operating Expenses															
Editorial Salaries	$1,250	$1,250	$1,250	$1,250	$1,250	$1,250	$1,250	$1,250	$1,250	$1,250	$1,250	$1,250	$15,000	$15,000	$0
Production Salaries	$800	$800	$800	$800	$800	$800	$800	$800	$800	$800	$800	$800	$9,600	$7,500	($2,100)
Advertising	$1,250	$1,250	$2,500	$1,250	$1,250	$1,250	$1,250	$1,250	$2,500	$1,250	$1,250	$1,250	$17,500	$20,000	$2,500
Marketing	$1,500	$1,500	$4,000	$1,500	$1,500	$1,500	$1,500	$1,500	$3,500	$1,500	$1,500	$1,500	$22,500	$15,000	($7,500)
Sales	$1,500	$1,500	$1,500	$1,500	$1,500	$1,500	$1,500	$1,500	$1,500	$1,500	$1,500	$1,500	$18,000	$15,000	($3,000)
Fulfillment	$700	$700	$700	$700	$700	$700	$700	$700	$700	$700	$700	$700	$8,400	$14,000	$5,600
Manufacturing	$600	$600	$600	$600	$600	$600	$600	$600	$600	$600	$600	$600	$7,200	$12,500	$5,300
Complimentary Copies	$250	$250	$250	$250	$250	$250	$250	$250	$250	$250	$250	$250	$3,000	$700	($2,300)
Office Expense	$2,500	$2,500	$2,500	$2,500	$2,500	$2,500	$2,500	$2,500	$2,500	$2,500	$2,500	$2,500	$30,000	$27,500	($2,500)
Utilities	$300	$300	$300	$300	$300	$300	$300	$300	$300	$300	$300	$300	$3,600	$3,500	($100)
Rent & Insurance	$750	$750	$750	$750	$750	$750	$750	$750	$750	$750	$750	$750	$9,000	$9,000	$0
Total Expenses	$11,400	$11,400	$15,150	$11,400	$11,400	$11,400	$11,400	$11,400	$14,650	$11,400	$11,400	$11,400	$143,800	$139,700	($4,100)
Contribution to Profit (EBITDA)	$9,858	$5,841	$6,498	$6,000	($779)	$2,906	($458)	($2,710)	($1,942)	$4,452	($1,876)	($4,035)	$23,755	$21,900	($1,855)
Depreciation/ Amortization	$300	$300	$300	$300	$300	$300	$300	$300	$300	$300	$300	$300	$3,600	$3,200	($400)
Interest	$200	$200	$200	$200	$200	$200	$200	$200	$200	$200	$200	$200	$2,400	$2,400	$0
Taxes	$1,972	$1,168	$1,300	$1,200	$0	$581	$0	$0	($388)	$890	$0	($4,535)	$6,723	$6,000	($723)
Net Profit	$7,387	$4,173	$4,698	$4,300	($1,279)	$1,825	($958)	($3,210)	($2,053)	$3,062	($2,376)	($4,535)	$11,032	$10,300	($732)

$$\text{Net Sales} + \text{Returns} = \text{Gross Sales}$$

If net sales is 100% (and it always is), and if you have 10% returns, gross sales will be 110% of net sales. This reflects the major factor that returns play in the industry.

Following these line items, we'll have another revenue line that reflects other monies that have been received, whether from subsidiary rights (see chapter 10) or from some other source, such as interest income. For this reason, some publishers label this line other publishing income, instead of just subsidiary rights. Whatever you decide to call it, it forms a fourth line item.

Total sales, then, equals:

$$\text{Gross Sales} - \text{Returns} =$$
$$\text{Net Sales} + \text{Other Publishing Income} =$$
$$\text{Total Sales}$$

As you can see (and as I'll discuss in more detail later) because net sales always equal 100%, the addition of other publishing income can provide a significant boost to your total sales line. It will take your 100% net sales figure to something greater than that percentage, which gives you a running start when you begin to deduct expenses. Once you have the sales line totaled, you can move on to expenses.

The first kinds of expenses that you must recognize are those that relate to the cost of your products themselves; that is, your cost of goods. These consist of three elements:

1. Your actual *development costs*, including editing, copy editing, permissions, photography, design, getting the manuscript into printable form, etc. These one-time costs are also called *plant costs*. Plant costs can be written off, or amortized, completely in year one, or proportionately over a few years. Ask your accountant about how yours should be handled. (See the Title P&L discussion in chapter 7.)
2. The cost of actual paper, printing, and binding
3. Royalties

Totaling all of these and subtracting them from your total sales tells you your gross margin. After subtracting direct provisions, the result is your gross profit. Most trade publishers work on a gross profit of around 50% excluding other publishing income; 57% including other publishing income. In today's world, trade publishers should strive for gross margins before other publishing income of 55%.

Following the gross profit line, we begin to list our direct expenses and operating expenses.

Subtracting these operating expenses from the gross profit provides your contribution to profit line. This is also called EBITDA; that is, Earnings Before Interest, Taxes, Depreciation, and Amortization. Remember our discussion of cash flow? This is where many publishers mislead themselves. They look at this line and tend to forget about the lines that come next, including *taxes*. They think that because they have a good contribution to profit or operating profit, they'll be able to fund their growth internally.

But subtracting taxes from contribution to profit leaves you with significantly fewer dollars than you had before you paid the tax man. Subtracting the taxes leaves you with your net profit. And while this is an extremely important figure, I recommend that publishers focus on the contribution to profit line. You won't pay taxes if you don't have earnings.

Isn't this contradictory? Didn't I just say publishers get into trouble by focusing on contribution to profit and ignoring net profit? The answer is yes *and* no. Yes, if you're talking about funding your own growth from internal funds. Net profit is *crucial*, because this is where the net funds for such growth can come from. At the same time, you must manage to get your contribution to profit line as high as possible. If you do this, the impact of taxes may still leave you with a net profit. If you don't manage to maximize the contribution to profit line, taxes will diminish that line even more, leaving you with even less to plow back into your company.

In short, you must manage to increase your operating profit *and* decrease your taxes. This is why you need a wise financial team, which is an absolute must for every publisher.

This is the essence of the income statement. As you make transactions throughout the year, they find their way onto your income statement in one guise or another. The impact of every sale or expense is totaled, and your profitability is determined.

The key to the income statement, as I've said, is to use it as a primary management tool. Constantly benchmark your position against others in the industry. Use the figures from the Association of American Publishers (AAP) and those from the Huenefeld Surveys. Compare your ratios to those of other publishers, both large and small. How does your cost of goods percentage compare with the industry? How does your expense percentage for fulfillment compare? For marketing? For income from operations? Ask for the annual reports and 10ks of publicly owned publishers and study them. Read, especially closely, the footnotes, where much of the financial explanation and detail can be found. Study the financial statements of Barnes & Noble, Borders, Books-A-Million, and Amazon.com and get to know their financials and the dynamics of their businesses. The more you learn about them and about the industry as a whole, the better you'll manage your own company.

The more you work with, and become familiar with, income statements, the more they'll inform you about your company. The more they inform you, the better you'll manage your business.

The Balance Sheet

As noted above, the balance sheet tells us what the company looks like financially on a specific date. For many, the balance sheet is much more important than the income statement because it reflects every transaction that occurs in the business.

What the balance sheet really does is to summarize three factors that tell you where you stand as a business:

- Assets, or what you own
- Liabilities, or what you owe to others
- Owner's Equity, or capital, which is the difference between assets and liabilities, and which reflects the owner's share of the business

How does the balance sheet summarize this? It balances the three elements above in an equation:

$$\text{Assets} = \text{Liabilities} + \text{Owner's Equity or Capital}$$

Assets are things you own. They are primarily tangible. The only intangible asset for accounting purposes is goodwill.

Assets include

Current Assets
- Cash
- Accounts Receivable
- Inventory
- Prepaid Assets (work in process, advances, etc.)

Long-Term Assets
- Plant and Equipment
- Goodwill

Liabilities include

Current Liabilities
- Accounts Payable
- Royalties Payable
- Taxes Payable

Long-Term Liabilities
- Notes Payable

Owner's Equity consists of
- Stock
- Retained Earnings
- Year-to-Date Profit

Because of the intricacies of the balance sheet, I will not go into them in detail here. The details can be learned from your accountant, or a good book on accounting. I will limit my discussion to a few key elements that you should recognize.

Assets. This is what you own. Assets are listed in order of their liquidity, that is, by how fast they can be converted to cash.

    Cash. First, note the amount of cash on hand. This is real and tangible. At the same time, recognize that too much cash on hand may not be the best use of that cash. It might be better invested and earning money, put into new product development, or put into inventory.

    Accounts Receivable. A/R is another key asset. This is the result of the sales you've made that are yet to be collected from your accounts. Some A/R probably won't be collected and you need reserves for returns and for write-offs of uncollectible accounts. Still, if your business is growing, your accounts receivable will also be growing. The key is to keep control of your accounts receivable and not to let them go too far out. Try to keep your accounts paying as close to 30 to 60 days as possible. As a benchmark, the average for our industry is closer to 90 to 120 days.

Inventory. Here is your third primary asset. This is what you've produced and is sitting in your warehouse. This is money tied up. One of your primary goals should be to keep inventory to a minimum and to turn this inventory into cash, through sales, as soon as possible.

Cash and accounts receivable are usually called *liquid assets* because they are or can be turned into cash relatively quickly. Inventory, on the other hand, may not sell and could sit for years.

Liabilities. This is what you owe.

Accounts Payable. This is the primary liability account used every day. These are all of the bills that people send you for services they've provided. Manufacturing bills, rent bills, office-supply, bills and all the others.

Royalties Payable. These are the royalties accrued and owed to authors for books you have sold.

Taxes Payable. These include unpaid taxes of any kind, particularly payroll taxes.

Notes Payable. If you've borrowed money from a bank or from any other person or organization and you've signed a promissory note to pay that loan back, then you will have a loan payable on the books. Loans payable almost always require the payment of interest. If you've borrowed heavily, the loan payments can become extremely burdensome. These can either be long-term or short-term notes.

Owner's Equity. Owner's Equity is composed of three elements:
- the value of common stock outstanding
- retained earnings from prior years
- the year-to-date net profit

Using the Balance Sheet

For most publishers, working with the balance sheet entails looking at key ratios that tell how your business is doing.

Working Capital is the difference between current assets and current liabilities.

Current Assets - Current Liabilities = Working Capital

If positive, this means that the company should have money available after paying all its outstanding invoices and notes for investment in additional inventory, promotions, or other growth investments. This assumes, of course, that you will quickly collect accounts receivable and turn the inventory so it can generate additional accounts receivable and cash.

Conversely, if your working capital is negative, you won't have the funds necessary to cover your liabilities and will have to borrow more money, which will raise your interest payments.

Working capital is critical to your company. You must monitor the balance sheet to be sure that your working capital is in good shape.

Current Ratio is simply the total current assets divided by the total current liabilities:

$$\frac{\text{Current Assets}}{\text{Current Liabilities}} = \text{Current Ratio}$$

Most financial institutions look closely at this ratio before deciding whether to make loans. The reason is that it gives an indication of whether or not a company will be able to pay its bills when they are due. The more your current assets are greater than your current liabilities, the more cushion you should have to pay them.

A current ratio of 2:1 is considered good.

Quick Ratio is similar to the current ratio, but only takes into account those assets and liabilities that can be converted to cash quickly if a crisis hits. Thus, it includes cash and accounts receivable, but not inventory, because inventory can often take many months to sell and may not be worth to a buyer as much as it is worth to you. The Quick Ratio, therefore, tells you how much you can quickly convert to cash to pay your liabilities. Again, the greater the ratio the better, with 1:1 being a minimum.

$$\frac{\text{Current Assets (excluding inventory)}}{\text{Current Liabilities}} = \text{Quick Ratio}$$

Return on Equity (ROE). Any stockholder (and every business owner is a stockholder in one way or another) wants to earn a profitable return from the business in which he's invested. The return on equity measures this ratio of income to the stockholders' investment. Thus, the ratio is:

$$\frac{\text{Net income}}{\text{Stockholder's Equity}} = \text{Return on Equity}$$

In publishing, a return of 15% or more is considered very good. In other words, if you have net income of $15,000 on an investment of $100,000, you're doing well. Does this make sense? Yes, if you consider the alternative of keeping that $100,000 in the bank and earning a miserly 3–5% interest on that money. If, on the other hand, you can earn 30% a year by putting your money into a fund that matches the Standard & Poor's index of 500 stocks, as many did in the 1990s, then 15% looks somewhat less attractive!

Return on Assets (ROA) basically measures that which you can earn on your assets by using them in the business. The comparative would be that rate that you can earn on your money in the bank or in any other investment. This ratio is measured as:

$$\frac{\text{Operating Earnings Before Interest and Income Tax (EBITDA)}}{\text{Total Assets}} = \text{ROA}$$

In addition to these elements, you should again benchmark your percentages for each asset and liability item with those of your competitors and those of the industry. See how you stand up against them. And see how you stand up against the benchmarks you've set up for yourself. Only you, as the manager of your business, can set the hurdle rate you must achieve, or that rate at which you want your profitability to be. And only by monitoring and acting on the various items in your income statement, balance sheet, and cash-flow statement—by using them for strategic direction and action—can you achieve that rate.

Don't be intimidated by all of these accounting devices. The more you work with them, the more familiar they'll become and the easier they'll be for you to use. And the more you work with them, the more meaningful they'll be to you and your business.

Create a Board of Directors

An excellent way to keep control of a small or midsized company and to keep perspective on it is to establish a board of directors. This should consist of no more than five people (you don't want too many because it is difficult to get them in one place at the same time, and meetings can be difficult to manage) who bring outside expertise to bear on your company. Board members should be chosen not because they're friends, but because they can help focus your business. Some may be publishing experts; you may want a lawyer, an accountant or banker, a marketing expert, a manufacturing expert, or another businessperson you admire for her management skills. You want people who can look at your business on a regular basis and tell you what's going right and what's going wrong. Choose people who can tell you how to correct deficiencies or who have the expertise to guide you as your company grows.

A board of directors should have regular meetings, probably two per year. Each meeting should be well structured and planned far enough in advance to give those attending the chance to review materials and think about them. In advance of the meetings, you must provide a synopsis of the company in the form of income statements and balance sheets, but also in the form of up-to-date budgets and cash-flow charts. Where do you stand in relation to your budgets? You should be able to talk about the implications of these statements and what they mean in terms of running your business.

You'll probably want to have your functional managers talk about their areas, and inform the board about how sales are doing and other matters that may need to be evaluated objectively.

Don't be defensive. You don't want your board to be yes-people. You do want them to be active participants in the management process. And that means they'll tell you things your staff won't. This is exactly what you should request of them. If your management technique needs refining, let the board tell you. If you need help getting a bank loan, let the board give you perspective on it. If there are changes in the business environment, let the board help you reposition the company to address these issues. In short, create a board that will help you manage for growth. Let them be objective. That's what you want them to be.

CHAPTER 5

Keep Your Staff Lean
(But Not Necessarily Mean)

With the mission statement, goals and objectives, budgets, cash-flow projections, and job descriptions in hand, you are ready to staff your company.

One common mistake made by many new business ventures is to *overstaff* in the hope that having enough employees will allow the company to get off the ground quickly. The theory is that if each member has special talents, with good experience and contacts, those attributes can be brought to bear on the new venture with the result that new authors and manuscripts, better production terms, expanded sales, and attentive publicity will result.

That's the theory. The reality is often the contrary. Good people cost good money—perhaps more than you've budgeted. Such people often come from larger companies with greater expense budgets and assistants—and may not have experience working in smaller, entrepreneurial organizations where every dollar counts and where the boss keyboards every letter. Furthermore, in the effort to get sales, an expert, eager sales manager may oversell, and the company may not have the funds to support such sales—resulting in returns and poor credibility.

The point here is to be careful, be conservative, and be cautious. Err on the side of frugality rather than excess.

On the other hand, don't wait too long to hire the staff you need to be effective. You don't want to scatter your own efforts so much that you begin to leave things half-done—or not get to them at all. There is a fine balance between having too much staff and not enough. Only you can make the ultimate determination. Use the staff and salary guidelines which follow to help make your decision.

How much does good staff cost these days? Three ways to find out are to look at the *Publishers Weekly* salary issue, usually released in August each year, the Heunefeld-PubWest Survey, or the AAUP's annual salary survey. According to the most recent *PW* 2005 survey (July 11, 2005, issue), and the 2004 Heunefeld-PubWest Survey, the average salaries are:

	PW Companies of $1–$10 million	**PubWest** Total Sample
Management: **Net Average: $91,729**		
President/CEO/Publisher	91,729	118,499
Executive or Senior Vice President	92,606	N/A
Vice President/General Manager	72,280	N/A
Vice President Finance/Controller	54,183	67,543
Business/Office Manager	N/A	N/A
Editorial: **Net Average: $59,980**		
Editor-in-Chief	72,326	78,699
Managing Editor	42,855	51,896
Editor	57,238	55,335
Associate Editor	N/A	N/A
Editorial Assistant	29,967	30,137
Sales and Marketing: **Net Average: $61,447**		
Vice President Sales and Marketing	122,190	90,326
Sales Manager	69,631	60,057
Marketing Manager	46,534	52,253
Publicity Director	54,250	36,877
Operations: **Net Average: $37,217**		
Distribution/Fulfillment Director	N/A	41,736
Production Director	48,625	57,718
Accounting Manager / A/R Specialist	N/A	34,139
Rights Manager	N/A	39,394

How many people does a smaller publisher need to be efficient? Looking at the organization chart on page 35, we might focus on the top row of operating people, plus an assistant:

- President/Publisher to guide the business, acquire, and edit
- Sales & Marketing Manager
- Finance/Business Manager
- Production Manager
- Assistant

This certainly covers all of the functional bases. However, does it make sense given your current and future sales goals and budgets?

One general rule of thumb for staffing is that each staff member should be responsible for a minimum of $150,000 worth of net sales. That is, if you have four people on staff your company should be doing $600,000 in net sales revenue ($150,000 x 4). According to the 2001 PMA Salary Survey respondents, the average revenue per employee for the 207 responding companies was $157,895. If you are brand-new and don't know what your net sales will be, base your decision on your estimated sales, less a significant reserve for returns. Because you'll have no actual sales data, keep that reserve in the neighborhood of 40%. If you're pleasantly surprised, that's fine. You don't want to be unpleasantly surprised!

My own view is $150,000 is much too low for a start-up and for publishers in general. I suggest my clients aim for $200,000 to $250,000 or more in net sales per employee. Using this rule of thumb, the same company with the same four employees should generate a minimum of $800,000 to $1,000,000 in net sales to justify their presence.

What this means, of course, is that for those first critical years, your staff will be lean and mean. It must aggressively pursue and achieve significant productivity while minimizing expense—exactly the position you want to be in.

If you need additional help, you can find it temporarily by using freelance contractors who can be paid strictly for the work they do, without adding to your fixed overheads, without adding benefits, and without adding additional infrastructure. Three areas that lend themselves easily to the use of freelancers are design and production, manufacturing, and publicity. Each area has a wealth of expert freelance organizations available to do such work at extremely reasonable rates.

Talk with other publishers, contact the Publishers Marketing

Association and read its newsletter, read *Publishers Weekly*, and look at the *Literary Market Place* for advertisements and recommendations.

Freelancing design, production, and publicity allows you to concentrate on the two critical functions you need to ensure your success:

- Sales
- Editorial acquisition and development

No matter how small or large your publishing program, these are the two primary functions you should oversee and monitor in-house.

Does this mean that I recommend publishers do their own selling? Not necessarily—I'll get to that shortly. What it does mean is that every publisher must control and oversee its sales from in-house. Only in this way will the publisher truly understand where its sales are coming from and know what is selling. Without this essential knowledge, the company can't plan properly or understand the dynamics of its book sales and of the market itself. And outside sales personnel will simply not take the time to understand your books. That is your responsibility and it demands an in-house sales manager or coordinator.

Furthermore, an in-house sales manager or coordinator can help stimulate sales to nontraditional markets. She can spend time thinking about each book and where it will have the greatest sales potential. She can create marketing plans and coordinate an overall marketing and sales strategy. Again, this doesn't necessarily mean that person should sell to those defined markets. But it does mean that the person can intelligently direct sales—whether done herself or through the use of a commissioned sales staff or through a distributor—to the ultimate benefit of the book, the author, and the publishing house itself.

Given a sales and marketing manager and a president/publisher, I also recommend a finance/business manager. This person's role is to ensure that the publishing systems function smoothly and that financial parameters are in place and properly used.

The finance/business manager is the person who monitors or does Title P&Ls; works with the president/publisher to do the hands-on business plans, budgeting, cash flows; pays the bills; negotiates rent; monitors and pays royalties; and is responsible for other such business functions. It is this person's responsibility to raise red flags. But just as importantly, it's this person's responsibility to offer creative insight into improving systems to reduce cost, improve work flow and productivity, and control all financial matters in conjunction with your outside accountant, especially tracking cash flow, accounts receivable, and accounts payable.

If your in-house business manager is a constant naysayer who can't provide positive contributions to every staff member, then find a new business manager. Far too often people in these positions will readily tell you what won't work or what's not possible. The paradigm, as Steven Covey says, has to shift. You have to insist upon an approach that states "tell us what will work, and then help us do it!"

The fourth person who's generally needed in a smaller publishing company is an operations/fulfillment manager. This person's role is to set up and maintain the computer equipment, the warehousing and pick-pack-ship operation, the customer service function, and other such vital concerns.

Again, the actual fulfillment may in fact be done outside the company. But someone inside must understand the needs of these critical functions. It may be that the business manager can act as operations/fulfillment manager for a short, initial time. My feeling, however, is that the fulfillment manager is so important to the success of the company that the role should be filled at inception.

One last person generally needed at start-up is an assistant—someone who can do whatever is needed, when it's needed. This doesn't mean someone who just does menial work.

Rather, the assistant's role is to do that work that must be done—whatever it is, from helping with the business plan to providing sales assistance to packing books. The more responsibility this job gets, the greater understanding of the company the person will gain. As greater expertise is developed, this person can take on more and can ultimately be promoted. And promoting from within is the best way to develop staff continuity and team loyalty. By doing this you will facilitate the development of understanding and loyalty toward the company among your employees.

Another benefit of making this job wide-ranging is that there is very little opportunity in most larger companies for cross-training a staff member to learn more than one job and gain an overall knowledge of the company's functional areas. Giving an assistant varied jobs and experiences allows that person to learn how a publishing company integrates procedures and roles in the effort to create new books. This overall knowledge can be invaluable later in that person's career and will provide your company with backup when needed.

Staffing, in short, is just one aspect of your business that is as much art as science. The basic point is simply to keep your staff level under control at all times. Most smaller publishers don't need more than one or two editors or salespeople. Having said this, there are always valid reasons to make an exception. When doing this be sure it's a well-considered decision, not just a rationalization based on a whim.

The other significant point to recall is to base your staffing decisions upon sound goals and objectives. If you're about to hire an editor, for instance, what kind of books, and how many books, will she be responsible for bringing in? What sales figures should these books generate? What subject areas will that editor be responsible for?

People cannot, and should not, have to operate in a vacuum. The more a role is defined objectively, the easier it is for the person doing the job to know if he or she is succeeding or not. The easier it also will be for you to evaluate that performance objectively—be it success or failure.

People have an innate desire to do what's expected of them. Your job, as the manager, is to make absolutely clear what is expected, to provide your staff with the tools to do the job well, and to monitor performance and achievement periodically—guiding and correcting as necessary.

Staff and corporate loyalty have been damaged severely in this era of downsizing. Publishing in general has traditionally been an industry of high turnover where promotion comes through the acceptance of a new job with a competitor, not primarily from internal recognition. I continue to believe that this high rate of turnover is ultimately detrimental to the company, if not the individual.

Good management encourages people to grow within their roles and to learn more about the company as a whole. Ultimately, it allows good employees to expand those roles and take on new ones as they develop the necessary expertise. If you concentrate on these principles, the benefits that will accrue to the company will come in low staff turnover and an educated, knowledgeable staff upon which you can rely.

Don't forget, if someone comes to your company merely for a few extra dollars, that person will probably leave you for some other company offering still more money. It's up to you to provide other inducements that make your company unique, that make a staff member want to stay with you, and that breed loyalty.

CHAPTER 6

Protect Your Assets

Like all other businesses, publishing companies, whether one-book firms or Goliaths, are ultimately deemed successful or not by whether they are profitable and how much they are worth when they are sold. Every action taken within a company should be done with the ultimate goals of profitability, and company salability, in mind.

If you approach your business with these two key factors in mind, then every decision you make will help incrementally build your company for success, which can be defined as its positive future value. As Bill Fisher, founder of HP Books and Fisher Books, pointed out so well, your product is not just one book. It is much more than that. Your product is your company itself. To build the value of each, and both, you must protect every asset of your business. (The only exceptions to this overriding strategy toward profitability are those books published, or services rendered, for ulterior, clearly defined, motives, especially those done for pro bono reasons.)

What are the assets of a publishing house? As we saw in relation to the balance sheet, they consist of

- Cash
- Accounts Receivable
- Inventory

- Prepaid Assets
- Plant and Equipment
- Intangible Assets

While protecting most of these—cash, accounts receivable, inventory, and plant and equipment—seems straightforward, protecting cash and accounts receivable needs some attention and intangible assets needs substantial explanation.

Cash and Accounts Receivable

While protecting cash and accounts receivable would seem obvious, it's always amazing to see how few smaller publishers actually have systems in place to ensure the security of these assets and how little thought is given to this critical task. While you want to believe in the honesty and integrity of your employees, I've personally seen, too often, outright theft and manipulation of the financial accounts. And it almost always could have been prevented.

Frequently, the same person will be responsible for invoicing, collection, posting to the accounts, taking the money to the bank, and reconciling the bank account. While it doesn't happen often, it is all too easy for that person to mishandle the funds or to siphon some off for her own purposes.

Your product is your company itself.

It is up to you, as manager of your company, to set up the procedures to secure your cash and receivables. These systems must account for opening the mail, handling cash, recording the receipt of checks and cash, getting that money to the bank, reconciling the bank account, and writing your checks. The key idea to remember is that the same person must not be responsible for all of these functions.

If you have employees and you are not personally dealing with all of the checks, cash, and accounts receivable, you must divide the work. One person tallies the cash and checks for deposit into the company's bank account, and another posts them to the accounts. A third person should then be responsible for tallying the same money and the two tallies should be the same. Your auditor or accountant will be able to reconcile your revenues with your bank deposits so you can be sure the two are equal. And, your auditor or accountant will be able to reconcile your receipts with your bank deposits so you can be sure the two are equal. Remember, the person writing the checks must never be the one reconciling the bank account!

Any person who is handling money or writing checks should be bonded or your insurance should be written to include protection against employee dishonesty. Your insurance agent can handle this. If your company is doing $5 million or more annually, seriously consider having a formal audit. While it's definitely more costly than a typical review, the audit will protect you better. And when you ultimately sell the company, the audit will provide you and the buyer with the historical and current documentation you need and want.

Intangible Assets

When discussing intangible assets, I should immediately say there is a difference between the accounting definition of intangible assets and the legal or everyday definition of this term. In accounting, as I noted in discussing the balance sheet, intangible assets refers only to what is called *goodwill*, or that amount received for the company when it's purchased, over and above its book value. This excess may derive from a variety of factors, including simply competitive bidding from other companies interested in purchasing the firm being sold. The legal definition of intangible assets is more commonly used in publishing. It refers to those assets that can't be readily valued by themselves (such as cash and accounts receivable) or by the initial value less amortization or depreciation.

The most important intangible assets for a publisher are contracts and copyrights, which protect the publisher's work from plagiarism and other forms of infringement. If filed properly, today's "new" copyright law protects the work in question, if written by an individual, for a period of fifty years from the date of the author's death—a substantial amount of time. Other time periods apply to different kinds of works, so be sure to check with the U.S. Copyright Office.

For this reason publishers must ensure they have contracts guaranteeing them the right to publish for the life of the copyright. Whether the copyright is in the publisher's name or the author's, the publisher must have the right to publish the work transferred to it through the wording of the contract. (See Contracts, page 98.)

How much are copyrights worth? That is a very tough question to answer. In some cases, if the book covered by the copyright isn't sell-

You need systems in place to secure your assets.

ing, it may be worth very little. On the other hand, if the book is a perennial seller, that one copyright alone may be worth more than the company itself would otherwise be worth.

One example of how important a copyright is, and how much it's worth, can be seen by looking at the history of Vanguard Press. This small, literary press, started in 1924 by a labor leader who wanted to publish inexpensive books for the working class, published a variety of books over a period of 64 years. During that time, it was responsible for publishing the first novels of authors who were to become extremely well known. These included Saul Bellow; Nelson Algren; James T. Farrell (author of *Studs Lonigan*); Pierre Boulle (*Bridge Over the River Kwai* and *Planet of the Apes*); Patrick Dennis (*Auntie Mame*); Joyce Carol Oates (*Them* and 22 other books); and the first two books of someone totally unknown in 1934—Theodore Geisel, better known as Dr. Seuss.

For a variety of reasons throughout its history, Vanguard remained a smaller publisher, never exceeding $1 million in annual sales. And like other smaller publishers, it had the same problem as most, trying to hold on to its authors when they became better known and attract-ed the attention—and advance money—of the larger publishers. Over time, Vanguard lost most of its better-known authors to the larg-er houses. So when the company ultimately had to be sold due to the owner's declining health, the question was, what was it worth?

Two factors were working in the company's favor: First, it pub-lished books under the theory that it would always keep them in print if at all possible. This gave the company a large backlist of contracts and copyrights that were still valid. Second, the company had what one other house coveted: the first two Dr. Seuss books. Random House wanted these two titles (*The 500 Hats of Bartholomew Cubbins* and *And to Think That I Saw It on Mulberry Street*) because it could then put all of the Dr. Seuss titles under its corporate umbrella. With this accomplished, Random House could market the entire Dr. Seuss library in any way it wanted.

In this case, these two books were worth more than the sum of all the other Vanguard titles combined. They, in fact, determined the selling price of the company. And for that reason, Vanguard Press decided to sell to Random House, who continues to capitalize fully on the Dr. Seuss books.

Your strategy as a publisher must be to build asset value.

Your strategy as a publisher must be to build asset value—and the best way to do that is to publish books that sell well over time. As the number of those books grows, your asset base grows—assuming you hold the contracts granting you publishing rights for as long as the book remains in print.

Many publishers think that a quick way to enter the publishing arena is to buy books from *packagers*, companies that create books and then sell them to publishers for publication. While this technique is fine for building revenue and profits (assuming the book is purchased for the right price in the right quantity, priced correctly at retail, and sells through to the consumer) almost all packagers retain copyright for themselves. Thus, when the publisher ultimately decides to sell to someone else, those packaged books will be excluded from the valuation of the company unless there is a transfer clause in the contract granting your company publishing rights.

I strongly encourage clients to create their own books or acquire books from authors because it ultimately accrues to the benefit of all. One can never tell what book may be the one that will be worth more than the others combined. But if the publisher doesn't have the intangible asset, whether the copyright or contractual right to the book, that publisher will surely regret it when he goes to sell the company. The publisher must always keep in mind why he's in business—to make a profit. Protecting one's assets, both tangible and intangible, is essential when pursuing that goal.

Copyrights

The best way to protect your copyright assets is to register your books with the Register of Copyrights at the Library of Congress. While registration is not required legally, such registration establishes a fixed date that you can point to if another party claims you've infringed upon their copyright or if you claim a third party has infringed upon your copyright. Legally, the copyright act of 1976 makes actual publication of a work unnecessary for copyright protection. Protection

You should register every book you publish and insert a copyright notice on the copyright page of your book.

begins with the act of creation. However, creation is a process that can take time. If someone else is also creating a work that happens to be similar to yours and doing so at the same time as you are, it may be difficult to verify that you created your work first. Registering your copyright with the Copyright Office helps avoid this problem.

Because the act of copyright involves any number of legal interpretations, you should leave it to your attorney to deal with the intricacies of the Copyright Act and how it can affect your company. Suffice it to say, you should absolutely register every book you publish and insert a copyright notice on the copyright page of your book.

How do you do this? It's explained simply in Circular 1, *Copyright Basics*, available directly from the Copyright Office at the Library of Congress. Get it. It's a simple explanation of those aspects of copyright that you'll need to know, and the publication is free.

The copyright notice can take a variety of formats but should contain all of the following, which is quoted directly from Circular 1:

> The notice for visually perceptible copies should contain all of the following three elements
> 1. The symbol © (the letter C in a circle), or the word "copyright," or the abbreviation "Copr."; and
> 2. The year of first publication of the work. In the case of compilations or derivative works incorporating previously published material, the year date of first publication of the compilation or derivative work is sufficient. The year date may be omitted where a pictorial, graphic or sculptural work, with accompanying textual matter, if any, is reproduced in or on greeting cards, postcards, stationery, jewelry, dolls, toys or any useful article; and
> 3. The name of the owner of copyright in the work, or an abbreviation by which the name can be recognized, or a generally known alternative designation of the owner. For example:
>   "© 2006 John Doe"

You can get Circular 1, *Copyright Basics*, as well as all the appropriate copyright forms you'll need to register your books by calling, 24 hours a day, the Copyright Office Forms Hotline at 202-707-9100 or by writing:

Publications Section, LM-455
Copyright Office
Library of Congress
101 Independence Avenue S.E.
Washington, DC 20559-6000

If you prefer, speak with an information specialist at the Copyright Office by calling 202-707-3000 from 8:30 A.M. to 5:00 P.M. EST Monday through Friday. The forms are online at www.copyright.gov/circs/circ1.html.

Also, download a variety of forms including **Form TX** (see pages 96–97), used for "published and unpublished non-dramatic literary works" by accessing the Library of Congress website at www.loc.gov/copyright. You'll need Acrobat Reader to view and print the forms, but that too is available free from the Adobe Systems website: www.adobe.com.

When you're finally ready to submit your book for registration, you must send in one package

1. A completed application form
2. A nonrefundable check for $30.00 per application made payable to the Register of Copyrights
3. A nonreturnable copy of each work you're registering. If that's a manuscript, you need only send one copy. If it's a book first published in the United States on or after January 1978, send two copies. If it's a book first published outside the United States, send one complete copy as first published.

One question that frequently arises in relation to copyright is who should register the work? The law stipulates that it can be done by either

1. The author
2. The copyright claimant, defined as "either the author of the work or a person or organization that has obtained ownership of all the rights under the copyright initially belonging to the author." This

Copyright Form TX

FORM TX
For a Literary Work
UNITED STATES COPYRIGHT OFFICE

REGISTRATION NUMBER

TX _____ TXU

EFFECTIVE DATE OF REGISTRATION

Month _____ Day _____ Year

DO NOT WRITE ABOVE THIS LINE. IF YOU NEED MORE SPACE, USE A SEPARATE CONTINUATION SHEET.

1

TITLE OF THIS WORK ▼

PREVIOUS OR ALTERNATIVE TITLES ▼

PUBLICATION AS A CONTRIBUTION If this work was published as a contribution to a periodical, serial, or collection, give information about the collective work in which the contribution appeared.   Title of Collective Work ▼

If published in a periodical or serial give: Volume ▼   Number ▼   Issue Date ▼   On Pages ▼

2 **a**

NAME OF AUTHOR ◀▼

DATES OF BIRTH AND DEATH
Year Born ▼   Year Died ▼

Was this contribution to the work a "work made for hire"?
☐ Yes
☐ No

AUTHOR'S NATIONALITY OR DOMICILE
Name of Country
OR { Citizen of ▶_____
     Domiciled in ▶_____

WAS THIS AUTHOR'S CONTRIBUTION TO THE WORK
Annonymous?   ☐ Yes ☐ No
Pseudonymous? ☐ Yes ☐ No

If the answer to either of these questions is "Yes," se detailed instructions.

NATURE OF AUTHORSHIP Briefly describe nature of material created by this author in which copyright is claimed. ▼

NOTE
Under the law, the "author" of a "work made for hire" is generally the employer, not the employee (see instructions). For any part of this work that was "made for hire" check "Yes" in the space provided, give the employer (or other person for whom the work was prepared) as Author" of that part, and leave the space for date, of birth and death blank.

b

NAME OF AUTHOR ▼

DATES OF BIRTH AND DEATH
Year Born ▼   Year Died ▼

Was this contribution to the work a "work made for hire"?
☐ Yes
☐ No

AUTHOR'S NATIONALITY OR DOMICILE
Name of Country
OR { Citizen of ▶_____
     Domiciled in ▶_____

WAS THIS AUTHOR'S CONTRIBUTION TO THE WORK
Annonymous?   ☐ Yes ☐ No
Pseudonymous? ☐ Yes ☐ No

If the answer to either of these questions is "Yes," se detailed instructions.

NATURE OF AUTHORSHIP Briefly describe nature of material created by this author in which copyright is claimed. ▼

c

NAME OF AUTHOR ▼

DATES OF BIRTH AND DEATH
Year Born ▼   Year Died ▼

Was this contribution to the work a "work made for hire"?
☐ Yes
☐ No

AUTHOR'S NATIONALITY OR DOMICILE
Name of Country
OR { Citizen of ▶_____
     Domiciled in ▶_____

WAS THIS AUTHOR'S CONTRIBUTION TO THE WORK
Annonymous?   ☐ Yes ☐ No
Pseudonymous? ☐ Yes ☐ No

If the answer to either of these questions is "Yes," se detailed instructions.

NATURE OF AUTHORSHIP Briefly describe nature of material created by this author in which copyright is claimed. ▼

3 **a**

YEAR IN WHICH CREATION OF THIS WORK WAS COMPLETED
This information must be given in all cases. ◀Year

b DATE AND NATION OF FIRST PUBLICATION OF THIS PARTICULAR WORK
Complete this information ONLY if this work has been published. Month▶_____ Day▶_____ Year▶_____
◀Nation

4

See instructions before completing this space.

COPYRIGHT CLAIMANT(S) Name and address must be given even if the claimant is the same as the author given in space 2. ▼

TRANSFER If the claimant(s) named here in space 4 is (are) different from the author(s) named in space 2, give a brief ststement of how the claimant(s) obtained ownership of the copyright. ▼

APPLICATION RECEIVED

ONE DEPOSIT RECEIVED

TWO DEPOSITS RECEIVED

FUNDS RECEIVED

DO NOT WRITE HERE OFFICE USE ONLY

MORE ON BACK ▶
• Complete all applicable spaces (numbers 5-11) on the reverse side of this page.
• Sn detaild instructions   • Sign the form at line 10.

DO NOT WRITE HERE
Page 1 of _____ pages

Copyright Form TX *continued*

EXAMINED BY	FORM TX
CHECKED BY	
☐ CORRESPONDENCE Yes	FOR COPYRIGHT OFFICE USE ONLY

DO NOT WRITE ABOVE THIS LINE. IF YOU NEED MORE SPACE, USE A SEPARATE CONTINUATION SHEET.

PREVIOUS REGISTRATION Has registration for htis work, or for an earlier version of this work, already been made in the Copyright Office?
n Yes n No If your answer is "Yes," why is another registration being sought? (Check appropriate box) ▼
a. ☐ This is the first published edition of a work previously registered in unpublished form.
b. ☐ This is the first application submitted by this author as copyright claimant.
c. ☐ This is a changed version of the work, as shown by space 6 on this application.
If your answer is "Yes," give: Previous Registration Number ▼   Year of Registration ▼

5

DERIVATIVE WORK OR COMPILATION Complete both space 6a and 6b for a derivative work; complete only 6b for a compilation.
a. Preexisting Material Identify any preexisting work or works that this work is based on or incorporates. ▼

b. Material Added to This Work Give a brief, general statement of the material that has been added to this work and in which copyright is claimed. ▼

6

See instructions
before completeing
this space.

—space deleted—

7

REPRODUCTION FOR USE OF BLIND OR PHYSICALLY HANDICAPPED INDIVIDUALS A signature on this form at space 10 and a check in one of the boxes here in space 8 constitutes a non-exclusive grant of permission to the Library of Congress to reproduce and distribute solely for the blind and physically handicapped and under the conditions and limitations prescribed by the regulations of the Copyright Office: (1) copies of the work identified in space 1 of this application in Braille (or similar tactile symbols); or (2) phonorecords embodying a fixation of a reading of that work; or (3) both.
a ☐ Copies and Phonorecords   b ☐ Copies Only   c ☐ Phonorecords Only

8

See instructions.

DEPOSIT ACCOUNT If the registration fee is to be charged to a Deposit Account established in the Copyright Office, give name and number of Account.
Name ▼   Account Number ▼

9

CORRESPONDENCE Give name and address to which correspondence about this application should be sent. Name/Address/Apt/City/State/ZIP ▼

Be sure to
give your
daytime phone
number

Area Code and Telephone Number ▶

CERTIFICATION* I, the undersigned, hereby certify that I am the   ☐ author
                                          Check only one ▶   ☐ other copyright claimant
                                                                     ☐ owner of exclusive right(s)
of the work identified in this application and that the statements made   ☐ authorized agent of
by me in this application are correct to the best of my knowledge.   Name of author or other copyright claimant, or owner of exclusive right(s) ▲
Typed or printed name and date ▼ If this application gives a date of publication in space 3, do not sign and submit it before that date.
_____ date ▶ _____

☞ Handwritten signature (X) ▼

10

MAIL CERTIFI-CATE TO

Name ▼

Number/Street/Apartment Number ▼

City/State/Zip ▼

Certificate will be mailed in window envelope

YOU MUST:
• Complete all necessary spaces
• Sign your application in sapce 10
SEND ALL 3 ELEMENTS IN THE SAME PACKAGE.
1. Application form
2. Application form $20 filing fee in check or money order payable to Register of Copyrights
3 Deposit material
MAIL TO:
Register of Copyrights
Library of Congress
Washington D.C. 20559-6000

11

*17 U.S.C. § 506(e): Any person who knowingly makes a false representation of a material fact in the application for copyright registration provided for by section 409, or in any written statement filed in connection with the application, shall be fined not more than $2,500.

January 1995-400,000 ♻ PRINTED ON RECYCLED PAPER   ☆ U.S. GOVERNMENT PRINTING OFFICE: 1995-387-237/34

category includes a person or organization who has obtained by contract the right to claim legal title to the copyright in an application for copyright registration.
3. The owner of exclusive right(s)
4. The duly authorized agent of such author, other copyright claimant, or owner of exclusive rights

The key point is that if the registration is not made by the author, then that author must transfer the rights to another party, who will then be able to file for copyright. This transfer is done by contract, not by a form from the copyright office. Almost all publishing contracts have wording that specifies that the author transfers the right to publish the work to the publisher for the duration of the contract.

Contracts

Every book you publish should have a signed contract giving your company the right to publish that book. Contracts provide the primary value to a publishing house because they give the house the many and varied rights needed to produce and sell the book in question. Without a contract, no publisher should publish a book, unless all aspects of the book are in the public domain; that is, if the time of copyright has expired and the book can no longer be copyrighted.

As we'll see in Part III, chapter 7, in a much fuller discussion of contracts, the basic contract between author and publisher spells out exactly who owns what, and the consideration, or who owes what to whom for the use of those rights. The broader the grant of rights to the publisher from the author, the greater the potential value to the publisher if those rights can be sold.

A key provision of most contracts stipulates that the publisher can assign that contract to any company that buys the assets of the publisher. It is the contracts that permit the publisher to publish, that give value to the publishing company. Without contracts, or the ability to assign those contracts to others, there is little of value to any purchaser. Thus it is absolutely critical to protect all aspects of your contracts and to get the broadest grant of rights you can.

One aspect of contracts often overlooked relates to publishers who are also authors. These are probably self-publishers, but may be sole owners, presidents of S-corporations or members of partnerships who are publishing their own work through their companies. More likely than not, these authors do not have contracts for their work between themselves and their companies. Who, they would probably ask, would we contract with? Why do we need a contract when we're working for ourselves or our companies are publishing our books? After all, we trust ourselves!

Publishers who are also authors should have a contract for each of their books.

The reason is straightforward. As we've seen, companies can buy and sell their assets to others. This includes inventory as well as contracts. If the author has no contract with his company for his book, then there is no way to determine what rights might be conveyed to the purchaser. There is no way to determine what the future royalty payments are, how long the grant of rights is for, and other such questions that are answered by the contract. If, on the other hand, the owner has a contract with his company, he can protect himself in the short term by paying himself royalties. In the longer term, he is protected because his contract will be assigned to any purchaser, along with others controlled by the company, who will then be legally responsible for fulfilling the provisions of those assigned contracts.

Although you may or may not earn much from your works, it's virtually impossible to know what the long-term success of a book might be. If you have a contract with your company and you sell the company, the company to whom you sell may well be bought by another company. It is common for one publisher to purchase the assets of another because *backlist* (which we define as those books that have already been sold once to retail or wholesaler buyers and have extended sales life) is a valuable commodity to those who want to start publishing companies, or to those already in business. If your book happens to sell well over the long term and your book stays in print, then you definitely want a contract that stipulates what you should receive for that publisher's right to sell the book.

I will discuss the overall publishing contract, and individual contract clauses, in detail in chapter 7.

Trademarks

While publishers are particularly interested in copyright because it extends to the printed, tangible word, other forms of protection extend to intellectual property as well and are available if your products meet certain requirements. They can protect words, symbols, designs (such as logos), or images that are actually used. Use, in fact, is one of the defining hallmarks of an item that is trademarked and trademarks can be lost if use is not continuous. Because trademarks can get legally complex, and because they don't usually refer to manuscripts or individual books (though a series, such as the *Chicken Soup for the Soul* books, may be trademarked), I will not go into a discussion of them here.

At the same time, if you have a readily identifiable image or mark or series title that you want to protect, and that you think contains value in and of itself, then I urge you to investigate trademarks and the possibility of registering your trademarks with the state or federal patent and trademark offices.

For further, excellent information about all of the legal aspects of publishing, read *Kirsch's Handbook of Publishing Law* (Acrobat Books), by Jonathan Kirsch, noted author, book reviewer, and publishing attorney, or Lloyd Jassin's *The Copyright, Permission, and Libel Handbook* (John Wiley and Sons).

PART III

Functional Organization: Strategy and Techniques

CHAPTER 7

The Editorial Process

Most of the time, the easiest way to manage is to *standardize the processes people use to make decisions*. If the result of that process allows people to determine quickly and decisively that something will or will not work, it makes them think harder and more fully about the underlying issues, while keeping it off of your desk in formative stages.

One excellent way to provide organizational structure to your staff is to set up templates that can quickly determine and illustrate whether certain functions meet the criteria that have been agreed upon. These templates can be formulated and used in every functional department throughout the company.

Editorial Category Planning

One of the most essential requirements for any publishing company is to know exactly what is being published and when it is due to be published. Surprisingly, many smaller publishers have no systematic way of looking at this function. These publishers live in a short-turn-around world where a manuscript literally comes in one month and may be published the next. Leaving enough time to publish properly is not an issue; just publishing is.

In publishing as in many other businesses, *there is a very fine balance between maximizing your revenue and optimizing your cash flow. Your editorial program (that is, your product development function) is, in effect, the basis of your cash flow.* You can easily reduce your cash flow by taking too long to find new products, by paying for the development and manufacture of your products too early, and by leaving sales opportunities either behind or too far ahead to generate the revenue you need to survive. Going to the other extreme, you can just as easily hold off on your development and production in an effort to conserve cash and fall prey to the difficulty of not having enough material far enough in advance to maximize your sales effort.

In publishing, cash-flow concerns are inextricably related to the acquisition process, which can, but doesn't always, necessitate spending money out of pocket for author advances and manuscript purchases. The fact is, author advances may be necessary years before a manuscript might be finally submitted. Because publishers don't like to offend authors and agents, authors writing trade books can usually get extensions on the time they need to write those books. In the professional publishing area, deadlines are almost always moving targets because authors are usually academics who, because of their teaching, consulting, and other related jobs, have concerns that impede their ability to deliver on time.

Given these situations, delays constantly occur throughout the entire process of publishing, which immediately impacts cash flow. Editorial staff, indexers, art and photography, permissions, all must be paid, in most cases, prior to the book's on-sale date. Paper, printing, and binding costs also must be paid on time to maintain one's credit standing with manufacturers. For many publishers this means payment within 30 days of completion of the job; for new or smaller publishers it can mean paying partially in advance of printing.

It is imperative, therefore, that every publisher plan its editorial program and flow as precisely as possible. This, in turn, together with the figures generated by the Title P&L described on page 112, begins to provide a realistic look at the future, both in terms of what your company should acquire, when it should acquire it, and the resulting cash flow that the program will generate. The primary planning objective is to allow enough time to write and produce your book while at the same time minimizing the time you are out-of-pocket for cash.

Your editorial program is the basis of your cash flow.

How much time is enough time? How much time should you leave between the time of signing the contract for a manuscript and the time it's published? At least 24 months. Do larger publishers work this far in advance? Some, but not all. Why should you leave this amount of time? That deserves a bit of explanation.

Between the time you sign a contract for a book and the time it's published, a variety of tasks must be performed to ensure that the book will generate as much revenue as possible. What has to happen within the time frame to maximize sales and orders?

1. Editors must have time to work on the book to ensure its accuracy and quality. This is pretty straightforward. If you don't have the final manuscript in final form, you won't have a very good book, if you have a book at all.
2. Sales and Marketing need to know exactly what books they'll be selling in the next season, and preparations for the next season usually begin 12 months in advance. (See chapter 2.)
3. Subsidiary-rights people must get manuscripts and jackets to begin to generate serial-rights sales and book-club sales. Serial rights sales are sales of excerpts from your book to magazines and others that are looking for editorial material for their own needs. Serial rights are broken down into first serial, those sold prior to a book's publication; and second serial, those sold after a book's publication. Both serial rights and book-club sales must fit the magazine's or book club's publishing schedules—not yours. You must work within the magazine's or book club's scheduling needs; if you can't, your competitors will—and they will get the sales.

How much time do magazines and book clubs need? Most magazines schedule their feature articles about six months in advance of publication. Book clubs determine main selections even further ahead—around one year in the best of cases. Alternate selections are usually chosen on a much shorter timetable, perhaps nine months.

Thus, as a publisher trying to sell these buyers, you must show them material six months to one year in advance if you are to be consistently successful. Ask yourself, then, how far in advance will you know the books you are to publish, and when will you have material to send to these buyers?

If we look at editorial acquisition as a flow chart, ideally it would look like this:

Mission Statement
▼
3-Year Editorial Plan
▼
Manuscript Solicitation
▼
Editorial Meeting
▼
Title Profit and Loss Statements
▼
Proposal Meeting
▼
Contract Negotiation

I have already discussed the mission statement, so you should have an understanding of its usefulness in focusing the company's broad strategy into a more narrow, targeted strategic approach, especially in defining that company's editorial thrust. The mission statement is the beginning of the editorial process. Once defined, however, you must begin to act upon that mission statement and focus the product line even more. This is where the 3-Year Editorial Plan comes in.

The easiest way to view your current and future editorial program is to do so by category. Remember, you aren't trying to be all things to all people—you have defined your program and are now focusing strictly on the categories in which you have special knowledge or expertise or on those in which you know there is particular opportunity. You want to capitalize on your strengths and the weaknesses of your competitors, which you have identified through your competitive research.

Begin your editorial planning by listing the categories of your publishing program down the left side of your template, and the current and future publishing seasons along the top of the template; see **3-Year Editorial Plan.** The time periods should conform to your selling seasons, which may be annual or semiannual, usually spring and fall. In some cases, especially if you happen to have the good fortune of being distributed by a large publisher, you may have three seasons.

When you've decided on the time periods, place those titles you already have under contract in the time period *in which they'll be sold.*

3-Year Editorial Plan

	Spring 2006	Fall 2006	Spring 2007	Fall 2007	Spring 2008	Fall 2008
			Spring 2006 – Fall 2008			
Category 1						
Category 2						
Category 3						
Category 4						
Category 5						
Category 6						
Category 7						
Category 8						

If you're unsure of the time period, make it later rather than sooner.

When you've completed this simple task, look at the results. What do they tell you?

- If you have only one book, it probably means you'll have to focus on finding distribution and finding new titles. Finding distributors won't be easy because most distributors or sales rep groups won't take on one-book publishers. Immediately, you have a major sales problem. (See chapter 9 on Sales and Marketing.)
- If you're publishing more than one title, are they in the same category? In the same selling season? Can you combine your selling and marketing efforts to achieve savings or maximum return for your promotional effort and dollars? How can you get other titles within the same category and how will you stagger their publication to ensure an ongoing presence in the marketplace?
- If you have books in more than one category, do you have the marketing budget to support each? Will you continue to acquire books in multiple categories? Keep in mind that to the outside world, your niche is defined primarily by the continuity of your editorial program. You may want to spread the publishing risk over various categories, but until you achieve a critical mass in each area, you will not achieve recognition or market penetration in any significant way, nor will you achieve economies of scale in your selling and marketing efforts.

In short, the 3-Year Editorial Plan allows you to see your overall program, by category, succinctly. With this in hand, you will know exactly what slots need to be filled and when you are long or short on books within categories, seasons, and years.

Comparative Book Template and Review

To identify promising areas and subjects for new books, areas that may be overpublished, and subjects to avoid, I recommend a simple technique. Drop into four or more of your local bookstores, both chain stores and independents. Supplement this with visits to online databases such as Amazon.com and BarnesandNoble.com. Review *Books in Print* and the Spring and Fall Announcement Issues of *Publishers*

Comparative Book Template

TITLE	AUTHOR/ORGANIZATION	PUBLISHER	HC/PB	Size	# Pages	# Colors	Price	Price/Page	© Date	Comments
Garden Style	Penelope Hobhouse	Willow Creek Press	HC	8" x 12"	216	4	29.95	0.14	1988	Packaged by Frances Lincoln
Growing Bulbs: The Complete Practical Guide	Brian Mathew	Timber	HC	6" x 9"	156	4	29.95	0.19	1997	ID Shots
Hardie Newton's Celebrat. of Flow	Hardie Newton	Storey	HC	8 1/2" x 11"	192	4	27.95	0.15	1997	By season. Memoir; Ideas
Heirloom Vegetable Gardening	William Weaver	Henry Holt	HC	8" x 10"	460	1	45.00	0.10	1997	3 - 8 pg. color inserts
Herb Garden Design	Ethne Clarke	Macmillan	HC	9 1/2" x 9 1/2"	144	4	25.00	0.17	1995	Packaged by Frances Lincoln
Horticulture: Well-Clad Windows Houseplants for Four Exposures	Tovah Martin/ Horticulture	Horticulture/Macmillan	HC	8" x 9"	212	4	27.50	0.13	1994	in assoc. with Horticulture
Ideal Home: The Planter's Guide	David Joyce	Conran Octopus	HC	9" x 10"	160	4	27.50	0.17	1995	Ideas.
Malcolm Hillier's Color Garden: A Year Round Guide to Creatg. Co	Malcolm Hillier	Dorling Kindersley	HC	9" x 11 1/2"	160	4	29.95	0.19	1995	
Martha Stewart's Gardening Month by Month	Martha Stewart	Clarkson Potter	HC	10" x 10"	360	4	50.00	0.14	1991	Idea book; not practical
The New Gardener: The Practical Guide to Gardening	Pippa Greenwood	Dorling Kindersley	HC	8 1/2" x 11"	176	4	24.95	0.14	1995	40 projects; 750 Illus.
The Patio Garden Month-by-Month	Michael Jeffers-Brown	David & Charles	HC	8" x 10"	144	4	24.95	0.17	1997	Nice idea; fair execution
Practical Small Gardening	Peter McHoy	Lorenz Books (Anness)	HC	10" x 10"	192	4	16.95	0.09	1997	Nice Photos, Illus. Step-by-Step
Pruning: A Practical Guide	Pater McHoy	Abbeville	HC	7" x 10"	240	4	35.00	0.15	1993	Packaged by Quarto
Rodale's Illus'd Ency. Perennials	Ellen Phillips	Rodale	HC	7 1/2" x 9 1/8"	533	4	29.95	0.06	1994	407,300 in print #6 Ingram Top 50
What Perenials Where	Roy Lancaster	Dorling Kindersley	HC	7" x 10"	160	4	24.95	0.16	1997	Well executed concept
What Plant Where	Roy Lancaster	Dorling Kindersley	HC	7" x 10"	256	4	24.95	0.10	1995	Well executed concept
A Year of Roses: A Month-by-Mont	Stephan Scanniello	Holt	HC	5 1/2" x 8 1/4"	190	2	25.00	0.13	1997	Very minor use of 2nd color
American Garden Guide Series Shrubs and Vines	Elvin McDonald, Series Edtr Holden Arb., Royal Bot. Soc; Chicago Bot. Gdn. Missouri Bot. Gdn.	Pantheon	Flexibind	6 1/8" x 9 1/4"	224	4	25.00	0.11	1994	Plasticized covers No Step-by-Step
Annuals										
Oriental										
Water Gardening										
Vegetables										
Average price per page:					235		28.94	0.13		

© Copyright 1997 Cross River Publishing Consultants

Weekly; review other publishers' catalogs. Approach all of these using a simple **Comparative Book Template** (see page 109).

The object of the template is to centralize and organize similar title information so trends become visible. I emphasize that this technique is *not* absolutely foolproof or complete. It is based upon those titles currently stocked on a random selection of bookstore shelves as well as those titles that are currently being sold and announced. Thus, some titles on the shelf will be brand-new. Others will be older titles. In essence, what you want to know is what titles are now selling. If they are older titles, it implies that they have shelf life, or longevity—which is because people buy them. (*Shelf life* is the length of time a book continues to sell and stays on the shelf in the store.) Titles with shelf life have become essential backlist. If they are new titles, you want to determine if a trend is beginning that will allow you to publish into it, or if there are already too many books on that particular subject to allow for easy entry of another new title.

Each Comparative Book Template should be used to focus on one subject category, using as many pages as needed. As the template is analyzed, you will have identified a variety of salient features including

- title
- publisher
- number of pages
- color or black-and-white
- copyright date
- format (hardcover; paper-over-board; paperback)
- author
- price
- price per page
- size of book
- special features

Once the template is completed, you can review it to see

1. Who are your competitors' current authors? Are they well known? Have they written just one book or many? Might they write a book for you if approached?
2. Is your subject category highly published, or are there few books on the shelf? If only a few, why? Is there lack of demand or have you found a niche that may be exploited?
3. Who are the dominant competitive publishers in the subject area? What are they doing right? What gaps can you see within their programs? (Get their catalogs and review them so you can

become intimately knowledgeable about their programs and books.) Are there strong brands you'll have to compete against?

4. What is the average retail price of hardcovers and paperbacks that are on the shelf? How should you price your book relative to this: higher, same, or lower? Why? Is there a large price difference between four-color books and black-and-white?

5. Is there a subject difference between four-color titles and black-and-white?

6. What is the ratio of hardcover to paperback books within the subject category? What does this tell you about the format you should use if you want to be competitive?

7. What is the average price per page (retail price divided by the number of pages)? Is there a multiple that stands out that will help you review your manufacturing and pricing models?

8. What do the jackets or covers look like? Are there similarities? Are they primarily type or do they use illustration, art, or photographs? What buzzwords are used on the jackets or covers that might apply to your books as well?

9. Is there a book size that is fairly standard (such as 6" x 9") or do formats vary?

10. How many titles have copyright dates that go back more than two years? Do books on the shelf have longevity or are most newly published titles? What distinguishes those that have been out for some time? Which are in second editions or higher?

11. Are there special features that are particularly attractive and that might work for your book? Some of these features might include spiral binding, maps tipped into the book, spot varnish on the cover, disks included, or other features.

After reviewing your findings, apply them to your own books. If you plan on publishing a book similar to one already out, how will yours differ? Can you identify areas that are fertile ground for new books? If so, you now know the category parameters for price, format, color or black-and-white, page count, and many other factors.

In short, now you can make much more informed decisions than you could before you started this simple, straightforward, rewarding process.

Editorial Acquisition

Because you are concerned primarily with internal strategy and management, I will not spend much time on the question of editorial acquisition. Many smaller publishers actually acquire (create) manuscripts through their own writing efforts; they are author and publisher together. Thus acquisition for them simply means finding another project to write and doing it themselves. A vast amount of material is available for every publisher if that publisher knows where to find it and how to acquire it.

As noted, one way to get manuscripts is to write them yourself. It's a simple method, but one you may or may not wish to pursue. I'm sure everyone who reads this book will have had the experience of going to a dinner party and talking about their occupation. In publishing, one hesitates to tell people what one does because it invariably results in someone saying "I've written a book about X, do you know anyone who might want to publish it?" Other than at cocktail parties, where else might you find manuscripts?

Unsolicited Manuscripts

Manuscripts come from a wide range of sources. If you've listed your company in various publishing resources (*Literary Market Place*, *Writer's Handbook*, and others) you will get manuscripts sent to you on an unsolicited basis. These may or may not work out for you. In the distant past, many larger houses actually read through these manuscripts (called affectionately the *slush pile*) and every once in a while found a gem. Today, larger houses rarely read unsolicited manuscripts, leaving it to agents to screen material for the house.

This leaves some room for the smaller house willing to spend time mining for gold. If you are willing to read a large number of unsolicited manuscripts in the hope that you can uncover something crystalline, then by all means let this be known. You will probably be submerged in short order. At the same time, there is always that one chance. . . .

Internally Generated Manuscripts; Work-Made-for-Hire

A second way to acquire a manuscript is to have an idea, flesh it out, and find someone to write it. This is very similar to the first way, except that now you're going *outside* the firm to have the book written. This is an excellent way to maintain control of the project, because the idea is yours. As usual, structure your contract to make sure you get what you want (see the discussion about contracts, page 125). Another way to accomplish this same thing is to do everything within your own company, creating the project as a *Work-Made-For-Hire*, which means you've paid someone on staff to write the book and your company owns the project's copyright and all other rights. This is an excellent way to ensure the growth of your intangible asset base, especially if the books are successful in the long-term. At the same time, it requires more internal cash to fund these projects because you need a staff to write the books and money to fund the research that will inevitably be required.

Meetings and Seminars
Another way to get manuscripts is to attend meetings and seminars on topics of interest to your publishing program. Here, you'll meet those specifically involved in your primary subject areas and can spend time discussing book ideas with those closest to the subject, with those who can write books for you. This is a very good way to keep abreast of new concepts in your subject area and to maintain a leading edge in your publishing program.

Agents
Agents are an excellent way to get material. Just as the larger houses now rely on agents to screen material, so too can smaller publishers who have proved their ability to survive and produce on a consistent basis. Don't forget that agents work for authors. It is the agent's job and responsibility to protect their authors from publishers who might not be professional, or from those whose survival is in question.

However, agents also must sell books to stay in business. If they can't get what they want from the big guns, then they must look elsewhere. And as business gets much tougher for the big guns, as it is as this book is being written, then those big publishers will become much more selective in what they buy. This, in turn, leaves more manuscripts on the market and agents must turn to legitimate smaller publishers as a viable alternative. This is certainly a fair position for an agent to take. If your company is professional and if you've been around awhile, then you are a legitimate target or customer for an agent.

How do you get manuscripts from agents? You simply let them know what kinds of books you are interested in publishing. You can do this by sending the agent a letter and a catalog, or you can visit the agent at his or her office. You can also call the agent on the phone. Whichever method you choose, get in touch. If agents don't know you're out there, they can't send material to you.

In any dealing with an agent, you must be realistic. Most agents will send most books to their larger clients because those larger clients may pay bigger advances than smaller publishers will. I say "may" because there is a feeling among smaller publishers that agents *always* get big dollars for their books. In fact, this is not at all true. Many manuscripts are sold for between $1,500 and $7,500. And while this may be a lot for some smaller publishers, for others it is well within reach. The key again is not to *overpay*. When you run your Title P&L, you'll know what you can pay and will be safe doing it. You can, in fact, compete with the big publishers on some books.

The main point is not to be gun-shy. If you don't talk to agents and try to work with them, you'll be limiting yourself. Try to find those agents with a stable of authors writing in your subject area. Make yourself known to those agents and others who have significant numbers of authors in their stable. As you become better acquainted with each other, you'll start to see more and better manuscripts. And somewhere down the line, you'll acquire a manuscript from an agent.

International Publishers

A fourth way to acquire manuscripts is to buy the U.S. or North American publishing rights from foreign publishers. The largest book fair in the world is the Frankfurt Book Fair, a huge international rights fair, held each October in Frankfurt, Germany. Here, rights to hundreds of thousands of titles on every conceivable subject, in every language, are available for copublication or rights purchase. You can purchase U.S. or North American rights to virtually any book in which you have an interest, if your price and terms are acceptable to the selling publisher.

As a smaller publisher, unless you speak a language other than English, you'll probably find it easiest to concentrate on working with other English language publishers, primarily based in the United States, United Kingdom, Canada, Australia, New Zealand, and South

Africa. In England alone, hundreds of publishers publish everything from craft books to sex books to academic books—all in search of publishers to either copublish or to buy rights.

Here is a firsthand example of how you can take advantage of this international arena.

When I first started in publishing, I worked for a small publisher without the resources to attend Frankfurt. Because of this, and our need for manuscripts, I decided to explore a market somewhat closer to hand: Canada. Even today, Canada is often overlooked by larger American houses who feel it too small a market with which to bother. This was certainly true at the time. And that provided a major opportunity. After a trip or two to Toronto to meet with a variety of publishers, after establishing rapport with them, and after attending a few Canadian Bookseller's Association trade shows, the manuscripts began to flow fast and furious. As a result, our small company got a very large reputation among Canadian publishers as being interested in their books and easy to work with. As we published more Canadian titles, it became easier and easier to make the deals. And shortly, we were also selling Canadian rights to our books to Canadian publishers.

If you make the effort to meet other publishers in other countries, you'll be surprised first at how receptive they are; and second at how it can pay off down the road. Finally, it's one of the benefits of this business that people are generally cordial in their own right, and you'll end up with a significant number of good friends in the process. Not a bad by-product of acquiring manuscripts and helping your company!

Editorial and Proposal Meetings

Once you've begun to generate a flow of manuscripts, you must apply your own editorial judgment to those submissions. You can't and don't want to publish everything that comes through the door.

The first step in this editorial process is to pass the manuscript to an editor for his or her review. If the editor agrees that the manuscript is worth pursuing further, then it should be discussed at an editorial meeting. This is simply a meeting at which all manuscripts considered for publication are discussed by the editors, basically from an editorial perspective. That is, how good is the manuscript? Is it well developed? What are the weak points? The strong points? Are there competitive books on the market? What are the author's credentials for writing the book? Other pertinent questions are sure to arise.

You can't and don't want to publish everything that comes through the door. In smaller companies, there may be only one editor responsible for making all decisions relative to what books are to be published. I strongly recommend, however, no matter how small the house, that other opinions be solicited on the merits of the various manuscripts being considered. One person's opinion may ultimately prevail, but having others around a table to provide input and feedback to the opinions of others can help shape a manuscript. This process also can help point out competitive titles of which the single editor may be unaware, and it will bring different perspectives to bear on the manuscript's ultimate acceptability.

In many smaller houses, the editorial meeting also functions as what we call a *proposal meeting*, which reviews the editorial merits along with the financial, sales, and marketing aspects all at once. The proposal meeting is similar to an editorial meeting but includes non-editorial people, especially sales and marketing staff. The difference between these two meetings is that the editorial meeting is preliminary to the proposal meeting and it doesn't take into account the economics of publishing the book. It is strictly dealing with the editorial merits of the manuscript.

The proposal meeting, on the other hand, augments the editorial meeting because at the proposal meeting, sales and marketing provide input into how the manuscript or proposal under consideration will fit into their programs. Discussion includes how it can be best positioned on the list, weaknesses of the proposal, sub-rights potential, and other sales and marketing issues that will impact the manuscript if it is acquired and sold. At this proposal meeting, the ballpark figures used to create the Title P&L are debated and refined, especially through added input from those selling the book, including reps and sub-rights personnel. Once these refinements have been made up or down, the Title P&L is rerun to make sure it still works.

However you decide to run your house, it is critical to have some separation between the editorial review and the sales, marketing, and financial review. In the final analysis, a publishing house survives only by publishing a preponderance of successful, profitable books. In conjunction with profitability, however, one must weigh the quality of the book. In the best of all worlds, these two criteria go hand in hand and support one another. Whatever is published should be as good a manuscript of its kind as is possible. This necessitates sound editorial judgment be applied to the manuscript. Too often a sales manager who says a book won't sell gets his way at the expense of a manuscript that may be significant. There is no easy answer to this uneasy alliance between editorial and sales. Ultimately, if an editor reviews those manuscripts that sell and feeds that back into his own judgment, the two functions—editorial and sales—will meld to the benefit of all (see Every Editor Should Be a Sales Manager, page 147).

Title Profit and Loss Statements (Title P&Ls)

A Title Profit and Loss Statement, or simply a Title P&L, should be completed for every book that passes the editorial meeting. By using this template, you can make informed decisions about estimated sales, returns, royalties, cost of goods, and ultimately, net profitability for that particular title.

If your company chooses not to use such a template, you put your entire company at risk because you will not know how much you'll make or contribute to profitability per book, and, as each book is added, to each list or to each year. It is crucial to complete this form prior to the proposal meeting because at that meeting the sales figures will be reviewed, as will the profitability. The Title P&L will be revised and rerun as a result of input at the proposal meeting.

Any book has the potential to break out of the pack and become a bestseller. Few actually do.

The Title P&L is the basis upon which most budgeting is done and also functions as the initial stimulus to knowing which books will be on what lists. The line items of the Title P&L, beginning to end, parallel those of the company's income statement. Thus, the figures derived from these Title P&Ls transfer, in their accumulated form, ultimately to the income statements and provide the basis for them. (See chapter 4.)

There are a number of essential ingredients to a Title P&L, but first and foremost, *conservatism is essential*. Any book has the potential to

Title P&L

TITLE: SAMPLE TITLE   ISBN: _____   PRICE: $22.95

SEASON: _____   NUMBER PAGES _____   HARD ____ PAPER ____

	TRADE		CONSUMER DIRECT		COMMERCIAL ACCOUNTS	TOTAL
GROSS UNITS	5,000		350			5,350
LESS RETURNS (UNITS)	1,000		18			1,018
NET UNITS	4,000		332			4,332
X RETAIL PRICE	$22.95		$22.95			
GROSS DOLLARS	$91,800		$7,619			$99,419
X DISCOUNT (50% AVG.)	50%		0%			
TOTAL REVENUES	$45,900	100%	$7,619	100%		$53,519	100%
LESS COST OF GOODS:						
DEVELOPMENT COSTS (BELOW)	$7,500		$576			$8,076
PAPER, PRINTING, BINDING	$2.50	$12,500	$2.50	$875		$13,375
ROYALTIES (%)	15%	$6,885	15%	$1,143		$8,028
FREIGHT IN	$200	$200	$100	$100		$300
TOTAL COST OF GOODS		$27,085	59%	$2,694	35%		$29,779	56%
GROSS MARGIN		$18,815	41%	$4,925	65%		$23,740	44%
LESS PROVISIONS						
BAD DEBT (1%)	$459		$76			$535
AUTHOR ADVANCE WRITE OFF (1%)	$459		$76			$535
INVENTORY WRITE OFF (3%)	$1,377		$228			$1,605
TOTAL PROVISIONS		$2,295		$380			$2,675
GROSS PROFIT	$16,520	36%	$4,545	60%		$21,065	39%

Title P&L *continued*

GENERAL & ADMINISTRATIVE COSTS (G&A)						
SALES COMMISSIONS						
MARKETING COSTS						
WAREHOUSE & FULFILLMENT						
RENT						
TELEPHONES						
SALARIES						
MISCELLANEOUS						
TOTAL G&A						
CONTRIBUTION TO PROFIT	$16,520	36%	$4,545	60%	$21,065	39%
DEVELOPMENT COSTS						
EDITING	$3,000				$3,000	
COPY EDITING	$2,500				$2,500	
INDEXING						
PROOFREADING	$1,000				$1,000	
TYPESETTING	$500				$500	
INTERIOR DESIGN						
JACKET/ COVER DESIGN						
PHOTOGRAPHER FEES						
PHOTOS						
ILLUSTRATIONS						
OUTPUTTING	$500				$500	
SEPARATIONS						
DATABASE SERVICES			$576		$576	
TOTAL DEVELOPMENT COSTS	$7,500		$576		$8,076	
YEAR 1 AMORTIZATION %	100%		100%		100%	
X AMORTIZATION % YEAR 1	$7,500		$576		$8,076	
TOTAL YEAR 1 DEVELOPMENT COSTS	$7,500		$576		$8,076	

break out of the pack and become a bestseller. *Few actually do.*

Typically most books, whether from small publishers or large, start with initial printings of around 5,000 copies. But in today's world of just-in-time inventory, initial print runs may be smaller than that. If this is the case, one would think that editors would use a conservative number for their initial sales figure. In many cases, however, they do not. Editors may use higher numbers because they

- don't have knowledge of the market and competitive sales numbers
- have higher expectations for the book than the sales force does
- are optimists
- have never been in a position where they had to sell directly to a retail or wholesale book buyer

Sales Figures

Whatever the impulse, sales figures must be realistic and conservative. Editors should consult with their sales and marketing associates to get an accurate assessment of the market and the sales figures that the sales and marketing department feels are appropriate. This doesn't mean that sales and marketing's numbers are always correct. But it does mean that you should consult them and evaluate their response before asking your sales team to try to sell more books than they believe is feasible. Editors should also become familiar with using BookScan to research comparable sales figures for use in their projections. (See page 329 for more about BookScan.) It is frankly unwise to try to force books out into the marketplace just to make your book look profitable on paper. Returns have killed many a good book, many a good title P&L, and many a good corporate P&L.

Realistic and conservative sales numbers are the only meaningful way to begin the process of looking at profitability.

Realistic and conservative sales numbers are the only meaningful way to begin the process of looking at profitability.

Returns

OK, maybe your book is the best book ever created. Maybe your reps will sell it in the tens of thousands. Maybe every single copy will be sold. Maybe you'll get no returns. And maybe the tooth fairy will come.

When it comes to returns, if you think your book and your publishing program is significantly different than other programs, your reasoning had better be good. In most cases, the only reason for low returns is low advance sales. What goes out in small numbers usually (but not always) comes back in small numbers. It's a mixed blessing to say the least.

The industry average for adult hardcover returns, according to the 2004 Association of American Publisher's statistics, is 31%, although the average for smaller publishers, according to the 2004 Huenefeld-PubWest Survey, is 11%. While this may be true, I think 11% is far too low for proper planning and urge you to use the higher AAP average. That means that for every 100 books you put into the marketplace, 31 will, on average, be returned. In most cases, it's safe to budget using this 31% return rate if your books are being sold to the book trade with normal 5,000 to 7,500 copy advance sales. If you plan on putting out more books, incrementally increase your returns rate to protect your company's profitability.

Don't fool yourself: You're more likely to have higher return rates than lower. So be cautious in the beginning. Let your experience over time be your guide to reducing the rate. And remember: If you are only publishing one book, you don't have an "average." Whatever the return rate is, it is—so be even more careful and conservative. (For a full discussion of returns see chapter 14.)

Cost of Goods
Cost of goods consists of

- those costs that are repeated each time a book is printed, primarily paper, printing, and binding
- royalties
- amortized development costs

In almost every case, cost of goods is a higher percentage when the quantity of books printed is smaller. Why? Smaller runs cost more to produce per unit than longer runs because the time and effort of getting the press ready to run is significant and essentially the same, regardless of run size. When this cost is distributed over a smaller number of books, it tends to become a larger cost per unit. As the run size increases and the make-ready charges get distributed over a larger quantity, the cost per unit decreases. For example, if your make-ready costs are $500 and you print 500 books, that cost is $1.00 per book. If you print 2,000 books, then the cost is only $0.25 per book. The same is true of paper costs; smaller quantities are generally priced higher than truckload lots.

Many people tend to think that this differential gives them latitude to increase their print runs to reduce the unit cost of their books. This seemingly logical reasoning usually leads to disaster.

On a per-unit basis, the more one prints, the less the cost per copy. However, this is only true *if those books are sold.* On a dollar basis, the more one prints, the more that printing costs in total dollars. Estimating higher sales figures to reduce the cost of goods and increase the gross margin is *self-defeating*—especially when those books ultimately don't sell or are returned in large numbers. In these cases, you are not only out-of-pocket for the costs of paper, printing, and binding, but you also may be unable to recover those costs later because the books may never sell, or may sell at remainder prices. Remainder dealers, to whom you may ultimately unload these extra books, make large profits at your expense. *Don't just think about cost per unit. Think, as well, about the total out-of-pocket cost and conserving cash flow. Never print more books than you realistically think you'll sell in a six-month period.*

> *Estimating higher sales figures to reduce the cost of goods and increase the gross margin is self-defeating.*

In today's world of modern printing, where printers specialize more and more in short-run presses and quick turnaround, it is in your best interest to conserve your cash and use it only when absolutely necessary. Every publisher should have the problem of having more orders than they can fill—but very few actually have that luxury.

Development or Plant Costs

Every time you create a book, you incur one-time costs. These costs are combined under the label *Development Costs*, or *Plant Costs*. Included among these costs are

- editorial costs: copy editing, developmental editing, proof-reading, and indexing expenses

- art costs: illustration, photo, and permission fees as well as transparency rental fees
- text costs: typesetting through preparation of copy for the printer
- design costs: jacket, cover, and interior text design
- separation and proofing costs

Development costs can be amortized or written off for tax purposes in various percentages over different periods of time, depending upon the kind of book it is and its expected life. Trade books are usually amortized over one year, but professional books or textbooks may have longer lives. Check with your accountant about the best way to take advantage of amortizing your costs. Again, the best way is to be realistic and conservative when looking at plant costs.

The most conservative approach to plant costs is to amortize them 100% in year 1, on the theory that trade books often have only one year of life expectancy. This immediately reflects all costs in the year they are incurred. (See chart page 124.) The net result of this strategy is to reduce your gross profit in year 1. In other words, if your net sales are $12,500 and your development costs are $2,000 and you choose to amortize all of it in the first year, then your gross profit is reduced in that first year by the full $2,000, meaning you make *less gross profit in year 1*.

Check with your accountant about the best way to take advantage of amortizing your costs.

If, on the other hand, you choose to amortize only 50% of the development costs in year 1, then your gross profit will only be reduced by $1,000, leaving you on paper at least $1,000 better off *in year 1*.

While this works fine in year 1, year 2 shows a different result: Because you have no remaining amortization left in the first case (you wrote off 100%), then using the same $12,500 net sale figure in year 2, you'll have the full amount of gross profit remaining. If, on the other hand, you only amortized 50% in year 1, then you'll be forced to amortize the other 50% in year 2—so you'll be worse off by $1,000 in that year.

Why does this matter? Because it changes the profitability of your company and may impact your ability to borrow and your overall credit-worthiness. It also impacts your cash flow. If you earn more, you pay more taxes, which reduces your cash flow. Which method is better?

How much is the right amount to amortize? Only you and your accountant can make that determination. Check it out.

Amortized development costs taken 100% in year 1:

	Year 1	Year 2
Gross Sales	$12,500	$12,500
Returns (20%)	2,500	2,500
Net Sales:	$10,000	$10,000
Cost of Goods:		
Royalties	500	500
PPB	2,000	2,000
Amortized Dev. Cost (100%)	2,000	0
Gross Profit:	$5,500	$7,500

Amortized development costs taken 50% in year 1:

	Year 1	Year 2
Gross Sales	$12,500	$12,500
Returns (20%)	2,500	2,500
Net Sales:	$10,000	$10,000
Cost of Goods:		
Royalties	500	500
PPB	2,000	2,000
Amortized Dev. Cost (50%)	1,000	1,000
Gross Profit:	$6,500	$6,500

From a management standpoint, amortization can make a difference in terms of taxes. If you strategically want to improve profits, you can postpone publication of books from later in this year to early in the next year. Conversely, if you want to reduce taxes, you can pull titles to be published early in the next year into this year, thereby allowing the company to take the expense for development costs this year.

Royalties

Royalties are usually a publisher's largest expense. The good news is that it's an expense you only incur if you sell books. If you don't sell, you don't pay—unless of course you paid the author a royalty advance greater than that earned through sales of the book. Then, indeed, you do pay—and you lose.

Many smaller presses don't pay royalties because their authors are in fact the publisher. The royalty, in essence, becomes the profit left over when all expenses have been paid. As noted in chapter 6, Protect Your Assets, this is *not* the best way to handle this situation for a number of reasons. Yet another reason to pay yourself royalties becomes clear when viewing royalties in the context of cost of goods: if you don't pay yourself royalties, you will understate and fail to recognize the actual cost of your book and therefore a major cost of running your business. In short, if you are the owner-publisher, it makes sense to recognize and pay yourself appropriate royalties.

Royalties are usually a publisher's largest expense.

The fact is, most publishers recognize the integral, essential partnership that exists between publisher and author and do pay royalties. Paying royalties allows publishers to get manuscripts a bit more easily because they can offer the author some compensation for his creative effort, which is only fair.

The major questions with royalties are what the basis of payment is and how much one should pay. Let's start with the basis of payment.

If you are the owner-publisher, it makes sense to recognize and pay yourself appropriate royalties.

Royalties are figured or based on either the *retail price of the book* or on the *net amount received by the publisher* after discounts (and excluding freight). The choice of one method or another can result in significant savings or expenditures depending on the rates being used. According to the 2004 Huenefeld-PubWest Survey of Financial Operations, perhaps the only survey to ask the question, 9% of their 75 reporting publishers paid royalties on list price; 84% on net price.

In most cases, the "standard" royalties on hardcover trade books, when based on retail price, are 10% to 5,000 copies sold; 12.5% to 10,000 copies sold; and 15% thereafter. It should be immediately stated that *no royalty rate is written in stone. This is a major area for negotiation when negotiating your author contract.* There is no reason, for instance, that you can't offer a flat 10% on all copies sold or 10% to 20,000 copies or higher. Or offer less than 10%. As noted, 10 to 12.5 to 15% are standard for some, usually the major publishers.

Not necessarily for you! According to the Huenefeld-PubWest Survey, the average percentage paid on list or retail price is 9%.

In many cases, royalties are paid on the net amount received after discounts. For instance, if you have a $20 retail price and you sell to an account at a 50% discount, the net dollar amount you receive is $10. If you base your royalty on this amount, and offer 10% to 15%, you can see the immediate difference between this amount and that based upon the suggested retail price. Taking 10% of the retail price, one would pay the author $2 per book; taking 10% of the net received, one would pay the author $1—a saving of 50%. Huenefeld's average royalty paid on net received is 11%.

Which one is better? It depends. As the economics of publishing are squeezed by higher costs all along the line, more publishers are trying to negotiate royalty payments based upon the net amount received. Business and professional books are trending more and more in this direction. At the same time, better (that is, more well-known, not necessarily qualitatively better) authors can command higher royalty rates and advances against royalties, usually based upon list or retail price. It's my feeling that this will continue indefinitely. There are always some authors whom publishing houses are more willing to pay for than others. These authors will receive royalties based on retail prices. Others will not.

As a publisher, you should almost always try to create a situation in which you pay the lowest possible advance and royalty but create a win-win situation with your author. One of my clients does this by paying no advance royalty but keeping the author's book in print much longer than most other publishers would, and putting more promotional effort into their selling.

This conserves the publisher's cash, yet keeps its authors happy. The key is to negotiate, know your limits, and *stop when necessary*. As the president of one major publishing house said—and with whom I totally agree—"there's no deal you can't walk away from."

How much should you pay your authors as an advance against royalties? The question really comes down to how many copies of that book do you expect to sell. Remember the Title P&L? Once you've estimated this number, you certainly don't want to pay royalties on more than that quantity, because you'll then be paying royalty in advance for books you don't think you'll sell. At the same time, you want to leave yourself leeway just in case you don't sell what you've estimated.

A good rule of thumb is to *pay no more than the amount the author would earn if one-half of the edition is sold*. If, for example, you've estimated that you'll sell 3,000 copies of a book at $20; then you should pay an advance of no more than $1,500 assuming you're paying a royalty of 10% of the net amount received.

This would be determined as

Retail price of book	$20.00
Average discount	x .50
Net amount received	$10.00
x Royalty rate: 10%	x .10
Equals royalty per book	$1.00
x Estimated sale quantity	3,000
Equals total royalty	$3,000
Divided by 2	$1,500

Of course if you can get the book for less, then by all means do so. Every dollar you save up front goes towards financing those cash-flow needs you'll certainly have.

Gross Profit

The amount remaining after subtracting royalties, cost of goods, and the appropriate percentage of development or plant costs from net revenues is your gross profit.

As a benchmark, most trade publishers work on a gross profit of around 50%, most professsional publishers around 60–65%. More successful trade publishers, especially smaller publishers with little backlist, should try to maintain a higher gross profit—somewhere around 60%. If your direct costs and your General and Administrative costs (G&A)—those costs you incur every day running your business (such as telephone, rent, insurance, payroll)—are, in total, less than 60%, you will have a positive net profit before taxes. If they total more than 60%, then you will have a net loss.

Focusing on gross profit, rather than on net profit, is an excellent way to get editors involved in the day-to-day evaluation of profitability of potential titles without getting them bogged down in costs over which they have no control. Editors, through contract negotiation, can control royalty and should get input on sales and production costs prior to extending any contract. It is impractical for them to get involved in determining percentages for all other costs of running the business.

Instead, the editor should focus on those factors above the gross-profit line, while senior management, in conjunction with the accounting or equivalent department, should determine the G&A and cost percentages on an ongoing basis, probably every six months or so, and feed that information to the editors. In this way, they can factor these percentages into the P&L and quickly evaluate if the total expense percent is greater or lesser than their gross-profit margin percent. If it is greater, then either they must increase net revenue per title, decrease royalty and production expense, or both. At the same time, management knows it must contain or reduce expenses to achieve greater profitability.

This methodology allows editors to work through Title P&Ls quickly, yet with a good understanding of profitability.

Subsidiary Rights
Remember that I just said that some successful trade publishers are profitable while maintaining a 50% gross margin. The reason is usually related to subsidiary rights income, which often shows up as a line item just after net sales. Subsidiary income is

Subsidiary rights income is extra revenue generated by selling the subsidiary right to publish your book to someone else.

called many things, but what it comes down to is *extra revenue* that is generated by selling the *subsidiary* right to publish your book to someone else. Subsidiary rights includes sales of

- serial rights
- book club rights
- foreign rights
- audio rights
- movie rights
- electronic rights
- merchandising rights
- and others

The average large publishing house, with a net profit of 10%, usually shows a subsidiary rights percentage of 7 to 8% of net sales. Given this, and assuming the line is above your gross-margin line, it's tantamount to increasing your net sales by that percent. Thus, if a trade publisher is working on a gross margin of 50%, including sub-rights income at 7% brings the gross margin to 57%—much more in line with our parameters for profitability.

At the same time, smaller publishers usually show nowhere near the 7 to 8% sub-rights income. Again, according to the Huenefeld-PubWest 2001 Survey, smaller publishers typically show between 1.2% and 2.3% additional income on this line. Thus, if a smaller publisher is running at 50% gross margin, 1 to 2% doesn't do much to help its profitability.

One question you may be asking is should you factor sub-rights income into your profitability analysis? My answer is simple and categorical: *No!*

Many publishers make the mistake of thinking they can predict sales to book clubs, audio publishers, foreign publishers, and magazines. The fact is, unless one of these vendors agrees in writing to take your book, you can't predict success. Many a publisher has inflated his Title P&L figures with income from these sources only to find that no purchaser is interested in his products, for whatever reason (and there are many).

Returning to the beginning of our discussion, be conservative. It's hard enough to predict sales to bookstores and libraries. Focus on these and let your sub-rights income be truly supplemental and incremental. (See also, a full discussion of subsidiary rights in chapter 10.)

EBITDA vs. Net Profit
The amount of money left over after all of the expense categories have been deducted from net sales is EBITDA (earnings before interest, taxes, depreciation, or amortization) or Operating Profit. How much should you expect?

The average operating profit for larger publishers is approximately 11.5%. This means that for every dollar of net sale made (that is, after returns) they can expect to earn 11.5 cents.

In relation to the total survey sample publishers, according to the 2004 Heunefeld Survey, money-makers had profits of 14.1%, while money-losers had losses of 9.3%.

A comparison of AAP with Huenefeld-PubWest statistics shows

some very distinct differences, *and some startling similarities*, between the AAP's larger publisher base, and the Huenefeld-PubWest base.

AAP and Huenefeld–PubWest Statistics

	AAP	Huenefeld-PubWest
Returns Percentage	31.0%	11.7%
Author Royalties	15.6%	9.0%
Paper, Printing, and Binding	39.1%	24.1%
Cost of Goods (Royalties & PPB)	54.7%	33.1%
Inventory Write-off	N/A	2.0%
Marketing Expense	13.8%	15.5%
Editorial Expense	5.7%	6.7%
Fulfillment	8.8%	8.3%
General Administrative	10.7%	9.7%
Operating Margin (Income from Operations)	11.5%	10.2%

AAP figures from the Association of American Publishers, Industry Statistics, ©1995, Association of American Publishers, Inc.

Huenefeld-PubWest figures from the Huenefeld-PubWest Financial Operations Survey, ©2004, courtesy of PubWest.

Contracts

Although I briefly spoke about contracts in Part II, this section focuses on those contract aspects of which every editor should be aware. Again, I caution that I am not an attorney and am speaking from a practical, not a legal, standpoint. That being said, I have also learned to take nothing related to contracts for granted. When you're just beginning to work with contracts, seek the guidance of a good attorney, especially one familiar with publishing traditions, norms, and language. When you become more familiar with contracts you should still get good legal advice for any clause or amendment about which you may feel uneasy or uninformed. Don't be afraid to ask for advice. A few dollars spent up front can save untold amounts later on. As noted before, *Kirsch's Handbook of Publishing Law* is an excellent reference for your shelf, as is Lloyd Jassin's *The Copyright Permission and Libel Handbook*.

Let's now look at those contract clauses that will have the most impact on you and your publishing company.

The contract, as has been noted, is one of the publishing house's prime assets. The grant of rights provided by the contract is key to every book you sign. Thus *it is absolutely mandatory that you have a contract for every book you publish.*

There are many boilerplate publishing contracts available, but remember: any contract you choose to use is a *negotiable* document. Nothing is agreed upon until you and the other party decide to do so, and nothing is agreed upon until the two parties (or more) have all signed the contract. Take nothing for granted when negotiating contracts—and remember, once again, "there's no deal you can't walk away from" if it doesn't meet *your* needs or criteria.

You must have a contract for every book you publish.

In most cases, the primary clauses on which you'll want to focus your attention are those relating to

- who the parties to the contract are
- description of the work
- format (hardcover or paperback)
- rights granted
- a "satisfactory manuscript" clause
- manuscript or disk due date
- territories granted and language
- term of the contract
- advance (if any) against royalties
- royalty rates and dates of payment
- subsidiary rights grants and splits
- defining who the copyright holder is
- author warranties
- defining who has responsibility for procuring and paying for artwork, illustrations, photos, permissions, index, etc.
- assignability of the contract
- reversion of rights
- any agency clause
- arbitration clause

While every clause is important, those above set the tone for the rights you, as publisher, have and may exploit. They delineate how much you'll have to pay for the project and to whom.

Let's work our way through these clauses while remembering a key fact: *Never go into a negotiation for a work without first running a Title P&L for that work. You must fit your negotiations into the parameters defined by the Title P&L.* If you go beyond the bounds of these terms, you run the probable risk of overpaying for the project.

Defining Who the Parties to the Contract Are

A contract must be between two or more parties. Thus, the first question you must answer is, with whom are you contracting? It's usually straightforward as to who the parties are in relation to a project. There's commonly one author (either a person or an organization) and you, the publisher. If this is the case, then it's simple. Sometimes, however, it becomes a bit more complex.

Frequently, there may be two or more authors. If this is the case, for ease of enforcement you should attempt to make the parties to the contract as few as possible. You should attempt to make one of the authors ultimately responsible for deciding various issues. The reason for this is twofold: First, if no author has ultimate responsibility for contractually related matters (and all publishing events should be contractually related), you run the risk of no one making a decision. The result is that incredible amounts of time can be squandered and the project's completion put in jeopardy. Second, I have been involved in too many contracts in which two or more people have been signatories, but in which the joint relationship between those authors has become strained or broken down entirely. In such cases, without the ability to have one author take responsibility, you run the very real risk of having the project canceled. One author tells you to do one thing and the others say the opposite.

Is an agent involved? If so, how is the agent involved and to whom is money paid? Do you need an agency clause?

Your job as publisher is to publish the best book in a timely way. The first step toward that objective is to define the parties with whom you'll be working—including any agent. You must know precisely who has the final contractual authority. Questions about the work arise at every turn—and you must know who can provide definitive, *legally binding* solutions to them.

Describing the Work

Every contract must state what it is you, the publisher, are buying and what the author is selling. Normally this is defined by a tentative title and a line or two of descriptive copy. There should also be a notice of how many words the Work will be, how many illustrations, and the format, whether hardcover or paperback.

In addition, you'll want to specify how the book should be submitted, whether as hard copy, disk, or both. As computerization and digitized production become standard to the industry, it's become common to ask for a printout and disks. This saves you the expense of rekeyboarding the manuscript, and helps to avoid (but does not completely eliminate) many errors that could occur in typesetting.

Rights Granted

Every contract provides for the ownership or licensing of specific rights that you, as the publisher, control. You must carefully set forth in every contract what those rights are. Virtually all publishing contracts provide the publisher with the right or license to publish in book form, but there are many other publications and licensing rights that can also be granted, such as audio book, dramatic (play or movie), merchandising, and more. All of these must be clearly stated in the contract.

One right should absolutely be clearly specified: electronic rights, whether e-book, database, or other. In the not-too-distant past, electronic rights were not specified in contracts because no one imagined such publishing would come into being. Thus, in those earlier contracts, grants for electronic publication were not mentioned, and it is now questionable as to whether the publisher or author holds those rights. Some publishers make the claim that because they control the print rights to the book they also control the e-book rights (that is, a book is a book is a book). This may or may not be the case (agents and authors in particular dispute this interpretation). In order to avoid controversy, such rights should be clearly specified in the contract.

Satisfactory Manuscript Clause

As the publisher paying for the privilege of publishing the author's work, you want to ensure what you ultimately get is what you agreed upon. Thus, you should insist upon a "satisfactory manuscript" clause stating that the manuscript submitted must meet your needs. In most cases, you'll want to keep this clause broad, giving you wide latitude.

Obviously the author wants to define this clause narrowly. In most cases, the courts have upheld the validity of this clause, and in most cases, based on a broad definition.

The real key to implementing this clause is to make sure you inform the author, *in writing*, exactly why his manuscript is not satisfactory, and give the author the opportunity to correct the deficiency. Many times, editors feel uneasy telling authors why they are rejecting a manuscript. Often, editors do so over the phone, in vague generalities. They never get around to putting their comments and reasons in writing. This is an open invitation to a legal suit. If you invoke the satisfactory manuscript clause, then do so in writing as precisely as possible. Give the author every opportunity to rectify the work and make it comply with your needs.

One of the author's fears in relation to the satisfactory manuscript clause is that it may be invoked unilaterally—for no reason or for any reason. In many cases a contract is signed long before the manuscript is delivered. It is signed in response to certain market conditions and trends that may change over time. Is this the author's fault? Probably not, and he shouldn't be penalized for this. Sometimes, however, publishers have canceled contracts for these reasons based on the specious application of the satisfactory manuscript clause. Thus authors and agents are rightfully concerned about the clause.

If you provide a mechanism for author satisfaction, then you'll be able to include a satisfactory manuscript clause. You definitely want it.

Due Dates

To plan your program (remember consistency and credibility) you must provide due dates that tie in to your publishing program. Thus establishing due dates that are reasonable and achievable is necessary. It does no good to try to force authors to meet dates that are unreasonable because all you'll get is

- a valid excuse when it isn't ready on time
- a poor manuscript that will take you even longer to edit and develop properly, thereby wasting even more time and money
- no manuscript at all and a frustrated author
- a damaged reputation among authors and agents

In short, be reasonable up front and everyone will look good later on. As already noted, your due date should be a minimum of one year from the time you plan to publish. You should ask for both a printout and a disk of the work. The disk should be in a word-processing format that your system and people can accommodate. Get a test disk before accepting the whole manuscript and make sure your equipment can read it. Be sure to stipulate that your authors keep a backup copy of the disk in their files.

If manuscripts don't come in on time, there is little you can do other than cancel the contract. Some creative publishers we've known have tried to use a late clause in the contract that pays a declining amount of the advance due on delivery or publication based upon how late the manuscript is. Of course if the manuscript is never delivered, the publisher should ask the author to return the original advance because the author failed to fulfill his obligation. Unfortunately, the author, in many cases, has already spent the advance and doesn't have the money available to repay. Or she will claim that she fulfilled her obligation, in which case the publisher would have to file a lawsuit to collect money due. Because lawsuits themselves cost substantial sums, in most cases the publisher will choose to forfeit his advance.

In this circumstance, one strategy a publisher should consider is to include a first-proceeds clause in the contract. This clause states that the author may retain any advance paid to date, but that such advance will be repaid to the publisher *if the author sells the manuscript to another publisher.* The first proceeds clause usually provides a mutually agreeable way for both parties to get what they want and need—though it may be over an extended period of time.

It is critical for the editors working on specific manuscripts to keep on top of their authors to ensure that their manuscripts are delivered. This is an editor's primary job. It's one every publisher should stress.

Territory
What territorial rights will you be acquiring? In other words, where will you be allowed to sell the Work? Your job as publisher is to sell the book in as many venues or countries as you can, thereby maximizing your revenue from the book.

In the best of all worlds, you'll get *world rights*—that is, the ability to sell the Work throughout the world in all languages, whether you publish the book in those countries or you sell the rights to others to publish. Start your negotiations asking for these.

Second, if you can't get world rights, you should ask for *world English language* rights—which gives you the ability to sell the book in the English language in countries throughout the world, or to other English language publishers.

As a third choice, you should ask for *North American rights*—that is, the right to sell the book in the United States, Canada, and Mexico.

Fourth, *United States and Canada only.*

Fifth, and last, *United States*

Again, you must negotiate for these rights and define them clearly.

Term of the Contract

This clause is fairly straightforward. For how long does the author grant the publisher the rights to publish the Work in question? In most cases the grant is for the *life of the copyright* with the proviso that the book must be kept in print and be available for sale. Of course, one must immediately ask how *in print* is defined? (Remember: when it comes to contracts, what's definite to you may be written in sand to others.)

In most cases, *in print* is defined obliquely; that is, as long as the publisher has inventory of the work available for sale to anyone who orders the book. This definition can cause conflict later. For instance, one of our clients sold a book to a publisher who is selling a few copies a year, but who also sold the book to a book club that uses the book as a premium for joining the club. Premium use, in clubs, results in a very small royalty, because the book is given away to new members. While this may be fine for the club, the publisher and the author receive little—yet technically the book is still in print according to the definition just given: that is, the book is *available for sale*. To avoid this conflict, define the term *in print* by placing a minimum on the number of books that must be sold over a certain period of time. Or, there could be a minimum amount of dollars of revenue generated, or the amount of royalty earned over a defined period of time. The time period might be one or two royalty statements. Thus, if the book sells or earns less than this amount, the author has the right, but not the obligation (in other words he has the right but may choose not to exercise the right) to ask for the publishing rights back; if it sells or earns more than this amount, the publisher retains the publishing rights. By basing the in-print definition on these criteria, there is an objective document—the royalty statement—upon which both publisher and author can make an objective judgment as to whether the book truly is in print.

Royalty Advances

Most authors write to earn money as well as to disseminate information. Thus, they expect an "advance against royalty" or an advance payment from the publisher that will be deducted from any royalty the author may earn from the sale of the Work. This is certainly a fair position for the author to take. After all, she has spent or will spend a substantial amount of time and creative effort writing the Work.

The question both you and the author must decide is how much of an advance is fair to both parties? Obviously, this ranges from nothing at all, if the publisher has no money to pay for advances, to millions of dollars for the superstars.

When negotiating advances there are three strategic scales to balance. First, you've run your Title P&L (Yes, you have!) and you should, therefore, know approximately how much royalty the book will earn based on the estimated sale, the projected retail price, and your projected royalty rate. Once you know this amount of total earned royalty, you don't want to pay more than that because you'll risk putting yourself in peril of not being able to earn back your advance. At the same time, you want to be fair to the author.

As I mentioned before, there are two rules of thumb from the publishing standpoint:

- Pay as little as possible.
- Pay at most one-half the first year's total earned royalty.

I subscribe to both rules. If you really want the book, you might start close to the one-half mark. But remember, you can always go higher in a negotiation; it's almost impossible to go lower. So start your negotiation on the lower side.

The second item that impacts your negotiation is the *market value* of the manuscript. If you are the only publisher talking to the author about the Work, you're in a better negotiating position than if you're bidding against five competing publishers. In many cases, when competition is involved, you'll find the author's expectations are large and the manuscript may be priced out of your range.

My advice is simple: never put your program at risk for one book. Stay within the bounds of your title projections. Remember: there will *always* be another manuscript available.

The third item that impacts your negotiating strategy is the author's need. While you want to be fair to your author, your other responsibility is to minimize the outlay of the company's cash so you can use it to pay bills, buy other new books, do research, and more. Just because an author wants a certain amount doesn't mean you have to pay that much. Again, work within the bounds of your Title P&L and start low. In a win-win negotiation your author will understand your needs, you'll understand his, and together you'll work out an amicable advance figure.

Royalty Rates and Payment Dates
Like royalty advances, royalty rates vary widely depending upon the stature of the author, the particular publisher, the category of book, and the market demand for the Work. There truly is no *norm*, but there are pretty good guidelines.

Royalty rates are those percentages of an agreed-upon dollar amount that the author will receive for the sale of each book the publisher sells. The rates define how much the author will earn for writing the book.

Royalty rates have a number of bases, but most publishers use one of two criteria:

- the suggested retail price of the book
- the net amount received by the publisher, meaning the retail price less any discounts the publisher may give an account

Most larger publishers within the established trade publishing community base royalties on the suggested retail price. Most smaller, professional, and college publishers base royalties on the net amount received. *Most*, however, definitely doesn't mean *all*. For example, many large publishers of business and computer books base royalties on net amount received; many smaller publishers base royalties on suggested retail.

Agents tend to like royalties based on retail price not because it means the author (and the agent) will earn more, but because the retail price is an objective criterion upon which to base payment. It doesn't change frequently. When royalties are based on the net amount received, there are multiple levels of calculation parallel to every discount level. Thus there may be five or more levels at which calculations must be made.

In actuality, it doesn't matter much whether you base royalties on retail or net as long as you can afford them and the author is happy accepting them. You can always equate the net to the retail by adjusting the royalty percentage and the quantity on which it is paid.

In other words, if we're looking at a 10% royalty on a $10.00 book being sold at 50% discount to a wholesaler, the author would receive $1.00 per book based on retail ($10.00 x .10), and 50 cents per book based on net ($10.00 x .50 x .10). You can see how significant the difference in base can be.

But if you wanted to equate the two, you could easily say that you'd pay 20% of net instead of 10%. Thus you'd pay $10.00 x .50 x .20 or $1.00 per book.

The point is to be consistent in how you base your payments. From an accounting and contractual standpoint it's much easier to use one base or the other, not switch back and forth between the two.

Are there standard terms for royalty rates? Again, it will vary, but in general, based on suggested retail price, common terms might be 10% for hardcover books, 7.5% for paperbacks. Many publishers add "escalation" clauses, which increase the royalty rate as more books are sold. Thus, it's fairly common to see 10% to 5,000 copies sold, 12.5% to 10,000 copies, and 15% thereafter. (I don't recommend these rates, but they are not unusual.) In this case, both the rate and the escalation points become negotiable (you see why you need a Title P&L that you can put on your computer!).

If royalties are based on net received, rates are commonly 10 to 15% on hardcovers and 8 to 10% on paperbacks. Again, escalation clauses similar to those above are common.

Once royalties are calculated, they must be paid. Most publishers pay royalties twice a year. Having said that, I know of many smaller publishers who pay more frequently, either quarterly or even monthly. The reason is that they want to keep their cash flow on a more level plane. If you pay twice a year you must ensure that you keep enough in the bank throughout the period to pay those royalties. (This amount, called accrued royalties payable, is recorded as a current liability on the balance sheet.) As we all know, however, there's always something on which to spend money. To be conservative, and to make sure that money coming in is paid responsibly to the author, some companies choose to pay royalties monthly.

The downside of paying royalties too frequently is that you may overpay. Don't forget, royalties are paid only on *sales* of books. But in this industry, *returns* are constant: what you put out today as "sales" can easily come back tomorrow as returns. So if you pay royalty on that sale today and then the book comes back tomorrow, you'll have to get your money back from the author—and that's a position I guarantee you don't want to be in. The only alternative you may have is to withhold royalty from future payment periods. But that assumes the book continues to sell. Yet, most trade books have a short life span with a trajectory that goes up fast and comes down fast. If you've paid royalties on the upside peak and then get caught in the downdraft, you've just spent too much.

The six-month cycle of payments allows the publisher some time to watch the trajectory and make allowances for it. As a publisher, you want to be sure to have a "royalty reserve" clause in your contract. This clause allows you to hold back a certain portion of "earned" royalty for future reserves against returns. I recommend a sliding scale that reflects reality: that is, a book's return rate declines proportionately to the time the book is on the market.

What's a fair reserve rate? I recommend a sliding scale of 30% reserve for returns in year 1; 25% in year 2; and 20% in year 3 and thereafter. In all the years I've used these rates, there has never been one complaint. The reason? The rates are fair and realistic based on the actual book market. Some mass-market publishers withhold 60% for the first few royalty periods, which tells you the state of that market. (See Returns, chapter 14.)

In sum, the royalty rates you pay are for you to determine. Keep an open mind, look at your Title P&Ls flexibly, and don't forget that authors are your allies. Without them, you have no books to publish. At the same time, if you run out of cash by paying too much of an advance, or too high a royalty rate, you won't be much help to any of your authors. Remember the first law of nation-states and business: survival first, everything else second (within ethical guidelines of course).

Subsidiary Rights Grants and Splits

As I've noted before, and will discuss shortly, subsidiary rights are extremely important to the publisher. They can absolutely mean the difference between profit and loss. So be sure to define the sub-rights that are granted, and the percentage of receipts that both the author and company will receive. While most splits are traditionally 50–50%, some, such as first serial, or foreign rights, may favor the author. A 70–30% split is not uncommon for first serial rights.

Who Holds Copyright?

As I've said, this too is important because it determines to some extent the value of your intangible assets. Today, copyright is usually held by the author, who transfers publishing rights to the publisher. This is fine as long as the transfer is contractually made. Be sure to define who is responsible for obtaining copyright from the Copyright Office; typically it's the publisher.

Author Warranties

One of the most important clauses in your author contract is the "author warranty" clause. In this clause, the author "warrants," or guarantees, a number of important items that make publishing his book more palatable, and safer, for the publisher.

First, the author usually guarantees the publisher that the work is his own, that it is original, hasn't been published before, and doesn't infringe upon any other author's rights, including, especially, any other copyright. In addition, the author usually warrants that the work is not taken from the public domain—in which case there would be no need for a contract in the first place. The author also should warrant that he will hold you, the publisher, harmless from any injury caused by the book. Injury, of course, can take many forms. It can be in the form of physical injury, for instance if a recipe in a cookbook proves poisonous (it's happened). Injury can also be legal; for example, the book may make slanderous or obscene statements or may plagiarize the work of others.

The fact is, given the litigious society in which we live, injury is in the eye of the beholder—and a lawsuit can be filed by anyone at any time. To protect against this risk, almost all publishing contracts require that the author state categorically that the book is not knowingly injurious to any party; doesn't contain any material that might prove harmful to the reader; and isn't obscene or slanderous. If a third party decides to file a lawsuit against the author, publisher, or both, then the author warrants, or guarantees, that he will pay for the cost of defending against the lawsuit, whether that defense is undertaken by the author or the publisher.

As a publisher, every contract you sign should have a strong author's warranty clause in it. If you are ever unsure about whether a manuscript might be more prone to a lawsuit than another, be sure to have your attorney review the manuscript to ensure that the author's statements are true and to try to alert you and the author to how the author's statements may be changed somewhat to mitigate the chance of a lawsuit. It's always better to be careful and safe than to be sorry.

Who Pays for the Artwork, Index, and More?

Small things can add up. Especially for the procurement of artwork, illustrations, and photos, all of which demand payment of permission fees, which depend upon the use you want to make of them (e.g., one-time use or multiple uses; U.S. rights only or world rights; color or black-and-white?). If the book in question will contain these items, make sure to specify who will pay for them. Most of the time, it is the author's responsibility. Sometimes the publisher pays for these items and charges them against the author's future royalties. In academic publishing, there are frequently grants paid to the author by the publisher to cover these costs. Indexes too are usually the author's responsibility, although quite often they are done by the publisher and the cost charged against the author's royalties. Be sure to specify who is responsible for these miscellaneous charges.

Assignability of the Contract

In today's world of mergers and acquisitions, the assignability of the contract is an important clause that should be in every contract. If

The assignability of the contract is an important clause that should be in every contract.

your company merges with another or is sold to another, part of the value of your company is determined by the contracts you have, and also by the assignability of that contract to the purchaser. If you don't have an assignability clause in your contract, you may not be able to include that contract among the assets you merge or sell to the other publishing house. If this is the case, then your intangible asset base is worth less than it would be otherwise. Make sure, therefore, that the contract allows you, as publisher, to assign every contract to another party. Your company will be worth more for your effort.

Reversion of Rights

Authors and agents always insist on a reversion clause for good reason. If the book isn't selling, the author (and agent) aren't making money on that book. And because they must make a living and earn royalty on each copy sold, it's in their best interest to keep the book in print. As a publisher, you don't want to give up, or revert, rights to any book if you can help it. You never know what will happen to that book over the course of many years. For instance, Vanguard Press, which I mentioned earlier, had a bestseller called *Auntie Mame* in the 1950s. Over the course of many decades, the book became a play and a movie. Anthologies constantly paid significant yearly fees for permission to include the work. If Vanguard had let the book go out-of-print and if it had reverted to the author, the company wouldn't have received this subsidiary income. Every publisher has such a story.

On the other hand, it's simply not practical to keep every book that one publishes in print, certainly not if they're not selling. There's a fine balance to maintain between being out-of-stock and out-of-print vs. having enough on hand to maintain the salability of the book. Computer books, which date fast because of new technology that renders the old obsolete, can probably be reverted relatively quickly. Fiction, on the other hand, probably should not be reverted quickly. Every publisher must make its own decisions based on the sales trajectory and future potential of each book. Consider each one carefully. You never know what the future may bring.

Agency Clause

If an author uses an agent, then the agent will request an agency clause that stipulates that the agent is empowered by the author to act for the author. This further states that all sums of money that will be paid to the author should be paid to the agent as the author's agent.

There is nothing in this clause of jeopardy to the publisher, but it should be made a part of the contract because you need the author's permission, which this clause grants, to send money to a third party. If the author has problems getting paid by the agent, that's not your problem.

Arbitration Clause
In most cases, publishers, authors, and agents enter into contracts with all good will intended. As I've already noted, while this is nice in theory, it doesn't always wind up this way in practice. An arbitration clause is almost always part of a publishing contract because it delineates a way to resolve disputes without the undue time and cost of a formal lawsuit. Normally, such clauses stipulate that any unreconcilable differences between the publisher and author shall be resolved by a panel from the American Arbitration Association, a nationwide group that specializes in adjudicating conflicts outside the courtroom. In most cases, decisions

Arbitration has its own costs plus those for the attorneys who are involved.

by the arbitrator are filed with a court and are accepted as a binding decision. In some cases, however, such arbitrated rulings may not be binding and a case could ultimately wind up in court. Check with your attorney about this clause and whether it benefits your company or not. If you do decide to include an arbitration clause in your contracts, specify the venue in which the arbitration will occur.

Contract Analysis Form

Finally, when you've negotiated the contract with the best terms you can, and when you've signed the contract and received a fully executed contract in return, have your editor fill in a **Contract Analysis Form** (see opposite). This is simply a summary of the contract's most important terms. These forms should then be filed in an easy-to-access place, so they can be conveniently found when contract questions arise. If you have a computer network, put them on the network.

Title Fact Sheets

Once the contract on any given book has been signed, a key responsibility of a good editor is to spread the word throughout the company

Contract Analysis Form

Stock # _____ Contract date _____   Publication date _____

Title _____   List price _____

Author _____   Price changes & dates:

Agent _____

Contract with _____   Advance:

Royalty Rates

Rate	Quantity	Discount	Regular Sales	Sheet Sales	Reprints	Foreign	Other

	To Author	To Publisher
1) Abridgement, condensation, or digest.	50%	50%
2) Anthology or quotation	50%	50%
3) Book clubs or similar organizations	50%	50%
4) Reprint	50%	50%
5) Special edition	50%	50%
6) Second serial and syndication (including reproduction in compilations, magazines, newspapers, or books)	50%	50%
7) First serial rights.	_____	_____
8) Sole and exclusive rights of publication in		
a) The United Kingdom	_____	_____
b) The British Empire and/or the British Commonwealth of Nations	_____	_____
c) Other foreign countries	_____	_____
d) Translations	_____	_____
9) The right to sell, lease, or license for use throughout the world:		
a) Dramatic rights	_____	_____
b) Motion picture rights	_____	_____
c) Mechanical and electronic reproduction rights.	_____	_____
d) Radio and television rights	_____	_____
e) Commercial rights.	_____	_____
f) Audio rights	_____	_____

Market: U.S.A. ☐   Canada ☐   British Commonwealth ☐   World ☐   Other ☐

Special provisions, including those involving payment, notification, control of rights, options, and illustrations.

about the manuscript that has been acquired. It's important, for planning purposes, to let everyone who needs to know, know that a new book has been added to the list and the pertinent specifications of that book.

The **Title Fact Sheet** (see opposite) serves this purpose. It concisely records the details of the newly acquired book in one place for all to see and reference. If your company is networked, put this sheet on the network for all to see. Otherwise, keep the sheet in an easy-to-reach editorial file. The information should be accessible to any interested party at any time. It can be used by all other functional departments for their planning purposes. Title Fact Sheets prove especially useful to sales and marketing personnel as sales conference and cataloging time approach.

A good Title Fact Sheet will have entries for

- title
- author
- ISBN
- publishing season and year
- format and size
- number of pages
- tentative price
- estimated initial print run (taken from Title P&L)
- content description
- author biographical details
- marketing plans and budgets (from Basic Marketing Plan Worksheet, page 204)
- directly competitive books
- blurbs, awards, citations

You'll find that over time this simple form will become a staple of your everyday publishing life.

Let the Industry Know About Your Book

Once you've signed the contract for your book, your editorial department should get preliminary information about the book to those who need to know, especially R.R. Bowker, who publishes *Books in Print* and *Forthcoming Books in Print*. These reference works are more impor-

Title Fact Sheet

Season _____ Year _____

Title _____

Author _____ Author Location _____

| Hardcover Price $ _____ | ISBN _____ | Projected Print Qty _____ |
| Paperback Price $ _____ | ISBN _____ | Projected Print Qty _____ |

Ship Date _____ Pub Date _____

Binding _____ # Pages _____ Trim Size_____

Illustrations/Photos: B&W _____ Color_____

Content synopsis:

Target market:

Promotional plans:

Author bio (include other titles, publisher, date published, sales history):

Competitive books:

Why should accounts expect to sell this book?

Endorsements/testimonials (for book or author):

tant today than they were before the electronic age. Not only do they make it easy for booksellers to look up your book to find out the title, author, publisher, and other salient details about it, but now, these sources provide an online database to online bookstores. This is how such online booksellers can advertise that they have immediate access to over 1,000,000 or more books.

Listing your books in *Books in Print* and *Forthcoming Books in Print* is easy: simply ask R.R. Bowker for Advance Book Information forms (ABI forms), which you fill out and return to R.R. Bowker. Bowker can be reached at 121 Chanlon Rd., New Providence, NJ 07974, 908-464-6800. Easier still is to fill out the form online at www.bowkerlink.com.

One critical element you'll need to complete the **Advance Book Information Form** (see opposite) is an International Standard Book Number, or ISBN, which identifies each specific edition of your book, including different formats such as hardcover or paperback. Once used, *it must never be reused,* even if the title goes out of print. The number itself is a series of ten digits, separated by hyphens, which identify the country of origin, the publisher, the title, and the edition of the book. The final number of the ISBN is a checking digit, which allows computers to determine quickly whether the full ISBN is "true" or not. As you can see on the copyright page and back cover of this book, the ISBN is printed on your book's copyright page and on the lower right corner of the book's jacket back or back cover. It is also placed on the back cover in an EAN barcode form to make scanning at the retail level quick and effective.

Publishers should note carefully, though, that as of January 2005, the ISBN standard will begin to migrate from the current 10-digit string of numbers to 13. This is happening in order to increase the available supply of ISBN numbers (who said publishers weren't publishing more and that more publishing houses weren't being started?) and to make the ISBN standard compatible with European standard numbering systems. All ISBNs in the original pool of numbers will be prefaced by the prefix "978" to accomplish this increase in digits. All new ISBNs will be given a "979" prefix. The ISBN International Regulatory Agency is also cautioning publishers to prepare themselves for 32 characters in the ISBN field.

What happens to an e-book or to a digital file? According to the U.S. ISBN Agency:

Advance Book Information Form

ADVANCE BOOK INFORMATION

R. R. BOWKER DATA COLLECTION CENTER
P.O. BOX 2068, OLDSMAR, FL 34677-0037

TITLE:

SUBTITLE:

SERIES:

Foreign Language: Translation □, from what Language:

AUTHOR(S):

EDITOR(S):

TRANSLATOR(S):

ILLUSTRATOR(S):

INTRO. BY; PREFACE BY; etc.

ILLUSTRATIONS   YES □   NO □

PAGES:

AUDIENCE (Select Primary Audience):

College Text □   Young Adult □: Grade:

Elhi Text □: Grade: Juvenile □: Grade:

Original Paperback □

Revised □   Abridged □   2nd Ed. □   Other.

PUBLICATION DATE:
Reprint □: if reprint, name of orig. publisher & orig. pub. date:

ISBN NOTE: Put full 10 digit number with hyphens in spaces below.
The system requires a separate ISBN for each edition.

ENTER PRICE(S) BELOW: INT'L STANDARD BOOK NUMBER

On short discount (20% or less) □

HARDCOVER TRADE: _ _._ _ _   ISBN _ _ _ _ _ _ _ _ _ _

If juv., is binding guaranteed?

LIBRARY BINDING: _ _._ _   ISBN _ _ _ _ _ _ _ _ _ _

HARDCOVER TEXT: _ _._ _   ISBN _ _ _ _ _ _ _ _ _ _

PAPER TRADE: _ _._ _   ISBN _ _ _ _ _ _ _ _ _ _

PAPER TEXT: _ _._ _   ISBN _ _ _ _ _ _ _ _ _ _

TCHRS. ED.:   _ _._ _   ISBN _ _ _ _ _ _ _ _ _ _

WKBK: _ _._ _   ISBN _ _ _ _ _ _ _ _ _ _

LAB MANUAL: _ _._ _   ISBN _ _ _ _ _ _ _ _ _ _

OTHER: SPECIFY: _ _._ _   ISBN _ _ _ _ _ _ _ _ _ _

LC#

PUBLISHER (Not Printer):
Address

Telephone

DISTRIBUTOR, if other than publisher
(If you distribute foreign books you must be their exclusive U.S.
distributor. Please send us a copy of your documentation
for exclusivity)

IMPRINT (if other than company name):

THIS WORK IS ESSENTIALLY (Check one):

□ FICTION   □ TEXTBOOK

□ POETRY   □ BIOGRAPHY

□ DRAMA   □ OTHER_____
                              Specify
□ CHILDREN'S FICTION

□ ESSAYS

PRIMARY SUBJECT OF BOOK
(Be as specific as possible):

□ MEDICAL (MB)   □ SCIENCE/TECHNICAL
                           (ST)
□ CHILDREN (CB)

□ LAW (LB)

□ OTHER (Specify):

1. Format/means of delivery are irrelevant in deciding whether a product requires an ISBN (if the content itself meets the requirement, it gets at ISBN, no matter what the format of the delivery.)
2. Each format of a digital publication represents a new edition and requires a separate ISBN.

For Print-on-Demand titles, an ISBN is needed and should be provided by the rights holder of the On Demand edition *only if,* according to the ISBN organization, *your product fits one of the following three categories:*

1. A copy of some edition of the title reproduced on demand via rudimentary photocopy, the text of which is exactly the same as the edition copied, while physical aspects of the book are different.
2. A copy of some edition of a title, reproduced on demand via the new reproduction technology, by a publisher that has bought On Demand rights to another publisher's title.
3. A copy produced via the new technology by an organization other than the publisher on behalf of the publisher (i.e., no rights have changed hands), where the On Demand edition takes the place in the market of the publisher's printed edition in the same format (e.g., trade paper to trade paper).

For more information on these situations or ISBNs in general, go to the Book Industry Study Group's website, www.bisg.org, or the U.S. ISBN Agency's site, www.isbn.org.

Remember, every ISBN identifies a unique book, so even if you revise an edition of your book it will require a new ISBN. The number must be preceded by the letters "ISBN" and the hyphens in the number must be used. To get your company's pre-assigned ISBNs, write to: International Standard Book Number Agency, 121 Chanlon Road, New Providence, NJ 07974, 908-665-6770. Request their *Title Output Information Request Form* and their *User's Manual.* An **Application for an ISBN Publisher Prefix** is on pages 152–153, or, easier still, fill out the form online at www.isbn.org.

In addition to the ISBN, you'll want to file for Cataloging-in-Publication (CIP) information. This information, printed on your copyright page, allows libraries to catalog your book immediately in correct

Dewey classification. CIP information can be obtained from the CIP Department, Library of Congress, Washington, DC 20540, 202-707-5000; or, for smaller publishers, from Quality Books, 1003 West Pines, Oregon, IL 61061, 815-732-4450.

Finally, you'll also want a Library of Congress Catalog Card Number, which identifies each book placed on a library shelf. This number must be requested before you publish your book, so it's important to file for this early in your publishing process. Contact the Library of Congress, Washington, DC 20540 and request the *Procedures for Securing Preassigned Library of Congress Catalog Card Numbers*.

Managing and Revitalizing Backlist

If you're a successful publisher, over the years you've probably developed one or more core titles that have become signatures of your backlist. These are the titles that sell best for you over time, year in and year out. These are the titles that maintain your revenue stream, cushion your cash flow, and help ensure your ongoing profitability and survival.

And while good backlist can continue selling indefinitely—especially fiction and children's books—even the best backlist inevitably slows down.

Through the simple, effective strategy of backlist management and revitalization, you can

- generate new frontlist titles
- increase revenue
- strengthen and prolong your backlist book's life
- keep your authors happy
- meet your editorial budgets and goals

When you create your yearly editorial budgets, a primary goal of every editor should be the *revitalization* of backlist books and sales. These books are probably the editor's easiest acquisition source. Authors are known; the books are done, only in need of updating; and the book's passage through editorial and sales approval is almost always guaranteed because these books have already proved their worth. In addition, the ultimate sale of the book to the wholesale and retail accounts is straightforward and simple: if your revisions are sub-

ISBN Application Form

INTERNATIONAL STANDARD BOOK NUMBER--UNITED STATES AGENCY
International Standard Numbering System for the Information Industry
630 Central Avenue, New Providence, New Jersey 07974
TEL: 908-771-7755 FAX: 908-665-2895 Email: isbn-san@bowker.com

International Standard ISO 2108   R.R. Bowker LLC, a Cambridge Information Group company

APPLICATION FOR AN ISBN PUBLISHER PREFIX

FOR AGENCY USE ONLY

SYMBOL: _____

PREFIX: _____

PLEASE PRINT OR TYPE:

Company/Publisher Name: _____

Address: _____

Phone Number: _____ Do Not Publish: ___

Fax Number: _____ Do Not Publish: ___

Toll Free Number: _____

E-MAIL: _____ Do Not Publish: ___

Web Site: _____

Fax-on-Demand: _____ Toll Free Fax: _____

If P.O. Box Indicated, Local Street Address is Required:

Name of Rights & and Permissions Contact: _____

Title: _____ Phone Number: _____

Name of ISBN Coordinator/Contact: _____

Title: _____ Phone Number: _____

Division or Subsidiary of: _____

Imprints: _____

PAYMENT: A NON-REFUNDABLE PROCESSING SERVICE CHARGE
          PRIORITY PROCESSING SURCHARGE $75

ISBN PREFIX BLOCK	REGULAR PROCESSING FEE	PRIORITY PROCESSING FEE
10 ISBNs	$225.00	$300.00
100 ISBNs	$800.00	$875.00
1,000 ISBNs	$1,200.00	$1,275.00
10,000 ISBNs	$3,000.00	-

Fee Waiver:
Applicants requesting a fee-waiver MUST provide a list of titles and
formats along with 501(C3) and mission statement documents.
Failure to provide this title list will delay Agency processing.

ISBN Application Form *continued*

__ Charge: ____ American Express ____ Visa ____ Master Card

Card Holder Name: _____

    Account #: _____ Expiration Date: _____

Total amount enclosed or charged: _____

Authorized signature: _____ Date: _____

* **Note**: **Credit Cards are the preferred form of payment**

PUBLISHING INFORMATION:

1. Indicate year you started publishing: _____

2. Indicate what type of products you produce (circle):

    Books   Videos   Spoken Words on Cassette/CD
       Software   Mixed Media

    Other - Please specify: _____

3. Book Subject Area (circle):

    o Children's
    o Law
    o Medical
    o Religious
    o Sci-Tech
    o Other - Please specify: _____

DISTRIBUTION INFORMATION:

1. Do you distribute for, or are you distributed by, any other company?
   Yes: _____ No: _____. If yes, please provide full company name,
   address and ISBN Publisher Prefix (if any):

_____
_____
_____

PROCESSING INFORMATION:

Your application for an ISBN Publisher Prefix will be processed ONLY if you include the following:

1. Completed application
2. Payment

* **Note: Credit Cards are the preferred form of payment**

The ISBN U.S. Agency will not provide an ISBN by telephone or fax. Processing time for an ISBN application is 10 business days (Saturdays and Sundays and holidays are not business days) from the date of our receipt of the completed form. This means that the application is inhouse for that length of time; ISBNs will be mailed to publishers after this processing period is completed (provided there are no problems with the application).

PRIORITY PROCESSING:

If you intend to ask the agency for a faster turn around time, a priority charge of $75. applies and must be added to the service charge fee. Priority service includes return, within 48 business hours of receipt, of your ISBN Publisher Prefix and ISBN log book (provided there are no problems with the application).

If you are requesting priority service and would like your ISBN log book e-mailed, please provide the e-mail address to where it should be sent: _____

Please Note: The priority service is either by e-mail or courier service, but NOT both.

WAIVING OF THE SERVICE CHARGE:

Your firm may apply for a waiver of the service charge if your firm has been granted a 501 (C3) charitable/philanthropic tax exemption status & your firm can supply a statement of your charitable/philanthropic mission. Your firm must supply documentation on BOTH to be eligible for a fee waiver. If you request a waiver of the service charge and require priority processing, a charge of $75.00 does apply.

Return the application and payment to:

ISBN U.S. Agency
R.R. Bowker
630 Central Avenue
New Providence, NJ 07974
isbn-san@bowker.com

stantial, especially when they include a new cover or jacket, the buyer will review the sales of the original book and either use that figure as a base for a new purchase quantity or increase the number. He makes

When you create your yearly editorial budgets, a primary goal of every editor should be the revitalization of backlist books and sales.

this decision based on the fact that you've now repositioned the book as *frontlist*, and, in most cases, will be promoting it with additional marketing attention and budgets.

Another benefit of revitalizing backlist titles is that your authors will be delighted with your continued interest in, and support of, their books. This, in turn, makes you a more appealing publisher for the author's next book.

Every Editor Should Be a Sales Manager

"OK," your editors say, "I've done my job, now it's up to the sales-people to do theirs. I've gotten you a great book and made sure it's out on time, now it's your turn to sell it. And don't give me any excuses!"

Sound familiar?

The question is, what do an editor and a sales manager have in common? Yes, both probably work for the same company and yes, they both work hard. But what else?

The answer is, if they're good at their jobs, both the editor and the sales manager scour the sales reports and sales figures for insights into which titles sell best, where they're selling, and why they're selling.

As an editor, it's easy to remove yourself from the day-to-day results of your books' sales. Good editors are always busy talking to authors and agents, trying to find and procure new books, editing books, spending time in meetings, etc. They rarely have time to sit down and review results. And to a large extent, they presume to define quality in one way: content, without asking whether anyone else is interested in that content.

The best editors, however, reverse this process. They realize that the knowledge gained by reviewing their sales figures can inform their future acquisition efforts and help focus their efforts more fully on subjects and categories that are selling—that people want to read—and avoid those areas in which sales are weak.

Such sales guidance is invaluable and such a review should be de rigueur for all editors. As the manager of your publishing house, or as an editor eager to do the best job possible, you must make it your business to talk to the sales force; to review sales reports regularly; and to determine the strengths and weaknesses of your list. Are some areas and titles hot and heating up? If so, are there backlist books you can repackage and quickly re-release as frontlist? (See Managing and Revitalizing Backlist). Can you find new titles on the appropriate subjects that are well on their way to completion that you can acquire? Remember, the publishing process takes time, so unless the manuscript or work you acquire is close to completion, what's hot today may be stone-cold tomorrow!

Are there other areas of your list that are cooling off, and that you might choose not to pursue for a while? Recognize that every publishing decision is a trade-off of resources. You only have a finite budget with which to work, and if you use it to publish in those areas that are cooling off, or those areas in which sales are slight, you are sacrificing your own opportunity to build a bigger list with significantly higher results.

In the longer term, what categories of your list sell best over time? Can you augment them with other, new books?

The process of editing is a dynamic one: trends come and go; new authors and manuscripts are everywhere. Sales patterns shift in response to subjects and bookselling changes. For example, what publisher hasn't been dramatically effected by the rise of the large internet e-tailers, the dominance of the superstores, the decline of the independents, and the implementation of just-in-time inventory demands? Editors must be aware of, and respond to, these market forces or their programs will suffer.

Does this mean that an editor should abandon her traditional role of keeper of the flame of quality? Absolutely not. Whatever manuscript or work is brought in and published must be the best it can be. But given that, it must also contribute to the survival of the organization so that the organization can continue to publish other books. And in business terms, that means that the majority of books must be profitable enough to offset those that will inevitably achieve less-than-anticipated results.

And for books to sell, an editor must acknowledge that her books exist in an incredibly competitive sales environment with demands of its own. The more the editor understands this market and its demands, the more she can understand which of her own books will sell best in that environment, why they sell, and where they are selling. And the more she comprehends these factors, the more her books will sell. And that will only benefit the company and enhance its chances for long-term survival.

Evaluating Editors

Evaluating your editors to see that they are doing their jobs and doing them well is extremely important. Without competent editors who bring in new books, who make sure their books are edited on time and get to production on time, and indeed, that they are published on time, your entire publishing program may be at risk. You must, then, create systems to monitor your editor's ability to keep the pipeline full and to keep it flowing.

You must create systems to monitor your editor's ability to keep the pipeline full and to keep it flowing.

The best evaluation system I've ever seen with respect to editors is that used by John Wiley & Sons. As I've said before, the difference between large publishers and small is a difference of degree, not of kind. So when you find a system that works for the large house, it probably can be adapted to a smaller house.

Wiley's simple and effective system ensures continuous monitoring of four basic editorial functions:

- sales emanating from an editor's list
- number of manuscripts acquired each quarter and each year, with the emphasis on the yearly number
- number of manuscripts transmitted in complete and correct form to production
- number of manuscripts published within the year

Each of these elements becomes a target number, which is agreed upon between the senior management of the division and the individual editor. The editor's goals must tie in to the divisional goals, which are created by corporate management.

An editor's targets relate and flow from year to year. In other words, many of the manuscripts acquired in one fiscal year will go to production in the next, assuming that it takes a year to get something written and edited. Thus, a typical editor's targets, viewed at any particular time, might look and flow as the following examples.

FY 1999	Manuscripts Acquired	Manuscripts to Production	Books Published
Sales Target: $250,000			
Career Books	5	4	3
Personal Finance	2	1	1
Management	1	1	0
Total	8	6	4

FY 2000	Manuscripts Acquired	Manuscripts to Production	Books Published
Sales Target: $400,000			
Career Books	6	5	4
Personal Finance	2	2	2
Management	1	1	1
Total	9	8	7

FY 2001	Manuscripts Acquired	Manuscripts to Production	Books Published
Sales Target: $500,000			
Career Books	6	5	5
Personal Finance	2	2	2
Management	2	2	1
Total	10	9	8

Once agreed upon, the editor strives to meet her targets. Meeting the targets ensures a steady stream of new or revised manuscripts that get to production on time and that are published on time. During quarterly reviews, for each editor's list, management can spot deficiencies at any point within the publishing process and determine, in conjunction with the editor, what steps will be taken to meet the yearly targets.

The two targets that the editor has little control over are sales and the books published. In the case of the former, the sales staff is responsible; the latter, the production staff. What this means is that the editor must constantly look for material that the sales staff can sell. Going back to our last discussion, the editor must be a sales manager.

Similarly, the sales force is given targets that they must meet based on the kinds of books that the editors are bringing in. It's a symbiotic relation that works. If the books don't sell, neither the editor nor the sales force will meet their targets. It is important, therefore, that there be cooperation and understanding between the two areas. At the same time, the editor can publish revised editions of books to ease her acquisition burden. More importantly, backlist sales of books within the editor's program count toward meeting the sales target.

Thus, a good editor who reviews her list regularly and keeps it up-to-date, who works closely with her salespeople, who keeps on top of current market trends, and who has good acquisition contacts can meet targets without undue pressure. Those who wait to acquire, who let their backlist atrophy, and who procure new books without good feedback from the market will have a very tough time meeting their targets.

This is also true of the relationship between the editor and the production department. If production doesn't get material on time, the editor suffers. If that material doesn't come out of production on time, then both the editor and the production department staff suffer, because production is also evaluated on getting material out on time. Again, cooperation is engendered and communication between the two areas is necessary for each.

Wiley's system is also excellent because it's based on objective criteria. Each of the four elements noted (manuscripts acquired, manuscripts to production, manuscripts published, sales target) is determined at the beginning of the fiscal year. If the editor meets her targets, she gets a bonus that is also determined at the beginning of the fiscal year. Thus throughout the year, every editor knows exactly how much he or she can earn. If the editor doesn't meet her target, she gets a proportionately smaller bonus. If she misses the target by a substantial sum, she gets no bonus. On the other hand, if she exceeds her targets, she can earn proportionately more bonus.

What makes this reward system work is that it is established at the beginning of the fiscal year and is not changed. Editors can work towards completion of their targets at their own pace, as long as they hit the targets by the end of the year. The second element that makes the system work is that the bonus money is not discretionary. If the editor succeeds in meeting her targets, the money is hers. It doesn't rely on a manager's whim or on a subjective analysis of things the editor can't control. It is fair and it is objective.

Think about your evaluation system. Do you have one at all? If you do, does it make sense? Does it compel your editors to meet and exceed targets and discourage them from coming in less than on target? Do you set the goals and objectives for your editors or are they involved in the process? Does your system ensure that manuscripts will continue to come in on time, be edited and transmitted on time, and get published on time? If not, you might think about your system a bit more. If you do cover all this ground, then congratulations, you're definitely on the right track.

A final word about the editorial process. Much has been said in this chapter about the manner in which companies can streamline their editorial programs and make them efficient and responsive to various corporate needs. Very little has been said about actual editing. As I've mentioned earlier, most publishers have a pretty good editorial vision of the kinds of books they want to publish and the market niche they want to occupy. Many publishers, however, seem to have forgotten that there is more to the editorial process than just acquiring and publishing. There is also the need for true editing.

Many of today's publishers, large and small, don't truly do much developmental editing anymore. They rely on agents to work with authors to get material in shape, to pre-screen manuscripts and to review full manuscripts before they are submitted to the publisher. In-house editors tend to be acquisition editors, who focus on the competitive aspect of finding and signing books for the publishing house. While there is definitely room for the acquisition editor, what is missing more and more from today's publishing environment is the demand for and insistence on quality editing.

Whereas most publishers used to have proofreaders and copy editors on staff, today, fewer do. Larger publishers freelance much of their editing work to developmental editors who specialize in organizational and line editing. In contrast, smaller publishers, primarily to save money, tend to try to do this work themselves, almost invariably to the ultimate detriment of the book. As we've said before, some people are expert in one area of publishing, some in others. There is a true talent to line editing and copyediting, yet most who do this kind of work are underpaid and underappreciated. Every book you publish should go through the full developmental editing process, including proofreading and copyediting. You must insist on this kind of quality and quality control or your book will be fair game for any reviewer to shoot at. More important, nothing will work against your ultimate success as a publisher as quickly as a poorly written book. Remember: credibility is your best attribute. Credibility necessitates quality books—which are the result of excellent writing and first-class editing.

Insist, therefore, upon a substantive editing by trained professionals. The result will significantly benefit your company and your book.

CHAPTER 8

Production and Manufacturing

The functions of design, production, and manufacturing are as much art as science, especially when one considers that both interior design and jacket/cover design are usually found under this heading. In many publishing companies, design, production, and manufacturing are separate; in smaller houses, they are usually combined. For our purposes, I'll view them as one.

Production and manufacturing cover a lot of ground. Not only are these functional areas responsible for the transformation of manuscript or disk to finished book, but they are also responsible for a major expenditure of money. If a manufacturing run is marred slightly, correction of the error, or rerunning an entire print run, can have catastrophic financial implications.

Design, production, and manufacturing, in many publishing houses, are not considered as glamorous as editorial or sales, and may be looked upon as secondary. They should be viewed as quite the reverse. Design and production have saved innumerable editors by picking up time lost in the editorial process; helped more sales managers by creating striking, promotionally oriented jackets and covers that appeal to consumers, and salvaged many a list by getting books out on time. It has made more senior managers look good by ensuring profitability to numerous books by effectively controlling development and manufacturing costs.

The design, production, and manufacturing functions demand

increasingly technical knowledge of what printing presses run which sheets of paper most cost effectively, and now, what computer capabilities are and how these are related to, and integrated with, new prepress, printing, and binding processes. Design, production, and manufacturing are in the forefront of the computer revolution. Production managers must now be able to converse knowledgeably about the use and application of digitized data within their companies.

Production and manufacturing departments also must be expert in handling crisis situations because almost every action that goes on within their department is time-sensitive. Thus, it's critical to have strategic controls in place.

The Production Schedule

Although I will discuss production issues in more detail a bit later, to produce a meaningful cash-flow chart, in addition to your budget and sales projections you will have to create a Production Schedule. This is similar to the sales budget you've created, but precedes it. In other words, if you're going to sell 1,000 books, then you need to produce at least 1,000 books. The production schedule will tell you when that will happen, because it tracks the flow of the manuscript from the time it is fully edited to the time it leaves the printer.

Isn't this information contained in the sales chart because that chart tells you when a book is sold? Not really. That chart only focuses on the last moment of the production schedule. What goes before—the design of text and jacket or cover; the typesetting and page layout; the separation or digitization of photographs; the actual printing and binding all involve the use and flow of cash.

Thus, you must know when these events will occur to budget your cash flow realistically. One of the most important functions of your production manager or managing editor is to prioritize the work going through the production process. While this might seem simple, it is anything but. The reason is that the work going through the production department is constantly being disrupted by events that impinge on the orderly workflow. The department is constantly being asked to produce sales catalogs, advertisements, and promotional material—all of which are unrelated to actually producing books. To keep the flow of books on schedule, the production manager must maintain a tight rein on who's doing what and in what order it's being done.

Production Schedule

Editor / Designer / Production Manager — Title / Author / ISBN	Description / Size / # Pages / Price / Qty / BDG	Request for Quote	Prelim. Ms. to Designer	Disk / Ms. to Production	SCHEDULE	First Page Galleys IN	First Page Galleys OUT	Index & Misc. to Production	Revised Pages IN	Revised Pages OUT	Revised Pages FINAL DISK	Bluelines or Lasers IN	Bluelines or Lasers OUT	# Colors Art	Loose Blues In	Caption Copy	Color Proofs Blues or Lasers In	Color Proofs Blues or Lasers Out	Jacket/Flap Copy In	# Colors for Art	Sketch in OK	Jacket Layout	Proofs in	Final Disk	Die Mech. & Specs.	Sample Case OK	Off Press	Bound Book Date	Pub Date	Supplier	Quantity	Manufacturing PO

A sample **Production Schedule** can be simple. It is basically a linear calendar of events that records the inflow and outflow of production material throughout the production process. At each stage, you must attach a cost to the event, and then record the cash outflow 30 days (or whatever your vendor terms are) from the time of that event. This cash outlay must be recorded in your cash-flow projection.

Make sure that your production schedule has two rows for entry: one for the estimated date something will happen; one for the actual date it happens. The reason to record both of these dates is not to cast blame on someone whose project is slipping. Rather, it alerts all those who review the production schedule—which should be everyone involved in the process, from the editorial staff to the sales staff—that there is a problem to be resolved quickly to maintain the schedule. As a last resort, the book may be rescheduled, but this too should become clear using the production schedule.

Keep in mind one particular fact: the production department is all too often called upon to bail out a book that is late. Editors always feel that production can be sped up to compensate for late manuscript delivery; sales always needs books sooner, rather than later. Management wants to get a return on its cash in the shortest possible time. Thus all sides put pressure on the production department to produce books quickly.

The fact of the matter is, this is usually self-defeating. If the editorial process is scheduled properly, it should allow plenty of time to provide a fully edited manuscript to production. Editors should know exactly *what's* expected of them, and *when* it's expected. This involves a great deal of input from them. Thus, if they're late, they—not production—should bear the burden. Furthermore, production's needs are just as critical as any other department's. They must compete with a multitude of other publishers, all clamoring for low prices and quick turnaround from manufacturing vendors.

Production departments get very little respect—and they deserve a lot.

Production departments get very little respect—and they deserve a lot. Using your production schedule as a primary tool, your staff can be well informed about the status of every book going through the process and management can be better informed about the ebb and flow of its cash.

Production Meetings

To facilitate the creation of the production schedule and maintain that schedule, the production department must meet at regular intervals. Scheduling, as I've noted, is crucial, and anything that can alert production staff to problems in a timely way is desired. The production meeting should be in two stages: a weekly meeting between the editor of the book and the managing editor or person responsible for production; and another weekly meeting between the managing editor and the rest of the production staff.

At the editorial-production meeting, editors should be asked to update each manuscript on the list in terms of its completion. Will it still be submitted on time? Will it need any special production attention or specifications? Are there any significant changes or requirements for printing and manufacturing? All of these should be discussed. Editors and production people should be wary of authors who continually promise on-time delivery and then don't come through. Editors, frankly, tend to be optimistic when it comes to production schedules and their own programs. It's better to be realistic. If an author will be late, let the production department know about it as early as possible so it can make adjustments to the schedules. Perhaps a book that's come in early can be switched with another that's late. Seek anything that makes the flow simpler.

Production must be candid with the editors. Some changes are clearly unacceptable due to cost overages. Because production staff should to some extent be judged on the basis of how well they can control costs, if an editor suggests a change that would be too costly, production should state this is the case. In addition, production should have input into the Title P&Ls because it provides the manufacturing estimates for that form. If there is a substantial difference between that original estimate and the final specifications of the book, everyone must be alerted, because it may mean more books must be sold, the price must be raised, or another adjustment must be made.

Once the production people are informed by the editors of the weekly progress (or lack of progress) of their manuscripts, the production department must discuss the results among themselves to be sure everyone is aware of what is happening and how it impacts all the other books on the list. The production schedule should then be updated with revisions and passed out to all those involved in, or interested in, the process.

Production Checklist

In addition to the production schedule, to avoid oversights, I always recommend that a **Production Checklist** (see opposite) be kept in every book's production folder. This is simply a checklist of every part of the book to ensure that all the copy and elements needed for the book are in and accounted for, including bar codes, CIP information, and other important material. These production checklists should be given to the editorial staff, so they can gather most of this information prior to its being needed by production.

With the production schedule and the production checklist in hand, you can begin to push the production process forward with a good degree of assurance that you've got it under control. Until the next crisis hits!

Costing and Estimating

As I mentioned, the production function can be significant in terms of both incurring costs and saving money for your company. With paper, printing, and binding (PPB) averaging approximately 50% of the total cost of goods, it is a sizable amount of money. At an average 5,000-copy print run, with a PPB of approximately $2.50, every title you produce costs about $12,500. If you can save 10 cents per copy, you can save $500—a meaningful amount of money, especially when multiplied by numerous titles.

How can you ensure that your manufacturing costs are reasonable? The simple answer is to set up costing, or estimating, forms, also known as **Request for Quote** forms (see page 169) or RFQs, with the specifications for your job, and to send those sheets to a minimum of five manufacturers per job. These sheets don't have to be fancy, but the same sheet should be sent to each manufacturer you solicit. And specifications must be in accord with the final specifications of the product you'll be sending for production. It is meaningless to solicit preliminary bids from printers and then change the specifications on the final product. Not only will this cause confusion for you and the vendor, but it will waste time and effort.

Production Checklist

I. Text
- ❏ Title Page:
    - ❏ Title
    - ❏ Author's Name
    - ❏ Publisher's Imprint
- ❏ Copyright Page
    - ❏ CIP Information
    - ❏ ISBN Information
    - ❏ Copyright Date & ❏ Copyright Holder
    - ❏ "Printed and Bound in the United States"
    - ❏ Edition Numbers (1,2,3....)
- ❏ Acknowledgment Page (If any)
- ❏ Text Pages
- ❏ Appendices
- ❏ Index

II. Cover (Softcover or paper-over-board hardcover)
- ❏ Front:
    - ❏ Title
    - ❏ Author
    - ❏ Additional Copy (series name, foreword)
- ❏ Spine:
    - ❏ Publisher
    - ❏ Title
    - ❏ Author's Last Name
- ❏ Back
    - ❏ Title
    - ❏ Author
    - ❏ All Final Copy
    - ❏ ISBN
    - ❏ Price (U.S./Canada)
    - ❏ Bar Code (EAN and UPC)
    - ❏ Subject Category (shelving information)
    - ❏ Author Photo (if desired)
    - ❏ Quotes

III. Jacket (Hardcover) if flap (i.e., not paper over board)
- ❏ All of Above from Softcover
- ❏ Flap
    - ❏ Author Photo (if desired)
    - ❏ All Flap Copy
    - ❏ Author Biographical Material
    - ❏ Company Blurb

IV. Printer's cover or jacket specification sheet
- ❏ Hardcover, Including Spine Bulk
- ❏ Paperback, Including Spine Bulk

© Cross River Publishing Consultants, Inc.

Different printers and binders often have different printing and binding equipment. Because of these differences, some printers and binders will be better suited to producing your particular book at lower prices than will others. Some, for instance, may have only sheet-fed presses, which are typically more cost-effective on smaller print runs of 10,000 or less. Some may have web presses, which are more cost-effective on runs of 15,000 and over. A few printers have Cameron belt presses, which print and bind your book in one line operation. They were created to make short runs of 5,000 or so faster and more economical for the publisher.

Additionally, different manufacturers have different workflows, with some being busy at certain times while others have less work. You can take advantage of these differences if you bid your work to the various vendors. The point is, if your product is to be produced at the lowest price, you have to capitalize on finding the vendor whose equipment is best suited to your job, who has the time to do it, and who offers you the most suitable payment terms.

As an example, one printer offers a 5% discount for work done in the first quarter of the New Year. This is because the period is traditionally slow for this printer and it wants to keep its staff working and its presses busy. On our hypothetical book costing $12,500, scheduling within the first quarter can save $625, or 12.5 cents per book. And because every dollar saved at the unit cost level translates to $6 or more at the retail level, this 12.5 cents translates to about 75 cents at the retail level. In other words, if you were pricing your book at $12.95 prior to the manufacturing saving, you could now lower the price, if you chose to do so, to $12.20, which might make that book more appealing to buyers.

The Request for Quote begins with the title and the month the files will arrive at the manufacturer. The date is important for the reason just stated: it may be a slow time for that printer. This could affect the price quoted to you.

Following these details, the pertinent specifications of the book are listed:

- Size of print run
- Trim size
- Number of pages

Request for Quote

Date:

To: Vendor
        Address

Please estimate the following title for us:

Title:

Month to Arrive at Printer:

Expected Print Date:

Quantity:

Trim Size:

Number of Pages:

Number Hardback: _____   Number Paperback: _____
Stock: Binding:
    Text pages: Perfect:
    Endpapers: Adhesive Notch:
    Jacket/Cover: Smythe:
                                    Other:
Ink:
    Text Pages: Case Material:
    Endpapers: Stamping:
    Jacket/Cover: Headbands:

Cover coating: Miscellaneous:
    UV Coating:
    Film Laminate: Packing:
        Gloss: Carton Specification, Size,
        Matte: Weight, Labels & Marking:
        Spot: Pallet Specifications:
        Lay Flat:
                                Freight:
Preparation: FOB Warehouse?
                                    CIF Warehouse?
Proofs: Carrier:
                                    Special Requirements:
Manufacturing:
    Web:
    Sheetfed: Payment Terms:
    Cameron/Belt:

- Format: hardcover and/or paperback
- Type, weight, and bulk of paper required for text, endpapers, and jacket/cover (uncoated, coated, matte; white, blue, blue-white). Because paper constitutes about 50% of the PPB cost, different weights can have a major impact on the estimate you get.
- Color of ink (i.e., just black; four-color)
- Type of lamination on a paper cover or paper-over-board title
- Preparation
- Proofs desired (blues, matchprints, other)
- Type of press to be used
- Type of binding (perfect, adhesive-notch, Smythe-sewn, flexible, etc.)
- Packing requirements (including carton specifications, labeling, pallet size, banding, etc.)
- Shipping and freight costs
- Special requirements (head and/or footbands; shrink wrapping; thumb-notched index tabs; etc.)
- Payment terms

Every penny you know about in advance is a penny you can bid competitively to other vendors and factor into your Title P&Ls to ensure their accuracy.

Once you get your bid sheets returned from the vendors, make sure you're comparing apples to apples. Vendors typically send bids out in their own formats, which may or may not coincide with the way you've asked for them and will undoubtedly be different from their competitors.

One manufacturer may, for instance, provide bids using its stock paper, which may be 50#. (In paper jargon, # is the symbol for pounds.) Another manufacturer might quote using 60# stock. If this happens, the price for the paper will most likely be different, because 60# stock is heavier and generally more expensive. Because of the weight difference, it may make your book more costly to ship. If the terms quoted aren't what you asked for, don't hesitate to ask the vendor to re-specify the bid in *your* format or to your specifications.

In addition, be careful about the kind and weight of items like binder's board, which is used in hardcover manufacturing to provide the base over which the cloth or paper cover material is glued. Often, different binders use different thicknesses and weights—which cost different amounts. Similarly, check the type of cover material for paperbacks. Is your manufacturer quoting on 12-point (Pt.) cover stock, 10-point cover stock or some other weight? Pt. stands for the paper measurement term *point,* which is equal to 0.001 inch, or one thousandth of an inch. A 12-point cover is 0.012 inch or 12 thousandths of an inch thick.

In short, take nothing for granted. If you are unclear about a part of the bid, ask for clarification.

Once the information in your cost sheets is comparable, you can usually eliminate one or two of your five bidders fairly quickly. The other three may be competitive. If this is the case, I suggest you go back for another round of bids. It's remarkable how often manufacturers will be able to reduce their original estimates when they get into these competitive situations—especially if you've used the manufacturer before and have established good credit with the company. How do you rebid? By being honest with the vendors, telling them you have an equal or lower bid and asking them if they'd like the chance to rebid the job. In most cases, you'll get a reduced estimate. If the job is truly at a point at which the manufacturer can't make the profit it needs or wants, it'll simply refuse to rebid, make suggestions for modifying your requirements to reduce the price, or tell you point-blank that this is the lowest it can go.

> *The lowest price is not always the best. There may be circumstances that warrant paying a bit more.*

Don't get me wrong. The lowest price is *not* always the best. There may be circumstances that warrant paying a bit more. You may want to ensure better quality by using a printer known for its high quality; you may have a rush job that mandates paying more for faster service; you may want to use a manufacturer that is slightly higher in price but provides more favorable payment terms. You may want to use a printer you know you can rely on or one whom you've done business with before and who's easy to work with. All of these are legitimate reasons to pay more if you have to. But if you don't have to, then there's no reason whatsoever to pay more.

As I've tried to make clear, one critical element for most small-to-medium size publishers is *cash flow.* Because of the size of manufacturing expense, the cash-flow demands of the production and manufacturing function are probably greater than any other in the company, with the possible exception of the royalty advance. Thus, the way payment terms with manufacturers are structured must play a critical role in your analysis of which printer to use.

One client recently asked me to bid out a project for him. When I requested terms from a variety of printers, many were interested in bidding, but all bid on their own terms—which from my standpoint, and that of the client, were very harsh. Because the client was a smaller, relatively new publisher who hadn't established credit with any vendor, the payment terms required varied widely. One larger manufacturer, who spends hundreds of thousands of dollars courting smaller publishers for work, asked for 120% up front! That's right, 120%! Why? Because the manufacturer wanted to cover the risk that it was taking by working with this new publisher for the first time. The manufacturer wanted to be sure that if the work was rejected by the publisher for any reason that manufacturer would be whole. The extra 20% was for any overage that might occur, or any changes that might take place that weren't in the original bid.

A second vendor quoted the same price as the larger, but worked with the client, requesting much more reasonable terms of 50% up front, 50% 30 days from delivery.

Which manufacturer do you think was selected?

The point is that if you don't get a variety of bids, and ask specifically for the payment terms, you may not find the best manufacturer with the best price and terms.

If I could offer one piece of advice to smaller publishers in relation to production, it would be to *rebid, rebid, rebid*. Don't worry about offending the manufacturer—they'll tell you when they can't go any lower. It's only then that you'll have to make a decision. And then you'll be looking at the project from the best possible vantage point.

Money-Saving Tips

Because production expense is so large, it behooves every publisher to use every trick in the book to save money on this expense. In addition to the costing and estimating sheets noted in the previous section, other techniques can result in savings for your house. A few of those tips follow:

1. Use a book manufacturer to print your books. Do not attempt to use a commercial printer who only prints a few books a year. A book manufacturer prints hundreds or even thousands of titles every year. They are specially equipped to manufacture books. As a result, you will get a better, perhaps even more professional job—and usually at a much lower cost. Book manufacturers are listed in R. R. Bowker's *Literary Market Place,* a copy of which can probably be found in your local library.

2. Use the manufacturer's paper—don't even think about buying and inventorying your own. Manufacturers typically use enormous amounts of paper in various standard grades. They buy from paper mills in vast quantities, which results in extremely favorable prices for them. It is virtually certain that you won't be able to buy paper from the mills at the low price at which the manufacturer buys. So don't waste your time trying. In addition, when you buy from the manufacturer, rather than the mill, you pay only for the paper used—and no more. Thus, you won't have to pay for any paper that remains unused, and then pay again for storing it, and then pay when you write it off because it spoiled in the printer's warehouse. And you won't have to worry about managing your paper inventory, which can be a full-time job in itself.

3. Standardize your book sizes. Most manufacturers have presses that create fairly standard-size books: 5⅜" x 8"; 6" x 9"; 8½" x 11"; etc. Thus, it's most cost-effective to produce books in these sizes. If you start creating books in odd sizes—for whatever reason your marketing manager or editor suggests—you'll almost always pay more for that book. Most publishers stay within the standard formats. If you're smart and develop a good relation with a good printer that provides you with low prices, you'll begin to standardize your products to the size most efficiently run by that manufacturer.

In the example used previously, when my client decided to use the vendor with better terms (and comparable pricing), that vendor also told me that the client could save additional money if it changed the book size from 7" x 10" to 6½" x 9½", which their press could run faster, with less paper spoilage. In fact, the client saved 15 cents a book just by making this minor adjustment. Because every $1.00 of cost translates to at least a six times multiple at retail, this 15 cents translates to 90 cents at retail.

4. Use notch or perfect binding rather than Smythe sewing. In the "old days," Smythe-sewing was the only way to go. It was the strongest possible binding and glues just weren't up to standard. In the 1970s that changed. Glue was then, and is now, almost as strong as Smythe-sewing and significantly less expensive. No longer does glue dry out quickly with the result that pages come out easily. In most cases, the glue will remain strong and maintain the book's quality for decades.

Smythe-sewing may still be competitively priced if you manufacture your books abroad, especially in Europe and Asia. If you are manufacturing abroad, be sure to specify what method of binding you want or get bids for Smythe-sewn and perfect binding. You may actually get Smythe-sewn books for less cost.

Special bindings that allow the book to open flat are usually quite expensive.

Avoid spiral or plastic comb bindings. These do not permit a good identification for the book when it is shelved spine-out, which will usually be the case in the bookstore.

5. Reduce the paper weight. Because paper is such a large percentage of the manufacturing cost, in most cases, depending upon the grade being used, the less the weight, the less the cost. Keep in mind that your price still has to reflect a good *perceived value* at the retail level. And when you use lesser weights of paper you usually decrease the bulk (thickness) of the book—which could result in a loss of perceived value. It's possible, however, to find a point at which the trade-off to lower weight paper does not diminish the perceived value. Be careful, as well, in regard to the opacity of the paper—that is, the amount of see-through you get when using lower weight stock. Ask for samples of the paper if you are unsure of what a particular grade of paper looks like.

6. Use ultraviolet (UV) coating instead of glossy film lamination. While you won't get the same gloss as film lamination, UV lamination still protects the book from fingerprints and minor damage while saving a few cents per book. It does not have the same resistance to abrasion damage as film lamination. Matte lamination costs more than glossy lamination. "Lay-flat" lamination, though slightly more costly than regular lamination, tends to eliminate the curling that occurs when using UV coating or plain lamination in humid surroundings. Lay-flat lamination is available in both glossy and matte finishes. Lay-flat lamination is not the same as lay-flat binding.

7. Use "permeated" paper covers on hardcover books instead of cloth. While cloth used to be the norm, in today's cost-conscious world, strengthened paper covers have replaced cloth in a majority of cases. While it certainly doesn't have the wonderful tactile feel and strength of cloth, paper does have the benefit of lower price. And with a dust jacket over it, the public doesn't notice.

8. As an alternative to a full-cloth binding, or a permeated-paper case, use a three-piece case instead of full-cloth. This gives your book an elegant look without much more cost than a permeated-paper case. A three-piece case places cloth on the spine, which extends about 1 inch on each side of the case, and permeated paper is then pasted over the side of the case. This gives a bit more strength on the spine and hinges than a straight permeated paper, and it also looks more luxurious. The extra cost is minimal, perhaps 2 to 3 cents per book.

9. Don't overweight your cartons. Remember, shipping personnel, warehouse personnel, store clerks, and others have to carry cartons. If you pack too many books into a carton, it increases the chance the carton will be dropped, thereby increasing damage. In general, keep cartons under 40 pounds. 30 pounds is even better!

10. Pack your books in standard carton counts, so each carton contains the same number of books. Some customers, especially wholesalers, distributors, and non-traditional accounts, prefer to order in carton quantities. Packing in standard counts allows you to invoice and ship quickly and accurately.

11. Similarly, standardize your pallet counts. This way, the larger distribution centers can order pallet quantities and handle them, rather than multiple cartons. You'll save money doing this because of the dramatically reduced handling.

CHAPTER 9

Sales . . . and More Sales

If you're like most independent publishers, sales and distribution issues, along with marketing matters, are at the top of your list of concerns. Most of you entered the world of publishing because you had an idea, not because you wanted to sell your books. So you've been somewhat familiar with the editorial side of the publishing world because it's one in which you've taken an interest, whether as an author or publisher.

Now, however, you're faced with the reality of the marketplace, where your books have to compete with thousands of others for the buyers' time, for shelf space, and for media attention so that ultimately the consumer will know your books are available, will want to purchase them, and will be able to purchase them.

By now you'd better know how to sell and market your books.

What Sells Books and Who Buys Them?

If you ask people in the publishing business what sells books, they will give you a lot of answers: reviews sell books, jackets sell books, publicity and promotion sell books, price is important, and on and on. And they're right. All of these are important to some extent.

But if you ask the general public what motivates them to buy books, the top two answers in every case are subject/topic and author's reputation. According to the *1996 Consumer Research Study on Book Publishing* sponsored by the American Booksellers Association and the Book Industry Study Group, in almost every place that consumers buy books, whether in large chain stores, smaller chains or independents, on the internet, through mail-order sources, or discount stores, far and away the largest factor in the consumer's buying decision is *subject* and *author's reputation*. Over 44% of adults purchasing books base their decisions on subject and approximately 24% on author's reputation. Only 2% think price is important; 2% think cover art or endorsements are important; and less than 1% think having a book on the bestseller list is important. In fact, subject and author were so consistently mentioned, that the survey subsequently deleted them as options. In the 1999 survey, for instance, cover art is the strongest motivation, at 13%, followed by the book's price at 12.8%. Twenty-eight percent chose "other" from the list presented and as the survey notes, "although panelists are directed to not include the book's subject or author's reputation in the selection, some may still feel that it is those reasons that most influence their decision to buy and so indicated 'other' as their reason for purchase."

What this tells us is simple: both editors and salespeople better have a good idea of what subjects are important to consumers and they must find books by authors with credentials and good reputations. It also tells us that a lot of people working on publisher's editorial, sales, and marketing staffs are spending a lot of time on matters that have a marginal impact on people's book-purchasing decisions.

The same study also provides demographic information about adult book buyers. Of those buying adults, 33% have annual incomes of less than $30,000; 25% have incomes of $30,000 to $40,000. Another 30% have incomes over $70,000. Those with higher incomes are the heaviest book buyers, as are those with high-school and college educations.

You should know *where* people buy books. Over 40% buy them in traditional retail bookstores. However, of this 40%, where once the independents dominated, now the large chain bookstores account for 58% of unit volume at a minimum. Mail-order purchases (including book clubs and specific mail-order sales) accounted for 23% of all purchases. Discount stores account for 9%.

Of those books purchased, 51% was fiction, with no other category coming remotely close. The next largest category was cooking/crafts, which comprises 10% of units purchased, and general non-fiction, at 10%.

As you can see, once you start publishing nonfiction, your market share decreases precipitously, with many categories competing for every buyer's dollar.

Now that you know what you're up against and you're still willing to move forward, then how do you do it?

Distribution: Options and Issues

So OK. Your book's found, edited, and produced. Now what do you do with it? How can you move it from your warehouse (sometimes your garage or basement) into the wholesalers and retailers and ultimately from there to the consumer?

The fact of the matter is, if you've gotten this far through the process without giving thought to how you'll distribute your book, you're definitely in major trouble.

Sales and distribution are crucial to your survival as a publisher. And as we've already seen, much of the distribution process relates directly to wholesaling and retailing needs. To publish successfully, you should have already gotten your own situation and timing in sync with those of the marketplace. I hope you have. If you haven't, then you should go back and read this book from the beginning once more.

If you do understand the urgent and essential requirements of the market, and you're seeking information about sales and distribution options early in the publishing process, then well done! You're already one step ahead of the pack.

When reviewing your sales options, keep in mind that, however you ultimately choose to sell, every buyer to whom you or your distributor are selling will also see books from all of your competitors. These buyers have a limited amount of time to consider your book, usually taking only about 20 seconds or less to review your book's jacket or cover and hear your pitch for it. They have a limited budget and limited warehouse space to house your books. In short, you or your distributor must understand and adapt to the buyer's needs. You can't expect the buyer to adapt to yours.

With that in mind, let's look at the question of distribution and the various options available to you to sell your book.

1. The best way to sell books is to have a sales staff completely dedicated to the demands of selling your books—with no other interference—and to sell those books directly to accounts. What this means in reality is that optimally you might want to have an in-house sales staff whose sole means of survival revolves around the money they earn from selling your books, whether that be salary, commission, or both. With this in-house staff, you can be assured that your books will come out of their sales bag first on every occasion.

The two major challenges to having your own reps is paying all of them and being responsible for the back-end warehousing, fulfillment, and collection activities. The fact of the matter is, if you're not doing over $10 million in sales, it probably won't pay you to have your own force—and even then it would have to be a small staff. Furthermore, you may not want to bear the responsibility of bad debt—which in today's climate seems to be growing somewhat as a percentage of sales.

Why do I say you should be doing $10 million in sales to warrant maintaining your own sales force? Because to blanket the entire country, you'll need about 10 representatives (reps). Let's compare the cost of using commissioned reps versus the cost of house reps.

For simplicity, let's assume that commissioned reps are paid an average of 7.5%, which combines 10% on retail sales and 5% on wholesale, and that house reps get a $40,000 salary, plus 25% benefits, plus a car allowance of $200 a month, and travel and entertainment expenses of $100/day for 90 days. This totals to $61,400. I won't count bonuses.

Net Sales Dollars	% of Net Sale	Commission to Reps.	House Rep Total Cost	% Net Sale
$50,000	7.5	$3,750	$61,400	123
100,000	7.5	7,500	61,400	61
150,000	7.5	11,250	61,400	41
200,000	7.5	15,000	61,400	31
500,000	7.5	37,500	61,400	12
750,000	7.5	56,250	61,400	8
1,000,000	7.5	75,000	61,400	6
1,500,000	7.5	112,500	61,400	4
2,000,000	7.5	150,000	61,400	3

As you can see, the breakeven between commissioned reps and house reps comes at between $750,000 and $1,000,000. But this is for one rep! The fact is, you'll need more than one rep to handle your sales. At a minimum, you'll need three, which means you'll have to be doing about $3 million minimum to consider it. And if you want or need more than three reps, the sales threshold increases. Roughly, you'll need sales of $1 million for each rep you have in-house.

The number of reps it takes to cover the entire country adequately has declined considerably as the number of independents has declined. It has also gone down as the proportion of books sold to the major internet bookstores, retailers, and wholesalers has increased. But you still need a minimum of three to four reps to sell properly. And as you can see, paying for in-house reps does get expensive.

2. A second method of distributing is to use your own reps, but use an outside fulfillment house. This enables you to maintain your sales contacts in-house, but eliminates the need to maintain a warehouse or to deal with accounts receivable collection. In this scenario, the in-house reps take the orders but send them to a shipping and fulfillment organization that does all of the "back-end" work, usually for a variety of publishers. The fulfillment organization collects the money from the accounts and passes it along, minus the fulfillment fee, on a regular basis.

This is a good way to operate if you have the time to sell accounts yourself, or with your in-house staff. Because of the sales levels required by various accounts to get in the door, and the cost of hiring a few good in-house salespeople, this kind of distribution should only be done by those who are doing more than $500,000 with the chains and over $3 million overall.

One of the best smaller publishers, Fisher Books, now part of Perseus Books, operated in this manner. This kind of distribution and fulfillment arrangement enabled Fisher to produce high-quality books, but ensured that the company remained sales-driven because it could concentrate on the sales and marketing effort without having to do the day-to-day functions of invoicing, picking, packing, shipping, and collecting. There are many fulfillment operations available, including Clark, CDS, ResoDirect, Ware-Pak, Stackpole, and others.

3. A third way to sell your books is to use commissioned sales reps. These are freelance reps who sell your books as well as those of

numerous other publishers. The good news about commissioned reps is that they have to make a living. So if your books are the ones that look good to them, then they will probably sell them well. However, if their other publishers are putting out better (read more salable from the rep's point of view) books, then your books will get less attention. In addition, if one of their other publishers happens to have a book competitive to yours, in the same season, the most salable of the two will prevail—which may be to your benefit or detriment.

Commissioned reps usually get a 5% commission on wholesale sales and 10% on retail. Nearly all publishers now pay reps a percentage on the larger wholesaler sales as well, because much of a commissioned rep's sales go to wholesalers instead of going directly to the publisher. Commissioned reps can work very well. Workman Publishing, for example, a large, wonderfully creative, and sales-savvy company, used commissioned reps for years, because it knew that these reps would sell their books because they are good salable books and because they generate enormous income for the reps. Using commissioned reps also keeps fixed overheads down, since you only pay for what's sold and you don't pay benefits or travel costs.

4. A fourth way to sell is to use a distributor. Going back to the first chapter, recall that a distributor is an organization that warehouses, sells, and fulfills orders for a number of publishers. The benefit for the publisher is that all of the sales, shipping, and fulfillment functions, including accounts receivable and collections, are in the lap of the distributor, not the publisher.

Thus for many independent publishers, this kind of sales service is appealing because it frees the publisher to concentrate on what it normally does best (and prefers to do): find new books; edit them; and market them. At the same time the distributor provides the publisher with consistent cash flow and protection against bad debt as the distributor is usually responsible for that bad debt.

The downside in using a distributor, as with the commissioned reps, is the number of books they must deal with. Many distributors use commissioned reps themselves, so the sales problem is compounded: the reps report to the distributor's sales manager and are one more step removed from your own control. Furthermore, given the number of books that the distributor has, both the distributor and the rep will prioritize the lists and the individual books. Thus yours may be higher in priority or lower, depending upon their perception of your title. If your book is rejected by the first few buyers to whom the distributor's reps show your book cover or blad (a cover of the book bound with finished sample pages to give an excellent image of the quality of the finished book), it may well be that your book may never again come out of the bag.

Another downside to using a distributor is the inherent risk of entrusting your inventory and accounts receivable to an organization over which you have little or no control. There are many instances in which a distributor has been forced into bankruptcy and its combine of publishers have tried desperately to seek redress and to get their books out of that distributor's warehouse. The problem, as most have found out, is that this isn't easy. When a distributor gets into trouble, all of its member publishers suffer: all will be forced to share what little payout there might be; all will be forced to maintain their inventory at the distributor until the bankruptcy judge decides it can be released. In the meantime—and it can be a very long time—these member publishers will not be paid and cannot sell the inventory that is tied up. In short, using a distributor can be a very risky proposition.

5. Another method that smaller publishers use to sell books is to put books into the major wholesalers. In essence, the wholesaler acts as the distributor. There's one major problem with this strategy: the wholesaler is not actively selling your book. It is keeping a small amount of inventory to ship if it receives orders, but there is nothing in particular that is pulling that inventory out of the wholesaler and getting it into the retailer and ultimately into the consumer's hand.

If any demand is created through a review or an author's appearance, a store or e-tailer can get the book from the wholesaler, but again, the store or e-tailer will have to get demand before it orders. And given all of the other books that are in the stores, and that are readily available on the shelves, your book doesn't stand much of a chance sitting on the wholesaler's shelf. This is a method I strongly advise against using. If, in fact, this is your only option, you might reconsider your decision to publish the book in the first place, because it will be difficult, if not impossible, to publish it profitably.

Of course there is always the exception. One prime example is the

Merck Manual of Home Health, which used this method and sold 450,000 copies. The difference is that Merck committed $4 million to TV and other promotional efforts to drive consumers into stores and to build demand. The effort worked incredibly well.

6. Another way of selling is on the Internet, whether through your own website or through an online bookstore. This is an excellent way of doing business, with little overhead attached to it. The question that remains unanswered, however, is how many copies you'll ultimately sell.

The upside of Internet selling is that it is growing incredibly fast. Amazon.com, the largest of the online booksellers, had book sales of over $800 million in 2004. Yet, they posted a deficit of $96.0 million. Barnesandnoble.com, the next largest online bookseller, had sales of $320 million in 2000 with a net loss of $275 million. Other book vendors are selling on the Internet as well and surely others will join the pack. Amazon, according to good sources, now accounts for the sales of approximately 40–45% of all professional sales.

My own hesitation in terms of using online selling sources has nothing to do with the medium. My concern relates to the false expectation that publishers may have about their ability to sell large quantities of books online. If the publisher views these outlets as ancillary sources of sale, then fine. If, on the other hand, the publisher views these sources as its sole venue for sale, then I think it should rethink its sales strategy. Every publisher must maximize its channels of sale, thereby reducing the risk attendant upon any one source. While the Internet can and does provide additional sales, it's too early to know just how extensive the ultimate sales potential for any single title may be. *The Guinness Book of Records,* a *New York Times* #1 bestseller in 2000, sold 3 million copies nationally, but only a very small percentage through Amazon.com. On the other hand, Amazon and bn.com have both sold enormous quantities of the *Harry Potter* titles.

Given these sales options, which ones are reasonable for most smaller publishers? I think that using commissioned reps is feasible, as is using a distributor. If I had my choice and some funds, I'd probably opt for two in-house salespeople, one working on the major national accounts, the other managing a group of commissioned reps. Why do I feel this way? Because ultimately, your sales are your lifeblood and it is very risky to entrust them to someone outside of the organization who is not party to the daily needs and demands of your business.

Furthermore, I think it is incumbent upon every organization to develop the sales contacts that allow it to get direct feedback from the field when it's needed. That feedback allows you to establish personal rapport with buyers so you can get to know and understand their needs, which are critical to your own success. And, feedback allows you to be directly proactive, not reactive, to the whole sales process. The problem, of course, is that you may not be able to get in to see various buyers, especially those at the chains, because your sales volume is too small. They also require you to present five or more titles per category per visit. Ingram Book Company, America's largest wholesaler, will no longer work directly with small publishers.

In the last few years, this problem has diminished somewhat because of the various *vendor-of-record* (VOR) programs that are available. These programs allow publishers to present their books to the major retail buyers, but through exclusive arrangements with wholesalers, enable the buyers to purchase these smaller publisher's books directly through the wholesaler. This benefits the publisher because its books can get into the larger accounts; and it benefits the larger accounts because they can order from a small number of sources and don't get overwhelmed ordering from thousands of diverse, smaller publishers.

The only difficulty with VOR programs is that the publisher has very little control over actually getting orders. The buyer may well like a book, but because of a variety of internal problems, a store may never generate an order for the book. And the publisher will only find out months later—or never—because the direct order goes to the wholesaler, not the publisher. On the whole, though, vendor-of-record programs seem to work.

The comments above should not be taken as a refutation of the excellent role some of the better distributors play in the support of, and indeed even the very survival of, smaller publishers. In fact, I think extremely highly of some distributors and regularly recommend them. The difficulty, however, has been noted before. Additionally, a distributor usually requires a 27 to 30% distribution fee from its publishers and charges for other functions as well: returns, cataloging, sending review copies, etc. Ultimately, the fee can climb to 32 to 33% of net sales or higher, which makes profitability difficult if one is trying to price according to market demands.

One deservedly well-respected consultant to smaller publishers states outright that publishers using distributors *can't be profitable*. I disagree, but I also think that every book must be priced out very carefully and market needs must be judiciously addressed. If the market for certain books only exists at very low price points—résumé books, for instance—and only in the trade, with no chance of special or nontraditional sales, then it will indeed be difficult to make any money in this category. Smaller publishers must be price followers, not price leaders, especially in relation to low-priced books. If they are to err on one side or the other, they should err on the side of higher price and higher profitability and not try to be the low-price market leaders.

Although the decision of which sales channel is best is never a clear-cut one, a few timely questions may help you decide:

- How many people can your sales support now?
- Is it more important to you to acquire more books or sell the smaller quantity you now have more effectively?
- Given your budgets, can you support more people?
- How do you like to spend your time? Acquiring, editing, or selling?
- Do you want to bother with warehousing and fulfillment?
- Do you want to assume the risk of bad debt?
- Can you afford to have your books and your money tied up if a distributor goes bankrupt?

Sales Budgets

As you recall from the editorial section, each Title P&L contains a sales summary by sales segment. In effect, this figure should accurately reflect the sales you expect from each book. Thus, your sales budget per title—that is, the number of books, in units and dollars, that you expect to sell—should be set already. In the best of all worlds, this will be the case.

However, quite often the sales environment changes between the time you establish your sales estimates and the time of your actual sales activity. Thus, before reaffirming the original sales number, you must reconsider each factor that may have changed your perceptions of the book and the market, for better or worse.

What can make such an impact on the estimate?

- The finished editorial product itself. While every effort is made to get the book you originally commissioned or signed up, the manuscript that's actually delivered may differ somewhat from your expectations. It may have taken a direction that gives you a better marketing handle, or a worse marketing handle. It may be written poorly, in which case you can either wait and have it revised, or, depending upon your schedules and finances, choose to publish the book at a slightly lesser level.

- New trends in the market. A book takes time to write and produce. As we all know, fashions change, new information constantly emerges that renders older information incomplete or out-of-date, new news brings new opportunities. Given these changes, and their impact on market forces, a publisher's marketing plans and efforts may change to adapt to these new factors. This may mean greater opportunity, but it may also mean less if you're on the back edge of the wave. Whichever the case, sales estimates may change.

- Cash flow. Throughout the year, your own budgets must remain flexible and reflect your company finances. You can't spend what you don't have—no matter how much you'd like to do so. If you budgeted a certain amount of marketing dollars to push out books, and you find that you don't have the money on hand when needed, then your sales of the particular book won't be as strong as you'd like. Conversely, if you have better sales throughout the year and your financial position is stronger than budgeted, you may choose to put more effort into those books that have been successful or into new ones coming out. If so, then again your sales budget can change.

- Industry changes. Those who have published through the 1970s, '80s, and '90s have seen enormous changes in the number of booksellers selling books and the number of books on the market. There has been a major decline in the number of booksellers (but with an increase in the number of outlets) due to the emergence of the chains and superstore concept. Additionally, with better computer systems and wholesalers to access, bookstores need less depth of inventory on hand. They can order one or two copies of a title from the publisher and get reorders within a day or two from the wholesaler. Inventory control and inventory turn have become the critical elements of a bookseller's success.

What has this meant for publishers? Both greater and lesser opportunities. Greater, because the superstores carry a wider range of stock and therefore carry more titles from more publishers. Lesser, because the quantity of each title is less than might have been carried in the past. Instead of advance orders of 5 copies of a title per store, the norm is now probably closer to 1 or 2. This has had a dramatic impact on publisher's advance sales projections—which cascades down to marketing and sales budgets. It has also had an enormous impact on unit costs per book as well as dramatically impacting printing technology.

Any number of these issues, and many others, alone or in combination, can significantly drive your sales budgets either upward or downward. It's up to you, as the publisher, to modify your projections to take these factors into account. I recommend looking at, and revising, sales estimates on a quarterly basis and reviewing the effect such changes will have on your future efforts. The earlier you can identify such changes, the earlier you can begin to make adjustments that will ensure the continued balance of sales and expenses. Don't forget, *profitability* is the key to your success. And sales revenues ultimately drive those profits.

Title Launch Meetings

As I noted in the editorial section, the sales function relies upon the acquisition and timely delivery of books it feels it can sell. This doesn't mean that the sales force acts in isolation to determine the potential of a book just as it doesn't mean that an editor purchases every book he or she feels is editorially sound and meritorious. To establish an ongoing program that functions well throughout the publishing process, both editors and salespeople must be at ease with the acquisition selections coming through the pipeline.

One primary way to keep people happy is to keep the channels of communication clear and free by inviting feedback throughout the process from all functional areas. You have seen how this works in the editorial meetings, where some sales and rights people may sit in and give their perspective.

But once a book is acquired, there are many more people involved in the publishing process who must know what's being published, and who will certainly want to mold that book into something they can ultimately sell better.

The title launch meeting, usually held every six months, is for just this purpose. Here is the time and place for everyone involved with a book or a list to sit down together for the purpose of discussing various points about that book:

- Purpose of publishing the title
- Market niche
- Title
- Cover—both art and text
- Sales points
- Marketing thoughts and initial campaign outline
- Sub-rights angles and needs
- Production aspects

The title launch meeting is one at which the editorial staff usually takes the lead in presenting the books. But the editor's real role is to simply talk a bit about each book before opening it up to other functional areas for comment. Here, it does the editor no good to try to defend his book, because it's already been acquired. Now the editor must be sure to answer all of the questions that arise in this meeting because they're sure to come up again either from the firm's own reps or the distributor's reps or, more importantly, from buyers in the various accounts.

The most effective strategy for title launch meetings is to invite all participants to air all of their thoughts, vent all of the deficiencies they perceive with the title, and accept these good comments with equanimity. As with all good brainstorming sessions, accept the comments for what they can do to help clarify editorial and marketing thoughts, not as negative idea killers.

With the meeting's comments in hand, the editors, salespeople, and everyone else should retire to consider what's been said and to act on the information to

- move forward quickly those points that work well
- revise or reorient those areas that seem to be problematic
- clarify positioning
- define title marketing and sales budgets within the context of the entire new line
- coordinate functional schedules for each title.

Pre-Sales Meetings

Following an initial title launch meeting, where the new list is first presented and where other early stages of sales and market planning take place, comes a pre-sales meeting. As its name makes clear, this meeting is held prior to the sales conference. At pre-sales, the final touches are put on all phases of the sales and marketing effort to ensure the most accurate and complete information is available for the sales reps. Included in this effort is everything needed to give the reps the strongest possible sales material, including

- a handle—the gist of every book in one sentence
- a complete title fact sheet
- fully fleshed out marketing plans and budgets
- finished jackets or covers
- author information
- publicity and promotion plans
- sub-rights sales or plans
- visual aids

Again, keep in mind the purpose of this meeting: to prepare all the materials to sell every book and to be sure you can communicate all of the information necessary to accomplish this goal.

This is the final practice before the sales conference. So use it not just to test what you have, but to listen closely to comments from the sales director, the marketing staff, the rights people, and others on the sales end who will have to work with the material provided. If necessary, now is the time to restructure presentations and material to get it right. If you've done your work well, you should find it easygoing in the actual sales meeting.

Sales Meeting

Here is where your six months of practice and preparation pay off. Given a successful title launch meeting and a good pre-sales meeting, the sales conference should be a piece of cake.

Now you can sit down with your sales reps and present every title on your list *from a sales point of view*.

But before you start to present any books, make sure you have put together a sales kit for each rep to look at as you make your way through the presentation. This way, the reps can make notes on each page that corresponds to each of the books you're presenting. They can then be sure to present all of the important information you provide to them as it relates to each title.

What goes into a good sales kit?

1. A jacket or cover of the book in color. This is absolutely essential. Without the jacket, the rep has nothing visual to show the buyer. And because books must be visibly seen on the shelves to sell (in most cases), this is a key point for the buyer.
2. A **Tip Sheet for Sales Reps** (see page 193). This is almost identical to the Title Fact Sheet, but it also has space for a concise handle and information about advertising and promotion. This sheet should be filled in before the pre-sales meeting so it can be reviewed and discussed at that time.
3. Advance quotes praising the book, if any
4. A list of competitive titles on the shelf that might pose a problem and ways to answer those questions
5. Tour or promotional schedules
6. Anything else that can help the rep sell the book

With this in front of him, the rep is ready to get on with your sales meeting.

It's always a simple matter to spot those who present books effectively from those who don't. The truth is that those who don't almost always focus on the editorial aspects of their books and almost always drone on about them for too long.

For sales reps, the time it takes them to present books to buyers, whether retail or wholesale, is money. If they can make a sale, then you and the rep will be happy. If they don't make a sale, then you've both wasted time and lost money.

To complicate matters, buyers have a limited amount of time to see reps. They have limited budgets to buy books each month (called *open to buy*, in which a buyer's purchasing budget is allocated monthly; once spent, or allocated, the buyer has no additional funds for purchasing other books that month). And, every buyer has a limited attention span (not necessarily in that order!).

Reps don't want to know a book's full history or every aspect of every chapter of each book. They don't want to know every nuance of the author's life. Even if they knew all this, they wouldn't have time to convey it to the buyer because each title is usually presented in a minute or less. Information fatigue syndrome truly gets in the way.

The sales conference is the place to present the information that is important enough to ultimately provide the key points of each book. How much is this? Obviously, it depends on the book and its place of importance on your list. For a lead title, such information is greater than that for a revision of a classic—for which the mere mention of such revision is usually sufficient.

So follow these four rules and you'll be OK:

1. Be accurate.
2. Be succinct. Spend no more than two to five minutes on a title unless it's truly extraordinary—and more frequently err to the side of two minutes.
3. Be sales and marketing motivated.
4. Resolve all prior sales issues before the meeting.

Last, in relation to your conference as a whole, be creative and upbeat. Remember, sales reps go to a lot of conferences. Whatever you say about your books, they will get most excited about those they feel they can sell best, whether because they may have a personal interest in the topic or because they know the title will appeal to their accounts.

Your job is to give them the angles and the handle that will allow

Tip Sheet for Sales Reps

TITLE: PRICE:

SUBTITLE: TRIM SIZE/PAGES:

AUTHOR: ILLUSTRATIONS:

FORMAT: (HC; PB)   BOOKSTORE CATEGORY:

ISBN: PUB DATE:

DESCRIPTION:

SELLING POINTS: (List in priority order.)

HANDLE: (One sentence – what makes this book unique?)

ABOUT THE AUTHOR: (Include author's current city and state.)

ADVERTISING & PROMOTION PLANS:

PRE-PUBLICATION COMMENTS/BOOK CLUB/OR OTHER SALES:

them to do their job well. And the more creatively you can convey the information, the better chance they'll recall the book and the points you've made about it.

This doesn't mean your sales meeting has to take on circus overtones. But you certainly better not put your reps to sleep.

One other comment: don't cut off discussion too early—but don't let your reps totally dominate the meeting. Your sales reps are your front line—the eyes and ears of your organization. To a large extent, they respond from experience, so if they tell you a jacket stinks, or to take a different approach to a title, you'd better pay attention. At the same time, such comments need to be put into a constructive mode. If it stinks, why? What would make it better? What's missing? What's not getting across and what should?

Remember, every rep has an individual response and it's unusual to get consensus. When you do get it—good or bad—it almost always makes sense to follow such advice. But if you have one truculent rep (no, they're not all that way all the time!) who consistently argues every issue that comes up, you'll inevitably have to manage that person before he or she casts a pall over your meeting. This is a job for your sales manager.

Sales meetings should end with clear action plans. Reps should know exactly what works for them and what you as a publisher expect. Following the open meeting, hold a one-on-one no-holds-barred meeting restricted to the sales director and the reps. Let the pent-up emotions of the meeting out—on both sides—and let everyone come to the mutual understanding that is required for both sides to perform to standards to which they both agree. If you give your reps sales quotas—that is, target sales figures for them to meet—explain how they are derived and why they are fair. Great detail isn't required.

Be sure to mention any promotional offers that you are considering and solicit feedback.

Finally, don't be afraid to say that you don't have all the answers. If you don't know the answer to a question, admit it and get back to the rep quickly with an answer. Don't let questions that come up at the conference linger unanswered. Summarize the questions and send a follow-up memo responding clearly to each issue within a week of your meeting. This keeps the questions fresh in the rep's minds and shows them by your actions that you have an understanding of their needs. They'll respect you for your efforts.

Analyzing Your Sales

After your reps have sent you orders and they've been fulfilled, you want to know exactly what has sold and where it's sold. The reason for this is simple: if you're doing well in one or two particular areas, you want to go back to those areas again. Similarly, if one type of book is doing better than another, you want to publish more of those. On the other hand, if some accounts are doing poorly, you want to know why to see if you can correct the situation. If some kinds of books are doing poorly, you also want to know why, so you can correct the deficiencies or avoid making the same mistake twice.

Sales analysis could actually be a book unto itself so I'll only discuss a few of the ways to view sales. Once you begin to look at your sales, you'll see that one analysis tends to lead to another. See *Fiscal Year Sales Analysis by Channel* (page 196) for an example of a form that will allow you to compare both unit and dollar sales from one fiscal year to another. Also see *Frontlist/Backlist Analysis* (page 197) for a form that will allow you to determine what percentage of your sales comes from frontlist and what percentage from backlist.

Sales Ranked by Dollars
This is straightforward. You should always know what books are generating the most revenue. List every book you publish by declining dollar volume so you can see clearly what's selling. List as well, how many of each book you've sold so you can get an average selling price per unit. What are their subjects? Why are they successful? Can you emulate these books, or spin them off into a series of new books? How often can you revise these books? This chart would basically have the following headings.

Book	Gross Units Sold	$ Revenue	Units Returned	$ Returned	Net Units Sold	Net Sales $	Average $/Book

Sales Ranked by Units
This would be the same as above, except ranked by units. What titles are selling the most units? Why? Where? Are there any special customers that are buying large quantities of a particular title? Headings for this breakdown would be similar to those above.

Fiscal Year Sales Analysis by Channel

	Units Total FY2	% Total Units FY2	Units Total FY1	% Total Units FY1	Dollars Total FY2	% Total Dollars FY2	Dollars Total FY1	% Total Dollars FY1	Return Rate FY2	Return Rate FY1
Distributor										
Wholesalers										
Retailers:										
Chains										
Independents										
Internet e-tailers										
Foreign										
Libraries										
Special Sales										
Non-Traditional Accounts										
Direct Response Sales										
Remainders										
Sub-Rights Sales										
Total Units										
Total Dollars										

Frontlist/Backlist Analysis

	Units Current FY	% Total Units	Units Prior FY	% Total Units	% Change
Frontlist Sales					
Title 1					
Title 2					
Title 3					
Title 4					
Title 5					
Title 6					
Title 7					
Title 8					
Total Frontlist Sales					
Backlist Sales					
Total Sales					

Frontlist = Titles Published During Last 12 Months

Book	Gross Units Sold	$ Revenue	Units Returned	$ Returned	Net Units Sold	Average $/Book

Sales by Gross Margin

Those books that have the highest dollar revenue or sell the most units may not have the best gross margins. For instance, you may sell a large quantity of a $4.95 book, which will give you high dollar or unit sales, but you may have other books that sell many fewer copies, which are more profitable because they are priced higher and have low unit costs. The books that have the greatest gross margin are those you really want to look at and do more of. Gross-margin rankings measure the efficiency of your sale so rank them in descending order. Headings here would be

Book	$ Revenue	Cost of Goods	$ Revenue - COGS	GM$	GM%

Sales by Territory

This report shows where your books are selling. Which territories contain your best customers? To a large degree this will be determined by population density, but you may be surprised. You may find that certain books appeal to customers in certain areas you would not necessarily think of. In addition, this report allows you to see how strong your rep groups are.

Book	Territory	Rep Group	Units	Dollars

Sales by Customer

You should always know who your best customers are. In today's book world, Ingram or Barnes and Noble, Borders and Amazon.com are probably every publisher's number one and two customers, but you certainly want to be well aware of who the other top customers are. Once you're past the top five or ten accounts, which are usually the major wholesalers and chains, things can get interesting. Concentrate on these top accounts, because that's where the bulk of your sales will come from. But never forget the other accounts doing substantial business with your company. You may be surprised at who they are. You can definitely establish rapport and create new business with all of them.

Book	Customer	$ Revenue	Gross Units Sold	Units Returned	Net Units Sold	Net Sales $

In the end, you simply want to gain as much knowledge about your books and your customers as you can. And you can never have too much knowledge in this regard. Spend time with your sales reports and look for patterns. The more you know, the more you can repeat the process that resulted in the greatest, most profitable sale.

Sales Through a Distributor

If you use a distributor, in addition to tracking sales using each of the methods just described, you must also keep track of the larger picture. That is, how your gross sales, returns and net sales are doing, but also
- Costs that your distributor takes for its service
- Total due as accounts receivable to you each month
- Returns as a monthly percentage of your total net sales
- Percentage of total yearly sales each month represents
- Cumulative sales per month per year
- Comparison of this month's cumulative sales vs. last month's

The reason you need to do this is to keep track not only of sales, but of cash flow. This is because distributors usually pay their publishers 90 days or more after the month-end closing date for sales made in that month. In other words, if the distributor sells your books in January, it will usually pay you for those sales on April 30. Once the initial 90-day period—when you receive no payment—is completed, your cash flow begins and continues as long as you remain with the distributor, assuming you have positive sales each month.

In contrast to publisher payments, which the distributor wants to delay as long as possible so it can collect the accounts receivable before paying its publishers, the distributor will charge its publishers immediately for any expenses they incur and any returns of the publisher's books that customers make. The reason for these deductions against the publisher's account is simple: the distributor wants to reimburse itself quickly for any out-of-pocket expenses it may incur for its member publishers and recognize returns in a similar fashion, because customers will immediately deduct such returns from any accounts payable owed to the distributor.

The net result of these cash flows is that payments are delayed while costs are taken quickly. The **Distributor Sales Tracking Form**

Distributor Sales Tracking Form

	Jul '04	Aug '04	Sep '04	Oct '04	Nov '04	Dec '04	Jan '05	Feb '05	Mar '05	Apr '05	May '05	Jun '05	Total
Gross Sales	829.36	31,258.39	5,921.11	3,067.39	5,555.65	2,106.20	5,912.42	3,648.18	28,930.19	11,074.00	7,534.71	4,067.00	109,904.60
Returns	177.56	1,441.43	804.43	3,380.33	1,581.50	4,310.05	1,438.00	1,577.68	3,070.00	3,340.00	2,312.83	2,157.00	25,590.81
Net Sales	651.80	29,816.96	5,116.68	-312.94	3,974.15	-2,203.85	4,474.42	2,070.50	25,860.19	7,734.00	5,221.88	1,910.00	84,313.79
Costs	495.18	8,236.83	2,501.94	1,097.04	-111.33	944.58	1,596.35	985.01	7,811.15	2,592.00	3,436.00	0.00	29,584.75
Total Due	156.62	21,580.13	2,614.74	-1,409.98	4,085.48	-3,148.43	2,878.07	1,085.49	18,049.04	5,142.00	1,785.88	1,910.00	54,729.04
% of total	1%	35%	6%	-0%	5%	-3%	5%	2%	31%	9%	6%	2%	100%
Returns %	21.41%	4.61%	13.59%	110.20%	28.47%	204.64%	24.32%	43.25%	10.61%	30.16%	30.70%	53.04%	23.28%

	Jul '05	Aug '05	Sep '05	Oct '05	Nov '05	Dec '05	Jan '06	Feb '06	Mar '06	Apr '06	May '06	Jun '06	Total
Gross Sales	31,470.72	24,936.72	10,846.12	0.00	0.00	0.00	0.00	0.00	0.00	0.00	0.00	0.00	67,253.56
Returns	0.00	0.00	0.00	0.00	0.00	0.00	0.00	0.00	0.00	0.00	0.00	0.00	0.00
Net Sales	31,470.72	24,936.72	10,846.12	0.00	0.00	0.00	0.00	0.00	0.00	0.00	0.00	0.00	67,253.56
Costs	0.00	0.00	0.00	0.00	0.00	0.00	0.00	0.00	0.00	0.00	0.00	0.00	0.00
Total Due	31,470.72	0.00	0.00	0.00	0.00	0.00	0.00	0.00	0.00	0.00	0.00	0.00	31,470.72
% of total	47%	37%	16%	0%	0%	0%	0%	0%	0%	0%	0%	0%	100%
Returns %	0.00%	0.00%	0.00%	0.00%	0.00%	0.00%	0.00%	0.00%	0.00%	0.00%	0.00%	0.00%	0.00%
+/- '01 Mo	30,818.92	-4,880.24	5,729.44	312.94	-3,974.15	2,203.85	-4,474.42	-2,070.50	-25,860.19	-7,734.00	-5,221.88	-1,910.00	-17,060.23
+/- '01 YTD	30,818.92	25,938.68	31,668.12	31,981.06	28,006.91	30,210.76	25,736.34	23,665.84	-2,194.35	-9,928.35	-15,150.23	-17,060.23	-34,120.46

is a template that allows you to track the sales, returns, costs, and flow of funds from your distributor.

Using this form, you can chart your gross sales per month, and then, when the returns and costs come in, apply them to the appropriate months. For instance, look at May 2005. We see gross sales of $7,534.71 were generated in that month. This revenue is not paid until August, because this publisher is on 90-day payment terms with its distributor. *In August*, the publisher had $2,312.83 worth of returns, which were immediately credited against the account, reducing May's net sales to $5,221.88. At the same time, this publisher had costs of various kinds (stickering, advertising, etc.) of $3,436.00 that again were immediately deducted by the distributor from the amount due this publisher. Thus, the net amount paid to the publisher by the distributor was $1,785.88. As you can see, the net sale amount of $5,221.88 is 6% of this publisher's total net sales for the year. Its returns of $2,312.83 were 30.7% of the monthly gross sales. (Because this publisher is now into a new fiscal year, the sales lines that compare '05 to '04 are actual only for the first three months, July through September. October through June simply reflect the same numbers without '05 comparatives.)

Using this Distributor Sales Tracking Form gives a good feel for what your real net sales, returns, and actual net payments are over the course of the year. Using this form along with the other tracking methods described above, you can have a very good grasp of what your sales are, where your books are being sold, how much you're due and when.

In the end, you simply want to gain as much knowledge about your books and your customers as you can. You can never have too much knowledge in this regard. Spend time with your sales reports and look for patterns. The more you know, the more you can repeat the process that resulted in the greatest, most profitable sales.

Marketing Plans

In a classic business sense, marketing differs from sales because it concentrates on a multidirectional push-pull effort that takes into account the customers' needs and fulfills those needs. Sales, on the other hand, concentrates on pushing your products into the stores; it is more one-dimensional in its direction and effort.

There are many excellent titles available on how to market your book and titles that give you good marketing ideas. In particular, I suggest publishers read Dan Poynter's comprehensive *The Self-Publishing Manual* and John Kremer's excellent *Book Marketing Made Easier* and *1001 Ways to Market Your Books*. What I will say here, categorically, is that you can never do too much marketing on behalf of your book. You can spend too much money in pursuit of marketing, but you can never do too much marketing.

Many publishers, both large and small, find it helpful to set strategic targets for themselves in relation to their marketing efforts. These targets are carefully aimed at daily, weekly, and monthly tasks. For instance, a publisher might say that it will complete a certain number of phone calls to reviewers every day; send out one feature story each week; visit the various book clubs twice each year. Implementing such targets assures a consistency of marketing effort and builds the overall marketing momentum for particular books and for your program as a whole. It's a strategy that makes sense and that every publisher should use.

Financially, marketing, including selling expenses and promotion, should be about 13 to 16% of net sales. This is in accord with generally accepted percentages of most profitable publishing companies.

Once you've committed to a consistent marketing effort, you must plan and budget for it. In addition, you must be sure everyone on staff who needs to know what those plans are has a place to find such information quickly. I recommend that every book published by your company have a marketing plan in place. Such a plan should consist of

- marketing budget
- sales goals for years 1 & 2
- specific marketing targets for this book
- marketing strategy for the book
- publicity strategy for the book
  - bound galleys to pre-reviewers
  - review copy plans
  - publicity releases
  - author tours and interviews planned
  - feature stories planned
  - press parties; publication parties

- author questionnaires
- book exhibits
- advertising plans including co-op ad placements
- author seminars, lectures, speaking engagements
- in-store promotions
- library promotions
- wholesaler promotions
- textbook and/or school adoptions
- special sales prospects
- sub-rights sales prospects
- premium sales prospects
- mail-order catalogs
- specialty outlets (nontraditional outlets: hardware stores, lawn and garden shops, etc.)
- other plans

As you can see from the length of this list, sales and marketing issues are paramount and must be addressed as early in the publishing cycle as possible. Money can be easily spent and easily squandered if it doesn't result in a coordinated plan and the effective sale of books. For an example, see the **Basic Marketing Plan Worksheet** (page 204).

Focusing the marketing plan is critical to the success of your effort. If you've clearly defined your editorial niche, then the marketing you do for one book should help the marketing you do for other books on your list. For example, if you are selling gardening books, the media lists you generate to publicize one gardening book can be used for others you are publishing, thereby saving time and effort. If you have done a successful in-store promotion on one book with an account, that account will be more inclined to do more promotions with you on another book in the same subject area. If you do your research and compile a list of mail-order catalogs for one title and you are successful in getting your books into a catalog, you will know where to focus your efforts on subsequent books of similar nature.

While all of these things can be accomplished with a variety of books on eclectic subjects, focusing the effort saves time, money, and effort. I highly recommend you do so.

There are thousands of ways to creatively market your books. A few, however, demand your primary attention because they are far

Basic Marketing Plan Worksheet page 1 of 3

Title:
Author:
First Printing:
Estimated Advance Sale:

Marketing Budget:
Publication Date:
Warehouse Date:
Estimated $ Revenue for Title:

Sub-Rights

Book-Club Sales:
    Club Sold:
        Advance Due:
        Royalty Percent:
        Payment Dates:
        On Sale Date:

Reprint Sales:
    Company Sold:
        Advance Due:
        Royalty Percent:
        Payment Dates:

Serial Rights:
    Magazine Sold:
        1st Serial   2nd Serial
    Advance Due:
    Payment Date:

Foreign Rights:
    Company Sold:
        Advance Due:
        Royalty Percent:
        Payment Dates:

Audio Rights:
    Company Sold:
        Advance Due:
        Royalty Percent:
        Payment Dates:

Other Rights:
    Company Sold:
    Kind of Rights Sale:
        Advance Due:
        Royalty Percent:
        Payment Dates:

Publicity

Total Budget:

Press Release:
    Quantity:
    Total Cost:

Bound Galleys:
    Quantity:
    Total Cost:

Author Tour:
    Number of Cities:
    Specify Cities:
    Total Cost:
    Freelance Publicist?

Mailing List:
    Quantity Names:
    Cost:
    Postage for Mailing:
    Total Cost:

Radio Phoners: Yes No
    Number of Stations:
    Total Cost:

Feature Stories: Yes No
    Freelance Writer:
    Total Cost:

Author's Publicity Plans:
    Travel Tie-Ins:
    Lectures/Seminars:

Continues

Basic Marketing Plan Worksheet page 2 of 3

Advertising

Total Budget:

Trade Advertising:	Date/Cost	Consumer Advertising:	Date/Cost
PW:		Magazine:	
Amer. Bookseller:		Newspaper:	
Library Journal:		Catalogs:	
Booklist:		Other:	
Other:		Total Cost:	
Total Cost:			
		Telephone Campaigns:	Date/Cost
		Where:	
Support Advertising:	Date/Cost	Total Cost:	
Ingram:			
Baker & Taylor:		Electronic/Other:	Date/Cost
Barnes & Noble:		Where:	
Borders:		Total Cost:	
Other:			
Total Cost:			

Promotion

Total Budget:

Catalog:		Exhibits:	Date/Cost
Quantity:		Book Expo:	
Total Cost:		Frankfurt:	
		London:	
Sales Kits:		American Library:	
Quantity:		Other:	
Total Cost:		Total Cost:	
Blads:		Incentive Discount:	Yes No
Quantity:		Terms:	
Total Cost:		Total Cost:	
In-Store Displays:	#/Cost	Invoice Dating:	Yes No
Brochures:		Terms:	
Counter Packs:		Total Cost:	
Prepacks:			
Dumps:		Other:	Yes No
Posters:		Coupons:	
Slitcards:		1 Free with 10:	
Other:		Other:	
Total Cost:		Total Cost:	

Continues

Basic Marketing Plan Worksheet page 3 of 3

Direct Response

Total Budget:

Card Decks:
    List:
    Quantity:
    Total Cost:

Solo Mailing:
    List:
    Total Cost:

Other:
    List:
    Total Cost:

Special Sales

Total Budget:

Specialty Retailers:
Catalogs:
Government:
Professional Societies:
Seminar/Training Groups:
Other:
    Total Cost:

Other Marketing

Total Budget:

Specify:
    Total Cost:

less expensive, and yield greater immediate visibility and sales, than others.

Publicity

Publicity in publishing terms is the act of getting books and authors known through a variety of means, including

- sending books to book reviewers for review in various newspapers, magazines, and journals
- writing feature stories about your book or author and sending them to newspapers and magazines for direct, free pickup
- putting authors on tour for in-store book-related events or signings; radio and TV interviews; seminars; book fair appearances, and more

The good news is that publicity can be highly effective—and relatively inexpensive. It is the most efficient way to generate national publicity because the media nationwide—whether newspaper, magazine, radio, TV, internet, or others—have an insatiable need for informational material to provide to their viewers or readers. You, as publisher, fill a unique role in the world: you are information or content providers. And as such, you have the very material that these media outlets need for their own survival. It's a highly symbiotic and mutually beneficial system: you have what they need; they have what you need. The key is to use the system to build relationships so you become known as the source of experts who can consistently provide these media outlets with what they need when they need it. The more you do this, the easier it becomes to generate additional publicity and get your books known more widely.

Publicity can be done in-house, by your sales and marketing director or by a dedicated staff publicist if you have enough books to warrant such a person. At the same time, there are many freelance publicists who do excellent work at very reasonable prices. This is one of the few areas where I regularly recommend hiring freelance help.

Why do I always recommend using publicity as a first step? Because it is relatively inexpensive. As noted above, the cost for a freelance publicist is modest when compared to putting a person on staff to do the work, especially when you factor in benefits. Using a freelance person means that you get value for the specific job you need done and no more. Second, the major cost involved in publicity is the cost of your book and the cost of postage. In relation to the former, you're looking at the paper-printing-binding cost, which will probably be in the $1.50 to $2.50 range. In terms of the postage, you can send material priority or fourth-class mail, United Parcel Service, or some other way. Whichever you choose, it will run from about $4.00 to $6.50 per book.

Thus the primary costs you incur for publicity will be at least $4.50 per book and at most $9.00 per book. Probably somewhere in the middle. If you take $6.00 as an average and add in a publicity release done by a freelance publicist, proportionately costing $6.00 per book ($600 for the release divided by 100 releases sent out with 100 books) then your total effort will come to $12.00 per book for everything, or $1,200 total. Compare that cost to having someone on staff. Compare it to any other marketing effort you undertake and you'll see how well it stands up. To summarize

Book manufacturing (PPB) cost per book	$2.00
Mailing cost per book (minimum)	4.00
Publicity fee per book (writing release, sending 100 releases on labels provided by publicist)	6.00
Total per book	12.00
X 100 books = Total Publicity Cost	$1,200.00

If you want to do an author tour, the costs go up significantly depending upon the number of cities and the size of the cities involved. If, for instance, you want to do one medium-size city, the cost can be $1,500. If you want to do New York, Los Angeles, or Chicago it can be $3,500+. This would include travel, a press release, pitch letter, reply card, mailing the book out, and follow-up. It does not include expenses such as postage, phone calls, faxes, etc. Some publicity organizations will guarantee bookings on three or more shows or you won't pay. Others don't guarantee results. (For more about author tours, see page 217, Author Tours.)

In short, costs for publicists vary depending upon what you need and want done. But overall, if you're only publishing a modest number of books each year, your costs will be lower if you use a freelancer.

How do you find a good publicist? Look for someone who is active in your subject category and who is knowledgeable about your kind of book; someone who has a list of contacts that can be immediately put to use for your book; and someone with excellent references who is willing to provide them to you. Call other publishers, Publisher's Marketing Association, or try the website of the Publishers' Publicity Association. Look at the publicity section of *Literary Market Place* as well.

An experienced publicist undoubtedly has the appropriate lists of reviewers, contacts at TV and radio stations, and other outlets already compiled, thereby saving you research time and work. Make sure that you are absolutely clear about the assignment in question, and make sure you have a letter of agreement spelling out everything the publicist is to do and the price agreed upon for each service provided.

One tip to keep in mind is to use freelance, or contract, publicists on a per job basis, and not on a monthly retainer. Most publicity work relates to individual books or to a defined project. Pay, therefore, a fixed fee, agreed upon in advance, to the publicist for an agreed upon set of services. We've seen too many publishers pay large monthly retainers for long periods of time with little result. No publicist can guarantee results. But by paying a fixed fee for a particular project, you, the publisher, can limit your risk and expenditures. If things go well you can always extend the project and engagement. With monthly retainers you may well end up paying much more than you'd like, with little to show for it.

If you do the research work in-house, be sure that the compiled list of reviewers is labeled and filed properly so it can be accessed in the future. You don't want to spend time compiling the same list twice. Also, be sure to categorize your lists as A, B, C in order of importance. If you want to send out a limited number of books, you'll want to send them out only to the most important reviewers for your particular subject. By placing the names in hierarchical lists, you will be able to quickly find those reviewers you need.

The Publicity Release

One of the most important items a publicist can provide is a publicity or **Press Release** (see page 210). A good release can be written for about $600. If the writer is an expert and has been around for some time, the price may be even higher; if the writer is less experienced or

Press Release

NEWS Release

1716 Locust Street • Des Moines, Iowa 50309-3023

NEW BOOK ANNOUNCEMENT
November 15, 2001

For further information, contact:
Kae Tienstra, 610/395-6298
Cathy Long, 515/284-2415

Better Homes and Gardens®
NEW COMPLETE GUIDE TO GARDENING
**A complete revision of America's favorite gardening reference
includes comprehensive plant encyclopedia and
how-to information for every gardener.**

More than 1 million copies of the earlier editions sold!

Annuals, perennials, vegetables, trees and shrubs, ground covers, fruits, herbs, bulbs, and vines are all included in the <u>completely revised edition</u> of ***Better Homes and Gardens® NEW COMPLETE GUIDE TO GARDENING*** (Meredith® Books / November 15, 2001/$34.95 Hardcover).

Experienced gardeners as well as beginners will find everything they need to plan, plant, and harvest in this valuable reference.

"It's a wonderful marriage of a no-nonsense gardening how-to combined with a beautiful dream book," said Jim Blume, editor-in-chief. "It doesn't stop with beautiful pictures, plant descriptions, and cultivation needs, but goes that important one step further by showing readers how to coordinate the design of the yard and garden. Our readers have told us they need help in this area and we've made sure that this type of coordination is a primary ingredient of the book."

It's a plant encyclopedia with 270 pages of photos and descriptions of more than 550 plants. But that's just the beginning! The first part of this volume, "Designing Your Landscape and Gardens," tells homeowners how to translate basic information into specific solutions for the challenges they face in their own yards.

Readers will learn how to think about the elements of garden design: accessing strengths

(Over)

Press Release *continued*

and weaknesses of a particular yard and combining plants effectively; achieving color throughout the seasons; using structural elements in the landscape; working with shady areas; designing a woodland garden. This section provides inspiration and practical answers for a variety of gardening challenges and questions.

Part Two, "Selecting, Planting, and Maintaining Your Plants," is a basic reference tool providing at-a-glance information on more than 550 plants by type (roses, annuals, perennials, trees, shrubs, bulbs, etc.), all conveniently categorized in alphabetical order. Included is information on selecting, planting, and growing all the plants featured.

Part Three, "Sharpening Your Basic Gardening Skills," is the nuts-and-bolts section readers will turn to again and again to help with soil building, planting, propagating, garden tools, and starting and maintaining lawns. A glossary, zone map, and index round out the volume.

Of special interest is the emphasis on American gardens, with pages of photographs of gardens across the continent. "We want to show what Americans do in their gardens," said Cathy Wilkinson Barash, executive garden editor at Meredith® Books / Better Homes and Gardens® Books and spokesperson for *Better Homes and Gardens® NEW COMPLETE GUIDE TO GARDENING.* "This book is a celebration and reaffirmation of the great tradition of American gardening."

Better Homes and Gardens® NEW COMPLETE GUIDE TO GARDENING is available wherever fine books are sold.

For further information or to arrange an interview with Cathy Wilkinson Barash, executive garden editor, contact Kae or Jon Tienstra, KT/PR Marketing & Communications, 610/395-6298.

Better Homes and Gardens®-Books/Meredith® Books is a division of Meredith Corporation, a diversified media company involved in magazine and book publishing, television broadcasting, and residential real estate marketing and franchising.

Better Homes and Gardens®
NEW COMPLETE GUIDE TO GARDENING
Hardcover $34.95
November 15, 2001
ISBN 0-696-02573-6

just needs or wants work, the cost may be lower. When you add in the cost of one-time use of the publicist's labels of targeted reviewers, the cost will increase further. And costs go up as your needs expand. If you want to do a feature release, for direct pickup by news organizations (newspapers and radio mostly), the cost will be around $1,000.

A publicity or press release is a document that goes to book reviewers, talk show producers, and others. Its primary purpose is to immediately interest these influential people in your book. If successful, the reviewer will devote space to spreading the word about your book. This space is basically free advertising. If you were to try to buy the space, it would be extremely costly—especially in those newspapers and magazines that have a large presence either nationally or in their primary region. This is why it pays you to spend a lot of time and effort on publicity. You're trading off a few dollars per book to gain thousands of dollars of free advertising. Not a bad trade-off. In fact, it's the best trade-off you'll make.

What makes a good publicity release?

First, a clear, short, catchy headline. Think of yourself as writing for the major tabloids, or one of the influential papers of the world. Understand that you have one chance to catch your reader's eye. One second or less. What would that headline be? In essence, it's similar to the need to develop a sales handle for your reps, except that now you're talking not to a buyer, but to another media specialist. The pressure is on.

Once you've solved the problem of creating a headline that works, you must describe the book you're pitching without the heavy use of superlatives. Reviewers don't want your review of your book, that's their job. They are the arbiters of taste for their audience.

You must describe what is unique or new about your book, the angle that makes it different or timely, that will make the reviewer feel as if he'll be giving his audience unique or timely information that will interest his readers in the review. You need to be straightforward, honest, and clear. And at the same time, you need to be resonant. It's not an easy task, which is why good publicity people are so useful to publishers, and always in demand.

With headline and body copy in hand, you must provide the basics about the book:

- title
- author
- price
- size
- format (hardcover or paper)
- number of pages
- number of photos or illustrations
- ISBN
- publication date

Finally, and very importantly, you must provide a contact person and phone number and e-mail address in case the reviewer wants additional information about the book.

With all of these attributes included, your release will be read and used, your book hopefully reviewed.

Another comment should also be made. Sometimes, smaller publishers feel that reviewers pay no attention whatsoever to them or their books. As these publishers see books from the major publishers being reviewed day after day, they get frustrated that their books aren't reviewed, that they're being passed over. Based on experience, this isn't truly the case.

The fact is, very few book reviews are written each year. And, the number is declining as newspapers and magazines either go out of business or merge. At the same time, the number of books published each year continues to rise. Because the larger publishers are putting out hundreds of titles each, and smaller publishers are putting out a relatively small number of titles per house, it is only natural that the larger houses will have proportionately greater publicity success.

Most larger publishers have many publicists on staff to handle their greater volume of books. Most of these publicists ultimately establish very personal rapport with the people on their review lists. As in all other aspects of the publishing business (and other industries as well), the stronger the personal relation between two people, the closer those people will work together. Additionally, the more bestsellers published by larger, reputable publishers, the greater the chance they will get review space.

What this means to the smaller publisher is that you must be professional and you must be persistent. If you don't get reviewed the first time you submit a book, keep trying. If, after a while, you still don't begin to see reviews, don't be afraid to call the reviewer and ask what's wrong. It may be as simple as her not getting the books; it may be that she doesn't like what you're sending and you can get some good feedback; it may be that she just has what she considers to be better books to look at and review. Don't give up! And don't become antagonistic toward the reviewer. Establish a dialogue and rapport with her over time and your chance of success will rise.

Publishers often ask how many review copies to send out. The answer is related to how important the book is to your list. If it's your lead book, anywhere from 100 to 300 copies may be reasonable. The key is to be sure you account for, and budget, enough money to get books into the hands of the most appropriate reviewers. As already noted, publicity copies of your books are your least costly way of getting the word out.

At the same time, you don't want to send out a lot of your books indiscriminately to those who don't actually ask to see them. One way to avoid this is to put your press release to work, instead of sending the actual book. Send the release to your target list—or an extended list because the cost for mailing the release is only for printing, postage, and reply-card postage. Ask recipients to call, e-mail, fax, or mail back the reply card expressing their interest if they'd like a review copy of the book. Of course you should respond quickly when such requests are received, because you've qualified the recipient—that person actually wants a copy of the book. You needn't fear that legitimate reviewers will ask for copies of your book if they don't have true interest. Given all the books they get each year, the last thing they need is another that will just sit on their shelves.

Because this book is about strategic management, I will leave it to others to provide a list of key reviewers and press throughout the country. However, I would be remiss if I didn't provide the list of the four absolutely essential *pre-reviewers* that can help make your book successful: *Publishers Weekly; Library Journal; Kirkus Reviews;* American Library Association *Booklist.* These are the primary media that review books for the wholesale, retail, and library book market. Reviews in these magazines can mean thousands of copies sold. Be sure to send two copies of your material, which should be in bound galley form (this is essentially bound proof material) *four months in advance of its publication date*, which is the lead time these journals need to review your book (this is not to say they will review the book, but if you don't get it there in time, they surely won't). For the names of the current contacts, check each organization's website.

The addresses and phone numbers are (at the time of publication):

Fiction (or Nonfiction) Forecasts Editor
Publishers Weekly
360 Park Avenue
New York, NY 10010
646-746-6758
www.publishersweekly.com
As of this writing, to inquire about whether galleys have arrived at *Publishers Weekly,* or have been assigned for review, e-mail pwreviewstatus@cahners.com.

Book Review Editor
Library Journal
360 Park Avenue
New York, NY 10010
212-463-6819
www.Libraryjournal.com

Eric Liebetran (Adult titles)
Karen Breen (Children's and Young Adult titles)
Kirkus Reviews
VNU US Literary Group
770 Broadway
New York, NY 10003
212-777-4554
www.kirkusreviews.com

Book Review Editor
ALA *Booklist*
50 East Huron Street
Chicago, IL 60611
312-944-6780; 800-545-2433
www.ala.org

Feature articles

One interesting way around the problem of getting reviewers to review your book is to write a feature article that can be used by editors who write "off the book page" columns—that is, those columns that deal with subjects similar to yours. While this method is by no means guaranteed, it is an excellent way to augment your other marketing efforts.

For instance, if you're publishing a book on cars and you can't get the book reviewed on the book-review page, then write an article about the newsworthy content in the book, mention the book's publication, and send it to automotive editors as well as reviewers. This kind of piece differs somewhat from a regular press release because you want to focus on that information of primary interest to the particular specialist editor you've targeted. You should use catchy headlines, bullet points, and colorful adjectives and adverbs that will make your copy and release interesting to the editor and the editor's readers so that he can just pick up your material and run with it.

I know of one major TV network affiliate in a key market whose consumer affairs editor runs virtually every piece using *Consumer Reports'* film. The reason is that it's free and it's pertinent. It also mentions *Consumer Reports* in every segment! You can provide information about your books in a slightly different way to newspapers, magazines, newsletters, internet sites, and more with similar results. The key here is to keep in mind that the editors are not as interested in the fact that your book has been published as much as in the valuable information they can share with their readers. Now's the time to showcase your author's expertise. Try it; you'll see!

Tip: Because the large-circulation papers are inundated with material from their own reporters, syndicated sources, and others, one way to get better pick-up of your feature article is to try for smaller circulation papers, or even weeklies. These smaller papers frequently need material.

Working with Your Author

One of the most important sales and marketing tools you have, especially to publicists, is one that is often overlooked: your author. Because the author took the time and effort to write a book, she probably has an in-depth knowledge of the subject, those who are interested in it, and the environment in which the subject exists as well as the influential people who exist in that environment. Rather than starting your publicity efforts from ground zero, use your author to begin to focus your efforts and to help publicize the book through her own efforts and appearances, wherever they may be. An excellent source of ideas and suggestions for both publisher and author about how to work together to mutual benefit is Judith Appelbaum's *How to Get Happily Published: A Complete and Candid Guide* (HarperCollins Publishers).

Author Questionnaire

A good **Author Questionnaire** (see page 218) will provide an enormous amount of information for the marketing staff, especially for the publicity department. I believe this information is so critical to the ultimate success of the book that I recommend my clients insist upon the completion and return of the Author Questionnaire as a condition of contract signing. In other words, that the questionnaire is sent to the author at the same time as the book contract and that the questionnaire's fully completed return is mandated for the same time the contract is returned. Without the questionnaire, there should be no fully executed contract.

To be blunt, few publishers operate this way. Most complete a contract, and only later do they send out the Author Questionnaire. Unfortunately, many publishers either forget to send it, or forget to ask for its timely return. The result is that often the questionnaire is never looked at or never returned. Without the questionnaire, the publicity effort can be crippled. This is why I recommend the questionnaire be filled out at contract signing, when everyone is enthusiastic about the book and everyone is thinking about how best to promote it.

Author Tours

The last points I want to make are in relation to author tours.

Author Questionnaire

Book Title:

Anticipated Publication Date:

Author's Full Name:*

Author's Name on Book Jacket:

Author's Address:*

City: State: Zip:

Country:

Home Phone: Business Phone: Fax: E-mail:

Nationality:*   Date of Birth:*

1. AUTHOR BIOGRAPHY:
Please provide a concise biography, including current occupation and title as well as the location of your employer. Please include any past employment that would be pertinent to readers of this book.

Author education:
Please provide a list of colleges attended, degrees and honors. Also provide the name and address of any alumni magazines at these institutions.

Affiliations:
Provide the names of any organizations to which you are affiliated, including academic, professional, and/or governmental.

Previous books:
Please list any previous books you've written, including title, publisher, year of publication, sales history if available.

Other previous publications:
List any other published material that is pertinent to this book and to readers of this book.

*Required for registering your book with the U.S. Copyright Office.

Author Questionnaire *continued*

2. ABOUT YOUR BOOK:

Describe your book:
Please describe why you wrote this book, the niche it fills, its subject, and key editorial points that make it unique.

Describe the ideal audience for your book:

What are the primary competitive books on the market?
Please provide editorial similarities and differences, whether the competitive books are in hardcover and paperback, their prices, and any special elements (are they 4-color?).

Tell us about any special requests:
Would you like to make any suggestions or special requests about the book to the book's editors, designers, or salespeople?

Suggest two alternate titles for your book:
Please provide us with two alternate titles for your book.

3. SALES AND MARKETING:

Blurbs and endorsements:
Please provide us with the names of colleagues or other influential people within your field from whom we may solicit comments about your book. Please provide addresses if possible.

Advertising:
Please provide the names of those magazines, journals, newspapers, or other media in which you think an ad might be effective.

Educational sales outlets:
Please provide the names of schools, or professors, that might be interested in using this book for courses either as a textbook or as a supplemental text.

Sales outlets or media at which you are known:
Please provide us with the name of your hometown newspaper and any bookstores at which you may be known.

Your future plans:
If you will be traveling within the year following your book's anticipated publication, please provide the cities and states to which you will be going. Please provide dates of visits if known.

ANY OTHER IMPORTANT INFORMATION:
Please provide any additional information that was not provided above but that you feel is important to the success of your book.

Many authors feel that part of the glamour of publishing, and becoming a published author, is getting to go on a promotional tour. They think that doing autographings and TV and radio shows not only will help the sale of their book, but will also give them a forum for expanding their own expert image and their message. While both of these results may occur, they also may not.

From a publisher's perspective, putting an author on the road can be risky. As I mentioned, it can be very expensive depending upon where you want to send the author. Costs range from virtually nothing, if you put the author on local media in the town in which the author lives, to $5,000 and up per city if you choose to send the author to a large city, put him up in a decent hotel, and pay for food, taxis, and/or author-escort services, not to mention the cost of review copies, mailing, and phone calls. Satellite tours, in which the author stays in one location but is broadcast, via satellite, to numerous television or radio stations in a particular region or nationally, is also expensive, sometimes coming in around $10,000.

Furthermore, the competition from publishers to get their authors on a diminishing number of shows for free is fierce. All of the major publishers are trying vigorously to get their top and middle-level authors on those few shows with national reach: *Today*, *Good Morning America*, *Oprah*, *Regis and Kelly*, and more. Similar to book reviewers, the producers of these shows, the ones responsible for booking guests, are inundated with books, press releases, and phone calls about the various authors available. And again, if you are a smaller publisher with fewer books and fewer daily contacts with these producers, your chances of successfully getting your author on these shows is proportionately smaller.

At the same time, your book may be exactly what that producer is looking for at a specific moment in time. If you send your book to the producer and present it professionally; if you follow it up with a phone call or e-mail to make sure the producer has received it and to find out if she needs additional information; and *if she needs that kind of author for her show*, then your author stands just as good a chance of getting on the show as an author from the bigger house.

Remember the first chapter when I discussed commitment, consistency, and credibility? Well, these three factors are absolutely critical in the world of publicity, especially in the world of TV and radio, where timing is fast and exists in a world of real-time events. In this world, there is no time for delay. If you say you can have an author ready to appear on a show, then you had better produce that author at the studio on the right day at the right time. If you do, you'll gain substantial credibility and the producer will not hesitate to consider your next book and author for appearances. If you don't get your author to the studio on time, you'll have a very difficult time getting another one booked—and rightly so.

One factor that's important to review before sending your author anywhere is that author's presence on camera or radio and the author's ability to be at ease and to work well under stressful conditions. While every author likes to think he or she is the perfect human specimen, the fact is some are more photogenic than others; some speak better and with more assurance than others; some enjoy this kind of promotion and some find it anathema.

If your author is ill at ease in media situations, or has little experience doing programs or appearances, then it will probably make sense to invest a bit of time and money in media training for your author. Media trainers will help your author by teaching him or her what to expect and how to react before the author goes on the road or begins to work on your behalf. Through role-playing and taping, the author learns how to answer various questions easily; how to make an audience (and him- or herself) feel comfortable; and how to make the entire process work to the benefit of the show, the author, the publisher, and the book.

Do author tours work? It depends. As mentioned, tours can be very expensive, so you need to sell a lot of books to recover your costs. If you spend $5,000 to book one large city, you'll probably have to sell at least that number of books to break even. As we all know, that's not always easy to do. As you expand your tour, you have to sell a lot more books to be successful. This is why I recommend the less expensive publicity route.

There are, however, times when author appearances do pay off.

- If the show will pay travel and other expenses. Sometimes, if the book or author is important enough, and if news is breaking around that subject or author, the show will pay for the author's expenses. This makes sense for the publisher and the author and they should both accept the offer of exposure and paid expenses quickly. Don't look the proverbial gift horse in the mouth!

- If your author travels a lot on business and is willing to pay the travel, lodging, and meal costs, then you can probably tie in your promotional efforts to hit the media in each city at a very reasonable cost. You might even pick up one night's lodging and food cost, which would allow the author to stay an extra day, which he could devote to media appearances, interviews, or local in-store autographings (be careful about this; there's nothing more deflating than an autographing at which no one appears). This can well be an effective, low-cost way to gain sales and enhance your author's reputation at the same time.
- If your author regularly gives seminars in various cities, you can take advantage of the media promoting the seminars. You can also have the author or a local bookstore sell books before and after the seminar. This requires close coordination with the bookstore to make sure the books will be available. In some cases, the books may have to be carried in by the author. If this is the case, then be sure to get a purchase order from the store at the time of the event, and have the store sign for the books as proof of delivery.
- If your author doesn't travel, but lives in a larger city, then by all means book that particular city. Sometimes local networks provide national feed.
- Finally, in today's modern digital age, rather than sending your author out on the road, think about radio or TV-satellite tours, where the author goes to a local studio and that appearance is broadcast nationally or regionally as you may determine, without the author leaving the studio. This avoids the major travel costs of most author tours. The results can be excellent.

Of course there are hundreds of ways of getting free and low cost publicity and many books about how to do this. These methods are preferable alternatives to

- print ads, whose results are extremely difficult to quantify objectively (unless it's a coupon ad)
- co-op ads, which are mainly purchased with wholesalers to

assuage your buyer's feelings. They sometimes have an impact but usually don't.

- author tours, which can become very expensive very quickly

This is not to say that author tours, co-op ads, and other such promotional vehicles don't work. It is to say that they are much more costly and less consistently successful than straightforward publicity unless something else is happening to send buyers into stores. For instance, if you're publishing a book that's currently a feature film, print ads tied in with the movie, or co-op ads with retail accounts, can certainly work.

Finally, make sure you stay on top of current news. If your author has special insight about something that's breaking, or if your book happens to be related in some way to that event, then you should bring that pertinent information to the attention of the media. Because of the short turnaround time involved in breaking stories, the media may clamor for someone to help them interpret the event or give it a spin of some kind. Your author or your book may be perfect. Remember, though, that the reverse is also true: there are no guarantees. If you have an author booked to speak about a certain subject and an important event occurs, your author could be bumped. In publicity, timing is everything. Be sure to take advantage of it.

CHAPTER 10

Subsidiary Rights

The sale of subsidiary rights is essential to the success of your company. Why do I say this? Because as I noted previously, the net profitability of most publishing companies comes very close to that percentage of sale of subsidiary rights. Without that sale, most companies would barely break even. With it, they can be successful.

A subsidiary rights sale is any rights sale that is "subsidiary" or secondary to the actual right to publish the book. That is, it is any sale of the right to publish the book that you, as publisher, grant to someone else for a licensing fee.

If you view subsidiary rights as just that, something that is incremental or "subsidiary" to your regular publishing program, then you will put it into the proper framework. This area can be extremely lucrative, but the streams of income are relatively unpredictable. You might get lucky and get a movie option or sale, which could mean a one-time hit of a lot of money. You could sell mass-market paperback rights or electronic rights for a lot of money. A good sub-rights director can literally generate millions of dollars in fees.

The more usual pattern of selling sub-rights results in a modest stream of revenue that builds over time. Similar to the interest earned in a money-market fund through compounding, the more you sell to clubs, paperback houses, magazines, and other rights buyers, the more revenue you generate and, just as important, the more chance there is for those sales to generate additional revenue over the long term.

In many companies, the subsidiary-rights function is found within the sales department. I have put it into marketing because it is not directly a sales function, but rather fits within the scope of overall marketing. The fact is, it doesn't really matter who has responsibility for subsidiary rights, so long as it's done properly.

What constitutes subsidiary rights?

- Book club sales
- Serial rights sales
- Foreign rights sales
- Mass-market rights sales
- Audio book sales
- E-content sales
- Movie sales
- Stamp sheet sales
- Condensation sales
- And much more

If you think sub-rights is only for the large publishers, think again! Many independent publishers are highly successful in selling sub-rights. Years ago, when I took over responsibility for sub-rights at one publisher with a fair number of backlist books, within one year we were doing over $1 million in sub-rights sales. At a start-up publisher for whom I worked, I consistently generated over $200,000 per year in sub-rights sales with a very limited number of titles with which to work. One of my consulting clients, which had done a modest amount with sub-rights, increased their sales to well over $500,000 a year with just a little bit of effort that differed from what they were doing. While I'd like to think I was the one responsible for these sales, the fact of the matter was that I brought a process to bear on these companies that continues to this day. And in the long term, it's the process that's important, not just the person doing it. *You too can sell sub-rights if you do it properly.*

As with many efforts in the publishing industry, selling subsidiary rights necessitates a heavy dose of personal relationships with those who may be interested in buying rights to your titles. It also requires a clear understanding on your part of your potential client's business.

Let's begin our discussion of sub-rights sales with book clubs, because this is probably where most independent publishers focus their attention and have the most success.

Book Clubs

Book clubs are direct response vendors who sell a variety of publishers' books to the members serviced by the individual club. The service provided by the club is at least twofold: to provide an editorial selection for members, and to make it easy for buyers to purchase books they either might not find elsewhere, or which may be purchased at a reduced cost from the club.

As you can imagine, the clubs' worst enemies are higher postal costs and discounting bookstores, whether tangible or virtual. And yes, you're right, that's exactly what clubs are now up against.

The clubs are constantly fighting postal increases and rate hikes that have a dramatic impact on their profitability. The clubs also have very heavy costs associated with creating catalogs and doing their normal member marketing. As you'll see in the next chapter on direct response marketing, it is very tough to make a lot of money in this business. Like others, clubs are also using the internet to acquire members and to facilitate ordering. And like most who are using the internet, clubs are spending a good deal of money on technology and acquisition costs—some more successfully than others.

Despite these difficulties, which have resulted in the merger of some major clubs, many book clubs are still doing a good business. And the wonderful thing about book clubs is that they are varied. Some are highly subject-specific, which is one reason people join them. There are excellent clubs specializing in history, cooking, gardening, design, military history, and many other subjects. Other clubs are more general in their editorial selections, such as Book-of-the-Month Club, Quality Paperback Book Club (which is format-specific), and the Literary Guild.

One common dilemma for publishers revolves around the question of whether selling a book to a book club will cannibalize the publisher's sale of the same book in other markets. As far as I know, there are no hard statistics to answer this question. However, if one looks at the results obtained from publishers who do large-scale direct-response marketing on their retail programs, the fear of cannibalization can be alleviated. A test carried out by Rodale Press with Barnes & Noble some time ago shed some insight on this matter. According to Pat Corpora, then president of Rodale's Book Division, Barnes & Noble tracked sales of books that Rodale was heavily promoting through its direct marketing effort. Sales of those books increased at Barnes & Noble stores.

Other large direct-response publishers show similar results. *Reader's Digest's* direct mail efforts had a dramatic influence in creating traffic into retail accounts for their category-leading *Complete Do-It-Yourself Manual*. Meredith Books, which at one time also had its own book clubs, had no hesitation whatsoever about selling its books in those clubs.

What almost all publishers agree on is that selling books to the clubs is an excellent way to *increase* your book's exposure and sales and that selling to clubs has no negative impact whatsoever on sales through other channels. Most publishers agree that the more channels through which you can sell your book, the greater the overall sale of that book.

Once you've decided to sell your books to the clubs, how do you go about it? There are basically four key elements to sell book clubs successfully:

1. Target your book to the right clubs.
2. Get your material in early.
3. Establish rapport with the buyer.
4. Price your material correctly.

Let's review each of these factors in turn.

Target Your Book to the Right Clubs

It does no good to send your book to a club that isn't interested because the subject isn't right. Sending a cookbook to the Military Book Club is a total waste of your time and money. Use common sense and rigorously target every book on your list to the appropriate clubs that may be of interest. I say "may" with reason. Over many years of selling rights, I've found that you can't be certain of how a club will respond. Remember on your Title P&L I didn't have you include any revenue for book club sales? This is why. Book club selection is out of your hands. You can never predict how a club will respond to your titles no matter how often you work with clubs. So never say "never." Target your books, but if you're in doubt, either call the buyer or send the book. A few dollars spent on postage and PPB isn't too much to pay if you get lucky.

On the other hand, don't send books that are clearly inappropriate to buyers. All you'll do is make them angry with you. You must use your own reasonable judgment.

> **Tip:** No matter how frequently you sell clubs, every time you think about submitting a new title, always go through the list of clubs in *Literary Market Place* to remind yourself of what clubs are around and what clubs might be interested in your title. No matter how often you sell clubs, there are always some you'll forget about or overlook. It's a step that's simple to take—and can reap rewards.

Get Your Material in Early

As I've noted before, every part of the book industry has its own cycles and selling seasons. With clubs, there are between 13 and 17 cycles per year for most of them. (The reason for this is that the one-time head of Book-of-the-Month Club, David Sherman, was trying to find a way to mail more than once per month. He realized that if he mailed just short of every 30 days, or every 28 days, he could get an extra cycle into each year.) A *cycle* is the period between mailings of club catalogs to members. And that means that clubs constantly need new titles for use as Main Selections, that is, the primary book offered during a cycle, or as Alternates, other newly offered titles that members may purchase from month to month.

In most clubs, the main selection is automatically sent as a "negative-option" title; in other words, it is automatically sent to the member unless a reply card is returned by the member to the club telling the club not to send the main selection. Alternates are almost always "positive-option" books, which members see in the catalog and actually ask the club to send.

Because of the negative-option approach, main selections are almost always returned at a rate of about 40 to 50%. That is, for every two main selections sent out to club members, one will be returned.

This is because members forget or don't bother to return the negative option card and don't really want the month's selection; they don't like the book when they get it; or they just don't want to buy books that month.

Positive-option books, on the other hand, are returned in very small percentages because the people buying them actually request them. Members make a "positive" decision to buy the book before it is sent out. Thus, they have expressed an interest in the book to begin with.

Today, many clubs are turning away from offering one main selection, instead offering two or three titles from which members can choose. The reason is to provide more choice, but also to reduce the expense to the club that's inherent in high negative-option main selection return rates.

What is important to you, as a publisher, is to understand the rhythm of the clubs' mailings; what clubs usually buy; and therefore what they'll need. A good way to do this is to join a variety of clubs, get their mailings, see what they're selling, and buy books from them. Also, return books to them. This way, you'll get a good feel for the dynamics of the club: its editorial direction, its billing cycles and invoices, and its customer-service functions, including, if you'd like, their collection policies! There's absolutely no better way to get a feel for a specific club.

As a direct-response operation, clubs need a good deal of time to

- Select the books
- Contract for books
- Produce books
- Create the copy and direct response packages
- Create catalogs that are mailed or posted on their websites

Thus, to sell successfully to clubs, you must get your books to the clubs very early, so those books can fit into the clubs' schedules. If you don't do this, you won't get a book into a club. If, for instance, you send a Christmas cookbook to the Good Cook Club (one of Bookspan's specialty clubs) in September, you're too late. The book should have been there in March at the latest, and that's for an alternate. A main selection should have been there in January.

Having said this, different clubs have different needs and schedules. Like publishers, some work on a much tighter turnaround than others. I recently made a sale for one of my clients to a club that is working on a four-month turnaround, from contract to sale date. This is very tight, but the club is relatively small and because there aren't a lot of publishers publishing books in the specific subject category, the club's choice of books is somewhat limited. Also, some books contracted for inevitably are late or canceled. Thus clubs are always looking for a few books at the last minute and are glad to get them when they come in. This is the exception, though, and in no way the rule.

One nice attribute (among others) of clubs is that they are anxious to see material as early in the publishing process as possible. If you have a clean finished manuscript and a cover dummy, you should send it. If there are photographs or illustrations, send those as well. Don't send heavily copyedited material or a dirty manuscript. But do send a clean one as soon as you have it. If the club is interested in the material, it will either give you an immediate answer based upon that material, or ask for additional material. Use your judgment as to what you'd like to see if you were in the buyer's position. That's what you should send.

Establish Rapport with the Buyer

Once you've sent in your material, wait a few weeks before checking up on it. Some buyers just don't respond to material at all; others are very good about getting back to you. If, however, you don't get a response, do call to check up on the book. Don't, however, argue about the results. If the book is rejected, so be it. Don't fight it. If you can get some feedback as to why it was rejected, that's great. But don't be overly pushy. Buyers have too many books to review and too many buying options. Don't make an enemy of them or a pest of yourself.

Do, however, get to know the buyers. One of the big mistakes some independent publishers make is that they don't take the time or make the opportunity to see book club buyers or to talk to them on a regular basis. Again, this is a highly personal business. The more you get to know the buyer, and vice versa, the better your chances of selling a book to that buyer. The key is to keep in touch with the buyer and to be selective in your submissions. Don't send books that don't make sense to a particular club. If you are in New York, or whatever the city in which the club is based, try to get an appointment with the buyer of a particular club. Book-club buyers are usually open to such visits if they feel you may have books that will work for them. Don't be shy. Send a catalog or list of forthcoming books. Pick up the phone and call. The worst that can happen is that they'll say no—and they'll probably say yes!

Given time, you will more than likely be successful in getting a selection. And more than likely, it will be an alternate because main selections usually (but not always) come from the larger houses who have "brand name" authors. The good news is that in very particular subject areas, independent publishers can compete with the larger ones if they have established themselves as experts in their subjects. There are many such publishers who have been successful.

Price Your Material Correctly
Few publishers get rich on book-club sales. The reason is that, as we've seen, book clubs have very high costs of creation and mailing. Thus, they must purchase books from the publisher at very deep discounts, or print their own editions, to make the margins they need to operate successfully. How deep are the discounts needed? Depending upon the quantity purchased, around 60 to 80%. This is why the publisher doesn't make much money on club purchases. For this reason, some publishers feel that they can make more money selling to their regular accounts than they can to clubs. This may be true—if you ultimately sell all of your print run and do so in a relatively quick time period. But for most publishers, there is the risk that the books won't sell out, and that they won't do so quickly.

Why then sell to book clubs? Because

1. You can make incremental money on the sale.
2. You can save money on your own print run by adding the club's copies to that run. The money you save per copy by running a greater quantity of copies never directly shows up on your income statement as a by-product of club sales but is a primary reason for selling to clubs.
3. Selling to the club helps you turn inventory faster.
4. Turning inventory faster helps your cash flow because you can turn inventory into cash quicker and earn an amount greater than keeping the money tied up in inventory, and most likely

greater than that you can earn by simply keeping your money in the bank.

5. You get free advertising from the club's catalog, website, and print ads.
6. You get the prestige of being able to state on your book's cover or jacket, and in all of your press material, that the book is a selection of a club.
7. Your authors will be happier.

If you sell a book to a book club, then you should earn money from that sale or you shouldn't make it. You will cover your costs of PPB and earn some extra on your unit cost. In addition, you'll earn royalty from that sale. If the book sells successfully for the club, it will reorder from you, or reprint itself. Either way, you will get additional money for that reorder. As you sell more and more to the clubs, the chances of reorders increase. Thus, just as you build your original sales budget one book at a time and some titles become basic backlist, so too will some of the books you sell to the clubs become long-term successes. Each of these in turn throws off small amounts of incremental revenue and profit that build up over time. And as these build, so too does your subsidiary rights revenue line.

This is the beauty of subsidiary rights. As you expand your program, the incremental dollars will continue to climb so long as you publish books your sub-rights customers want. So look for the big hit, but be happy with the small, continuous sales. Over time, it adds up to a large amount that adds directly to your profitability.

Pricing for Book Clubs

A publisher can make money on book-club sales in two ways:

- on the unit cost
- on the royalty

If a club is interested in your book, the buyer will call you and ask for a quote on buying the copies they need, whether 200 or 2,000 or more. If the book will be used as an alternate, the club will probably need about 1,000 to 1,500. Some clubs are smaller than others. As this is being written, I have two clubs interested in using a client's title as an alternate. One club wants 200 copies; the other 1,000.

There are two ways clubs work with publishers: they either buy copies from your inventory or stock, or they will print their own edition. If a club buys copies from your stock, it will pay you both a unit cost and a royalty. Sometimes this is paid in a lump sum, with royalty included in the amount; sometimes (usually) royalty exclusive, with the unit cost being paid first, an advance against future earned royalty also paid up front, and the rest of the royalty paid as the books are sold. If the club prints its own edition, the club will pay you an advance on royalty and the remainder of the royalty as books are sold.

When you estimate your book for the club you must do so using their parameters. Again, this is not full book income, this is *subsidiary income*. The club's costs are high and it is a separate sales channel. You must establish a different costing method for it and provide the club with the discounted price that works for their market.

Let's work through an estimate for a club. See the following **Book Club Pricing Template**.

Begin with your retail price. Let's assume $29.95.

Discount your retail price by 20% to get to the club's sale price. A primary selling point for the club is that it offers its members editorial selection at significant savings. In most cases, this is a 20% discount from the publisher's retail price. Some clubs, though, are discounting much higher than 20% to compete with the chain stores and online retailers. This makes it almost impossible to sell to those clubs from stock. In almost every case, a club discounting that much to its members will have to print its own edition.

If you take your $29.95 price and apply the 20% discount, you'll get to a club price of $23.96, which would probably result in a rounded-off club price of $23.95. At this point, you should ask the club to tell you the price at which it will sell the book. The reason is that you don't know for sure what price makes sense to the club. For instance, you may think $23.95 is accurate because it's 20% off the retail price. However, the club is always trying to earn the greatest margin it can. Therefore it could easily try to earn more for itself by pricing the book at $24.95, which would still result in a significant $5.00 savings off of your retail price for the club member. Five dollars is an appealing discount for a member. As we'll see, determining the club price can make a substantial difference to the amount you can earn.

Book Club Pricing Template

SAMPLE BOOK #1						
	Book Club 1		Book Club 2		Total both	
					clubs	
Retail Price	$29.95		$29.95			
Discounted by 20%	$5.99		$5.99			
Club Price	$23.96		$23.96			
Divided by 4	$5.99		$5.99			
Royalty Inclusive Price to Publisher	$5.99		$7.75			
Less Royalty @ 6% Club Price	$1.44		$1.44			
Amount Available for PPB	$4.55		$6.31			
Publisher's PPB Cost	$2.24		$2.24			
Gross Contribution on Sale	**$2.31**	103%	**$4.07**	182%		
Less Agent's Commission						
@ 10%*	$0.60		$0.78			
Net Contribution on Sale	**$1.71**	76%	**$3.30**	147%		
Plus Pub's Share of Royalty	**$0.72**		**$0.72**			
Gross Publisher's Contrib.	**$2.43**	109%	**$4.02**	179%		
X Quantity Purchased						
750	$1,824.15		$803.24	200=quant.	$2,627.39	
1000	$2,432.20					
Total Gross from Club						
Royalty Inclusive Price x Quantity						
750	$4,492.50		$1,550.00	200=quant.	$6,042.50	
1000	$5,990.00					
Total Commission Payable,						
if applicable						
750	$449.25		$155.00		$604.25	
1000	$599.00					
*If there is no agent, your net						
will be the same as your gross						

Taking the club price, divide that by 4 to get to the royalty-inclusive price the club will offer to you. Effectively, this is the same process as dividing your retail price by 5, so why don't I just do that? Because I need to know the club price to determine the royalty amount that will be based on that price. So I must add that extra step to the process, as I did above.

Now you can also see why knowing the club price makes a difference to your analysis. If you divide $24.95 by 4 you get $6.24. If you divide $23.95 by 4 you get $5.99, a difference of $0.25 per book, a significant amount of money per book. From another perspective, that's more than the cost of the book's cover or jacket.

Once you have the all-inclusive club price, which covers both unit cost and royalty, you back out the royalty to see what the actual unit cost is and to see how it compares to your own unit cost.

Different clubs use different royalty rates, so again you should ask the buyer what the royalty rate is for that particular club. Rates range from 2.5% on dividend or bonus books up to a more usual 8 to 10% on hardcover books. For our purposes, let's assume 6%. In a rather macabre twist, from a publisher's standpoint, the lower the royalty paid the better, because it allows more of the total amount paid by the club to be allocated to the unit cost, which remains with the publisher. In most cases, by contract, sub-rights money is split 50–50% between the author and publisher. So if you received $5.99 per book total, and a 10% royalty was paid on $23.95, you'd receive $2.395 per book for royalty, which you'd have to split with the author, each of you receiving $1.198 per book. Thus, you'd be left with $3.595, which is equal to $5.99 – $2.395, for your unit cost. If you received a 5% royalty on the same retail price, you'd receive $1.198 in royalty, which again you'd split 50%–50%, which would leave you with a larger amount to be allocated to the unit: $4.79 per book, calculated at $5.99 – $1.198.

With this calculation completed, you can compare the club's unit cost offer for your book with your unit cost of paper, printing and binding.

Many smaller publishers feel the club should pay a proportionate share of their plant, or development, costs. Clubs don't operate that way. They know that you are publishing this book for yourself whatever they decide about it. In other words, if they didn't buy the book, you'd still publish it and incur all of the development costs in any case. The club's copies do necessitate extra paper, printing, and binding costs, they think, so the club should only pay for those. In fact, the club is correct. You would publish the book with or without them, so don't add in film or development costs when comparing your PPB costs to the unit price they offer.

Comparing the club's unit offer with your own paper, printing, and binding costs, what are the results?

- If your unit cost is less than that offered by the club, you're in good shape. Remember, this is incremental revenue, so don't look for huge profits. Go ahead and make the deal unless it puts you in a short stock position.
- If your unit cost is more than that offered by the club you shouldn't make the deal unless, and only unless, you want to get your foot in the door of the club and you are willing to accept a one-time loss to do so. I never recommend that a publisher lose money on a sub-rights sale unless it's for an extraordinary reason.
- If your unit cost is equal to the club's unit offer, then you'll make money on the royalty but must make a decision as to whether it's worth it to you to make the deal. I usually recommend that the publisher make the deal because it will earn royalty; it will gain advertising and prestige for the book. And, it will help you turn your inventory (depending upon your stock situation this may be good or bad).

Ideally, if you can print the club copies at the same time you're running your own, it will save money on your printing by reducing your own unit cost. This effect is very often overlooked by publishers because it never shows up in a revenue column. If you are printing 1,000 copies at $2.50 per book and the club wants 1,000 copies that you can add to your run, then that extra 1,000 copies will significantly reduce your unit cost. While the reduced unit cost will show up as added gross margin and contribution to profit, *it never shows up as contribution to profit resulting from club sales*. It is simply not viewed that way by most publishers, who look at sub-rights as a revenue line, not as a reduced cost of goods line. In fact, the savings engendered by the addition of the club's copies has saved you a significant amount of money on your own copies in addition to generating revenue. To look at the significance of book club sales properly, you must view it in this context.

What should you look for in terms of profitability or contribution to profitability? Every publisher has a different answer to this question and each must establish its own *hurdle rate* percentage. Remember, this is incremental money, *and the sale is nonreturnable*. If you can earn a rate that is greater than that you'd earn by keeping your money in the bank, then the deal probably makes sense. Thus if you can earn 10% on the unit you'd be doing well because current bank or money-market fund interest payments are running 2–4%. I usually look at the unit cost plus 20% as a starting point when quoting clubs.

At this point, you know your gross contribution to sales from this club purchase. If, however, you are using a sub-rights agent, you must factor in that agent's share, usually around 10% of the total gross dollar sale of finished books. Subtracting this from the gross contribution yields the net contribution on your sale—in our example, $1.71. But that's not all you'll earn.

Once you've made the unit comparison, don't forget to factor in your 50% share of the royalty. In some cases, if your unit comparison is equal, this could push the deal into profitability. In other cases, it's just icing on the cake. Net contribution plus your share of the royalty provides your gross contribution to sales. You can then multiply this figure times the number of units you're selling to show the total amount you'll earn on the deal, and do other calculations as well, depending upon what you want to reveal.

With this information in hand, you can respond to the club. More often than not, the club's price will be very tough to negotiate. It never hurts to try, though. And the more you can get for that unit, the greater the benefit to you.

I have been discussing the concept of a club buying from your stock, whether directly, or whether you print and sell finished books to them. The other way clubs buy is to purchase the right to print their own edition of your book. This is a frequent occurrence today.

In such cases, the club will make you an offer for an advance and royalty. The offer will almost always be based on a straightforward calculation. That is, the club's price times the royalty rate times the number of copies they project to sell, divided in half.

For example, if they print your $29.95 book and sell it for $24.95, the club pays a 6% royalty and thinks they'll sell 1,000 copies, then the calculation will look like:

$$\$24.95 \times .06 = 1.497 \times 1000 \text{ copies} = \$1,497 \div 2 = \$748.50$$

This advance is usually paid one-half upon the full execution of the contract and one-half upon the club's release of the book.

The advance and royalty deals are very clean. You provide the club with your original film (which they insure) or duplicate film (you can negotiate as to who pays for the duplication) and the name of your printer. The club contracts directly with the printer to do the work and pays the printer. Sometimes, if the unit-cost analysis doesn't work in your favor, it makes more sense to let the club print because then you gain royalty but don't have to worry about losing money on the print run. Sometimes, if you need inventory, you may be able to run-on with the club's edition. The club may be able to print at a lower cost, because they manufacture many more books and often get better pricing.

In sum, use the clubs to help your profitability, but don't view them unrealistically. Over time, working with the clubs can generate substantial income and incremental profits. And as we've seen, these profits can make the difference between corporate profitability and corporate loss or breakeven. Get to know the club buyers as well as you can. If you prove your commitment to them, work with them consistently and properly, then they will welcome your call and visit. And that will be beneficial to everyone—especially your company.

Serial Rights

Another subsidiary right that is relatively easy for smaller publishers to sell is serial rights. Serial rights refers to the sale of parts or all of your book to a magazine, newspaper, journal, website, or other media, which will then publish that excerpt of your book in the magazine or other media. The benefit of serial rights is again incremental revenue and free publicity for your book.

Like book clubs, magazines, journals, and most other media work on long lead times. Newspapers are the exception. They can publish very quickly and you can get material to them later than you can to others. If you want to work with magazines and journals, however, you must submit your material as soon as you have a manuscript. At the same time as you submit to the book clubs, submit to the serial rights buyers.

Basically there are two kinds of serial rights:

- First serial, which gives the purchaser the right to publish the material prior to its book publication
- Second serial, which grants the purchaser the right to publish after publication

First serial rights give the media publisher a "scoop" over others because it will have first access to your material, so the publisher can usually demand a larger fee for that use. In exchange the magazine may want an exclusive arrangement. This means that the magazine wants to keep its publication solely to itself and its readers—which can generate a lot of publicity for the magazine itself. If the magazine insists upon an exclusive, then you cannot sell first serial rights to another magazine or newspaper. Assuming you negotiate an agreeable fee for this, it's usually a fair trade-off.

Second serial rights are always nonexclusive and the payments to the publisher by the media for such rights range from zero to substantial sums. Some media don't pay publishers for this right, claiming that they are providing exposure for the publisher's book. Every publisher must look at the circumstances of these offers and make a determination as to whether it is a reasonable offer or not. If so, take the deal; if not, don't.

Serial rights can be nice incremental income. At the same time, you must look at the costs closely. Because you normally don't receive large payments for second serial rights, you must weigh the costs of postage and copying carefully. These can be significant costs, especially if you are sending out a large number of copies. Such costs can quickly eat up your profits. On the other hand, such sales can provide your book with a national audience, which can translate into book sales. Again, however, you can't track this directly unless there is some response mechanism at the end of the excerpt, an 800 number or a department number that the responding buyer can quote.

In the hierarchy of subsidiary rights, I recommend pursuit of serial rights second to book clubs. The nice part about serial rights is that they don't take a large amount of effort. Just as with book clubs, you target your list of media, send the manuscript, and follow up by phone or e-mail. That's about it. And just like clubs, as you begin to establish rapport with the rights buyers, you will become familiar with their needs, they will become familiar with you and your company's books. The net result—again, over time—will be ultimate success.

Foreign Rights

If you recall the comments made earlier about where to find books to acquire, and my discussion of foreign publishers (chapter 7), then the thought of reversing that scenario, and selling the rights to your books to foreign publishers will come as no surprise to you.

Just as U.S. publishers are always looking for new books to publish, so too are foreign publishers. And sales of your books to these publishers can be an excellent source of subsidiary rights income.

The key is to find those publishers who are publishing in categories similar to yours. Once found, it's an easy process to find an editor in that foreign house with whom you can correspond and who can express interest, or not, in your books. This expression of interest can come through perusal of your future list, which may consist simply of a list of titles you've purchased for future publication and which are now part of your rolling three-year publishing plan; your current catalog; or from looking at a finished book. In most cases, it will be all three.

The easiest way to begin the process of selling foreign rights is to make a commitment (remember that word) to this source of sub-rights income. You'll need this because selling foreign rights isn't cheap. You'll have costs of mailing, copying, and probably some travel. So you've got to make a commitment to it. This is a long-term situation. Accept that.

Once a commitment is made, find a copy of the *International Literary Market Place* (ILMP) published by R. R. Bowker. This is essentially the international equivalent to the *Literary Market Place* and lists publishers by country. As before, I suggest starting with the English-speaking publishers, just because it's a bit easier. Once you understand the process and get your feet wet, you should certainly move on to those publishing in other languages. Again, don't hesitate to contact these foreign publishers—almost all speak and correspond in English.

242 Functional Organization: Strategy and Techniques

Review *ILMP* to find those publishers who have interest in your subject area. Once found, write to the editorial director at that publisher. See the **Foreign Rights Request Letter** following. Enclose one of your catalogs and ask for one of theirs. Or, easier still, have them review your catalog online. Tell the editorial director you are beginning to explore rights sales and ask if he's interested in looking at any of your titles for possible rights purchase. If he expresses interest, then send a "reading copy" of the book to him for review.

If there is no interest, so be it. At least you've established a contact at that publisher with whom you can correspond. Keep him abreast of new titles far in advance, as they develop, and ask for an expression of interest from the contact. Only do this for books you're actually publishing. You don't want to use this editor as a sounding board because his perspective may differ radically from yours and that of the U.S. market. Do send periodic updates of new books on your list for his response.

If there is interest, then your deal will be similar to that of a book club: the foreign publisher will ask you for pricing as a run-on, if you will be going back to press soon, or for duplicate film costs so the foreign publisher can run its own copies. If the latter, then that publisher will pay you an advance amount and royalty, just as the book club will. Obviously, if you're selling to a publisher publishing in a foreign language, then you'll always have to quote an advance and royalty because there is no possibility of a run-on with your edition.

You can quote a run-on at both royalty-inclusive or royalty-exclusive rates. I always recommend trying to get a royalty-inclusive sale. The reason for this is simple: you then don't have to worry about how many books the foreign publisher sells. You will already have your money in hand. Obviously, the foreign publisher is aware of this strategy and will do its best to get a royalty-exclusive deal, because it doesn't want to pay you for books it might not sell. And therein lies the negotiation.

To quote a foreign run-on, you must know your own paper, printing, and binding costs. You want to quote that cost, plus the cost of any changes necessary for new copyright page information, new imprint information, a new jacket or cover if the publisher wants one, and other such minor changes. You should quote the unit at what's known as *cost plus,* that is, the actual cost plus a markup for your

Foreign Rights Request Letter

Date

Name
Title
Publisher
Street
City
Country

Dear (Contact Name):

I am pleased to enclose a copy of our most recent catalog, a list of future titles, and a rights availability list for your review. If there are books in the catalog or on the future list that you would like to consider for publication in (country or language), please let me know and I will be happy to send you reading copies of those books when they are ready.

At the same time, I would greatly appreciate receiving a copy of your catalog and a list of titles available for U.S. publication.

I look forward to your reply.

Sincerely,

Your Name

CROSS RIVER PUBLISHING CONSULTANTS
3 Holly Hill Lane, Katonah, New York 10536   Telephone 914-232-6708   Fax 914-232-6393

efforts. In most cases, publishers add 25% to their modified unit cost to cover administrative changes. You don't want to cheat yourself. At the same time, remember that publishers must price books competitively in their own markets. If you quote too high a fee for a run-on, you may lose the sale because the publisher will be forced to price it too high for his market. Ask the publisher what price he expects to sell it for in his market. If you divide that price by five (remember the clubs?) or six you will get close to what he can afford in his currency, royalty-exclusive. Then you'll have to figure out the exchange rate to see if that works for you. And don't forget, you're figuring on a moving target: that is, what the exchange rate will be sometime in the future when you deliver books and your partner publisher pays you. Many a publisher has ended up losing money because of exchange-rate fluctuations, so be careful and always specify that you are to be paid in U.S. dollars or your own currency.

Let's take a hypothetical case to see how this works in practice.

Suppose you have a base run-on price from your printer of $2.00 per book for paper, printing, and binding. Suppose your partner publisher wants to put his imprint on the title page, change the copyright page to reflect his needs, and do a new jacket. Let's say this costs 25 cents per book, bringing your revised unit cost to $2.25. Adding 25% for administrative work adds 56 cents, so the total unit that you will quote to the publisher is $2.81, *royalty-exclusive*. That is, the partner publisher will also pay you a royalty on his retail price. The question is, will this unit price work for your partner?

Let's say you're working with a British publisher who wants to publish the book in the UK for £8.99. This means that you should come close to a mutually agreeable price by getting your unit close to £1.80, or £8.99 divided by 5. At an exchange rate of about $1.60 per British pound, this would come to about $2.88 per book—very close to what you wanted to charge. In this case, the deal would probably work.

You can see, however, that if the British publisher wanted to charge less than £8.99 for the book in his territory, it would not work. It is important, therefore, for you to have some knowledge of what his market is and how it works; knowledge of his competitors; and knowledge about what other countries are selling similar books for.

For these reasons, and to meet with your counterparts in publishing houses throughout the world, ultimately it is important to attend some of the major conventions at which foreign rights are sold. There are four that you should consider, depending upon your schedules, publishing interests, and finances.

By far the largest international rights fair is held in Frankfurt, Germany, each year in October. In 2004, 6,691 exhibitors displayed their books, in every conceivable language, on every conceivable subject. The English language publishers have a major presence. This is the premier place to have your books shown and to set up meetings with your counterparts at those foreign publishing houses that will be interested in your books. If you don't know who those publishers are, then Frankfurt is an excellent place to find out firsthand. There is one caveat to working the Frankfurt Book Fair: you must set up your appointments, each limited to a half hour, well in advance, using the *ILMP* mentioned earlier to find the appropriate publishers and their contacts. Treat your first visit to the fair as *exploratory*. If you sell something, that's terrific, but your purpose in year one is to determine who the publishers are with whom you can work; to meet your counterparts at other houses; and to see what kinds of books work for foreign publishers and what don't. This is important to know, because you don't want to spend time pitching books that clearly won't work for the foreign publisher.

If, for instance, you publish business books, you can waste a lot of time trying to sell personal finance books that rely on U.S. laws. On the other hand, those same publishers will certainly be interested in books on global finance, corporate structure, and other business issues that impact the global market. If you're a cookbook publisher, you will quickly learn that measurements must be in imperial or metric measures if they are to work abroad, so think about putting both into your books when you do your original manuscript. Such issues become primary on the world stage, so preempt them early in your own creative planning stage.

The second place to go to sell foreign rights in the English-speaking world is the London Book Fair, held in London, England, in March of each year. Here you have direct access to most of the British publishers who sell books in the retail and academic markets. Over the years the London Book Fair has increased in size, in terms both of those who attend and those who display. Because it's in London, it is easy to get around and easy to work. Again, if you go, try to set up appointments well in advance.

The Bologna Book Fair, held in Bologna, Italy, each year in the spring, focuses on illustrated children's books. It may, in fact, be as important as Frankfurt for this category of books. If you publish children's books, you should certainly investigate this forum.

Lastly, you can do some foreign rights work at BookExpo America, the former American Booksellers Association meeting, held each year in the United States, in late May or June. This is America's largest gathering of booksellers and foreign publishers. While some foreign publishers attend, especially from the United Kingdom, as a rights fair it simply pales by comparison to Frankfurt or London. On the other hand, BEA is highly useful for doing other contact work at the same time, so you might want to attend to achieve multipurpose results.

The key to meeting with foreign publishers at book fairs, wherever they are held, is to do your homework before going. You must set up appointments to meet with the appropriate people attending the book fairs from the publishers of interest to you. Typically, appointments are made for half-hour sessions. You should begin to set up appointments, by fax, phone, or mail, with those you want to meet, three months in advance of the book fair. In your initial meeting request letter, simply ask if someone from the firm will be attending and suggest a date, time, and place (usually at your stand or theirs) for the appointment. The firm in question will respond to your letter. If you don't make appointments beforehand, you run the risk of being unable to get an appointment with those with whom you most want to meet, thereby wasting your time and money.

Another way to make your books available to foreign publishers at these conventions is to display them through one of the combined book exhibits. While these will never give you the results or the face-to-face direct experience that you could achieve by attending the fair, this method costs a fraction of the price.

One organization that does combined displays is Publisher's Marketing Association. PMA is well known to most smaller publishers as an organization that specializes in helping them in myriad ways. These range from disseminating marketing information to co-sponsoring a program with Independent Publishers Group to get books from smaller publishers distributed nationally. As part of its overall marketing mission, PMA also displays publishers' books at Frankfurt, London, and BEA. It is an excellent, inexpensive way to get your books shown and a good base to operate from on your first trips to these fairs.

Another organization that displays at various international fairs is the Combined Book Exhibit. This organization has been working book fairs for many years, displaying and cataloging the books that their publishers choose to enter. Combined Book Exhibit is especially focused on academic book fairs.

How much can you expect to make on foreign rights? It depends, obviously, on the kind of book you have. If it's an international bestseller, you can make millions. If it's a small book with limited interest, perhaps $1,000 or more. The range is vast. Remember too that your marketing expenses for selling foreign rights are typically deducted before royalty splits are made to your author. Costs for exhibit space, personnel, and travel should be fairly apportioned against those titles sold and deducted from any revenues received. Whatever you earn, though, is extra, incremental money to that which you had before. Remember, sub-rights income grows as your reach expands. It's your job, especially in relation to foreign rights, to reach far and wide.

Foreign Rights Agents

Many publishers, both large and small, rely on agents and foreign co-agents to handle their foreign rights sales. The reason is simple: foreign rights sales can be complicated by a variety of issues including the difficulty of keeping abreast of local market trends; the difficulty of keeping up with the constant editorial and personnel changes that occur within individual publishing companies; the difficulty of conducting business in a foreign language; not to mention the difficulty of dealing with foreign currency-exchange issues.

Agents, in the foreign rights context, are those who have expertise in the various foreign markets, or who have co-agents in these markets who have specific expertise in their markets. Such agents and co-agents work with your publishing company to sell your books, or more usually the translation rights to your books, to foreign publishers. Co-agents are those who are affiliated with the agent, working with the agent for part of the commission. Usually, co-agents are located in or near the countries or regions in which they specialize. For instance, an agent may be based in Prague and handle

Eastern Europe; Sydney and handle Australia and New Zealand; Barcelona and handle Spain and South America (where there is language affinity); London and handle England—you get the idea. It's this local presence that gives these agents and co-agents the expertise in their markets that is difficult to possess when you're 3,000 or more miles away from that local market.

How much do agents charge for their services? Most work on a commission basis and charge 10 to 15% of the sale price as their fee. When an agent uses a co-agent the fee to the publisher is usually 20%.

To find an agent or agents who can help you with foreign rights, start with the *Literary Market Place*. Browse the section on agents. You will find a variety of names of both U.S.-based agents and their affiliated co-agents abroad. Before doing anything, check *ILMP*. There you will also find a list of foreign agents and, within the listings, the countries or regions in which they specialize. With this information in hand, you can contact the agents who meet your needs and ask them if they would be interested in handling your particular line. You'll have to send a letter and a catalog to give the agent an idea of the kind of books you're publishing and the extent of your publishing program. But basically, with your list and program outline in hand, the agent can make a decision. (Again, alternatively, the agent can review your website.)

Most agents and co-agents handle foreign rights on an exclusive basis. That is, if you contract with an agent to sell foreign rights for your company, you must submit material to the agent, who then submits it to the foreign publisher and negotiates any arrangement for you. It defeats the purpose of using an agent if you negotiate directly with the publishers within the agent's exclusive territory. That's the beauty of using an agent; you extend the network of people working on behalf of your company; he or she does the work, and you limit the number of people with whom you work. All this, and you only pay if the agent successfully sells your books. This doesn't mean you can't have a personal relationship with the publishers in the agent's area of exclusivity. Quite the contrary. As I've already made clear, the more you meet with these publishers and understand their needs and the more familiar foreign publishers are with your list, the better you can target your submissions.

You can always send a catalog or rights list to foreign publishers (or they can view them online) and have them send their requests for reading copies and information to the local agent. This makes it easy for the publishers, keeps the agent in the loop, and fulfills your needs as well.

If you have a consistent, ongoing publishing program, I recommend that you use agents at least for foreign-language markets. At the same time, I would also advise you to monitor your agents and help them sell your books. Most foreign rights agents work with a variety of publishers so you must keep your agents informed about both your books and your expectations for your books if they are to sell your products. By providing your foreign agents with up-to-date information, they can provide you with excellent outreach and local expertise that you would have difficulty duplicating on your own.

Mass-Market Rights

The final part of sub-rights sales that I'll deal with are sales of paperback editions of your hardcover book to paperback reprint houses.

Most smaller publishers today are quite familiar with selling hardcover or trade paperback editions of their books into the traditional wholesale and retail markets. Both formats are readily acceptable and are sold the same way.

Differences do occur, however, when selling mass-market editions of your book. In this case, the traditional source of trade distribution applies to some of the accounts, but not all. Mass merchants, such as Wal-Mart, Target stores, and others, are serviced differently. In addition, the customers selling mass-market books usually need a regularly supplied program to keep them fully stocked with the latest bestselling titles. The fact is, most traditional publishers simply don't have the facilities or the sales force to service these accounts.

Because of this, many publishers attempt to sell mass-market rights of their books to a publisher who has a full distribution network for mass-market paperbacks. Because of the consolidation in the industry, there are fewer and fewer of these publishers. You can get a good indication of who these publishers are by looking at the bookstore shelves; and especially by looking at the racks of mass-market paperbacks in airport stores, supermarkets, drugstores, and other locations. Bantam, Avon, Berkeley, Fawcett, Pocket Books, New American Library

(NAL) are just a few of the imprints that stand out. These are major publishers with regular rack-jobbed programs. The mass-market environment is highly competitive. And the large publishers rule.

Selling your book to mass-market publishers is not as difficult as it sounds, so long as your book fits into the categories in which these companies publish and as long as the companies feel they can capitalize on your initial launch. Fiction is always in demand, especially category fiction in the areas of westerns, mysteries, and romances. Nonfiction is more difficult and depends a lot on what is currently selling. Today, books about diet, health, and business are strong.

The way to sell mass-market rights is exactly the same as selling any other sub-rights. Send your book, in finished form, to one of the editors at a mass-market house along with a letter stating your intent. Call before you send the book to see if the editor is interested in looking at it. The good news is that there have been some significant mass-market successes with small-press books recently, so these buyers are on the lookout for more such books. Don't think you can just send anything, though. You must show a track record of sales of your edition to support your efforts. If you can only sell 2,500 copies, you'll have to talk fast to make the mass-market house think they can do a lot better with your book. If you've sold 25,000 or 250,000, that's a different story. Then the mass-market house knows there's a market for the book and that publisher can put the strength of its bigger sales force, and its mass-market distribution, to work for the book.

Whatever your sale of a book, just like selling sub-rights to book clubs, never take a mass-market sale for granted. Just because you've done well with a book doesn't mean it's a sure thing. I recently tried to sell mass-market rights for one of my client publishers whose book is Ingram's number-one trade paperback bestseller in a specific category, a book that's sold over 600,000 copies in ten years, with sales increasing each year! Believe it or not it was turned down by every publisher to whom it was sent. Among the reasons: "We already have a full list of competing titles in this category"; "We're revising our own major book in this area"; "We've passed it to our editors and they don't feel this book is saying anything new"; "There's no room on the shelf for both a mass-market and a trade paperback at the same time"; and on and on. To say I was stunned by these rejections was an understatement.

Like every other sub-rights sale, if you do get a sale, the price paid by the mass-market houses for titles varies enormously. Bestsellers go for millions. Most books go for $5,000 to $50,000. Royalties range from 6 to 8% of retail (cover price).

Again, don't be shy. If you don't try to sell rights, you never will. Mass-market houses can only deal with those who show them books. If you don't, others will. So start now.

Tracking Sub-Rights Sales

Tracking sub-rights sales is extremely simple. The fact of the matter is, you just need to keep track of what you've sent where. Thus, keep a separate record for each book you send using eight columns (see **Subsidiary Rights Tracking Form,** page 252). The first column lists the company to which you've submitted the book. The second lists the person to whom you've submitted the book (this could differ within clubs, for instance). The third, the date requested (if requested); the fourth, the date sent. The fifth tells you whether the account wants an exclusive arrangement or will accept a nonexclusive arrangement. The sixth column tells you if the club or account wants an option on the book—that is, an exclusive period of time to consider the project before you send it to others. Often an account will pay you a fee for this option period. The seventh column describes the use the account will make of your book. If it's a club, it could be either a main selection or an alternate, for instance. Finally, the last column records the decision and facts about that decision.

If you get a sale on one of your books, record that sale at the top of your sheet. This makes referencing the sale easier if you need to look up the details at a later date.

At the same time, you should cross-reference your sub-rights by customer. For instance, you might have a page for the Book-of-the-Month Club; one for the Literary Guild; one for each foreign publisher to whom you've sent a book; one for each mass-market publisher. The reason for cross-referencing is simple. If a client calls you about a particular book, you can track it quickly either way. If you want to see how much you've sold to a specific client, go to the client page. If you want to check up on a particular book, then go to the book's individual page.

Subsidiary Rights Tracking Form

Title: _____ Author: _____

Publication Date: _____ ISBN: _____

Sub-Rights Sales:

Company	Date Sold	Contract Date	Contact at Client	Type of Sale	Price Requested	Price Received	Special Terms

Sub-Rights Submissions:

Company	Contact Person	Date Requested	Date Sent	Exclusive; Non-Exclusive	Option/Expiration Date	Use	Decision (If Yes, Specify Above)
Book Club							
Serial Rights							
Mass Market							
Other							

This kind of tracking template works for almost every type of sub-rights sale. Tying this kind of report in with a tickler file on your computer helps you follow up even better. There are many kinds of software programs that allow you to do this.

Once you've recorded the sale in your own templates, there is one further step you should take: make sure that those companies to whom you sell and/or license rights maintain accurate records of sales they make based on your products and on which you will receive royalties. Often, companies to whom you license rights will report their sales in lump-sum fashion. If you've only sold that company one title, this isn't a problem, because whatever is reported to you accrues to that title. If, however, you sell more than one book to any one company, it is quite possible—and indeed is fairly common—for that company to report all of these sales on one form and to send one check for the aggregate amount. In such cases, it's almost impossible for you to know how to allocate that payment correctly to the individual titles and authors. In many cases, the net result of this is that these sums sit in the publisher's bank, earning interest, but never being distributed to the authors.

In an attempt to resolve this issue, the Book Industry Study Group Advisory Committee (BISAC), which helps to set standards for the book publishing industry, has recommended that publishers do two things:
1. Include a clause in the contract of every sub-rights sales agreement signed with a third party, stipulating the following provision:
   "All payments and accounts due under the terms of this agreement shall be made by Licensee to Publisher whose receipt shall be a full and valid discharge of the Licensee's obligations hereunder only if each such payment is accompanied by documentation that includes the required information specified in Appendix 'X' (that is, the Subsidiary Rights Payment Advice Form) of this contract and if such payment clears."
2. Include, along with the contract, as Appendix X, a copy of the Subsidiary Rights Payment Advice Form (see page 254).

As you can see, the form requests an Unique Identifying Number for each product on which payment is being made. Thus, when you make a sale, you must assign such a number to each product sold. This

Subsidiary Rights Payment Advice Form

[Publisher's Letterhead]

This form must be completed and attached to your check or faxed to this number: _____ when you send payment pursuant to licenses granted by us to you.

Failure to do so may result in our inability to record your payments and prevent us from determining that you are in compliance with the terms of your license(s).

* Amount remitted: _____

* Check or wire transfer number: _____

* Check or wire transfer date: _____

* (for wire transfers) Bank and account number to which monies were deposited:

_____

* Publisher/agent payer's name: _____

* Title of the work for which payment is being made:

_____

* Author(s) of the work: _____

* Our Unique Identifying Number for the work, as it appears in the Appendix to the relevant contract. If none, the original publisher's ISBN number of the work:

_____

* The period covered by the payment: _____

The following information will be very helpful, so we ask that you also provide it:

* Reason for payment (guarantee, earned royalty, fee, etc.):

_____

* Payment currency: _____

* Type of right (book club, reprint, translation, etc): _____

* Summary justification of your payment:
  Gross amount due: _____
  Taxes: _____
  Commissions: _____
  Bank charges: _____
  Net amount paid: _____

is relatively easy. You can use the title's ISBN number, or any other number you choose. The key is to be sure the number allows you to know exactly what book and what author will receive its share of that payment. With these two simple steps, you will show that your company is in the vanguard of publishers determined to be in compliance with industry norms and trends, and which are also working on behalf of their authors. It will show, yet again, that your company is committed to the entire publishing effort.

In addition to the variety of ways I've mentioned, there are many other opportunities to generate subsidiary-rights income. The sale of movie rights can be highly lucrative; selling condensation rights is another way; selling electronic rights is another; selling audio rights or audio book-club rights is yet another, as is selling to anthologies. The possibilities are virtually endless. The more contacts you make in all of the various sub-rights areas, the more your income and profitability from these sales will grow. Start slowly, but start. It's only a matter of time.

To give you a real-life example of success, here's a true story. In the course of sending out books for sub-rights use, a small publisher sent out one of its books for consideration by *Reader's Digest* in its condensed book program, now called *Select Editions*. This is one of the *Digest's* major profit centers, which buys books from other publishers and condenses approximately five books in each volume. Only fiction is used in the programs. After about six months (the Digest rarely does anything quickly), the publisher received a call saying that indeed *Select Editions* did want to use the book. The offer was normal for the *Digest* at that time—about $40,000 advance guaranteed. And all for the cost of one book and postage—about $5. Not a bad return!

There are many such stories. You too can send your books to the *Select Editions* program at *Reader's Digest* and we urge you to do so. If you're passive, you'll never get any sub-rights sales. If you're active, you will get them over time. Keep at it. Don't give up!

The same exactly can be said for sales and marketing in general. The more effort you put forth in both areas, the more you will sell. The crux of the issue is to make sure that the effort is budgeted well and targeted. It's easy to spend money on sales and marketing, especially so when the buyers in every wholesale and retail account ask you to "support" their own efforts. The implication is that if you don't "support" them through paid advertising, they won't buy your book. It's straightforward. And to an extent it's true. If you won't work with them, there are many others who will. And that will get those others better buys, better placement in the store, and goodwill. Yet small publishers simply don't have the funds to compete against the big publishers in this realm. Smaller publishers must be smarter and more wide-ranging in their pursuit of publicity and promotions that are cost-effective and within budget guidelines. It's not easy to do. But nobody ever said publishing was easy.

Nobody ever said publishing was easy.

One final word of caution. If your book is in demand by more than one buyer in any sector of sub-rights, whether serial rights, book clubs, mass-market, or another, and you have more than one bidder for that particular right, you may legitimately go back and forth from interested party to interested party asking each in turn for higher offers. This can be done formally, as an "auction," on a specific time and date or informally. In such situations, each respective party will undoubtedly ask you what the prior party's offer is. While you may be somewhat coy, the unwritten rules of the game say that you ultimately must tell the person what the last bid figure is.

What you should *never, ever do is misrepresent what is happening.* Do not mislead an interested party into thinking someone else has given you an offer when they haven't. Even if you think they might make an offer on a book and even if you've discussed the amount of that offer. The fact is, if you don't have a valid offer in hand you don't have an offer. Period. End of discussion. Wishes don't make it a reality.

Because publishing negotiations are often verbal, publishers frequently base quick decisions involving large and small sums of money on what they are told. If what they are told isn't accurate, or isn't truthful, then they may well make offers that aren't necessary or that are greater than that which might be the case otherwise. If this happens, and if you've misrepresented offers made by others, you will be hard put to ever sell similar rights to others ever again. The publishing world is very small. Competitors at work are often good friends at home (some are husband and wife). They talk to each other regularly at industry events. And they talk especially about recent books they've purchased or lost at auctions. Bids become quickly known. And if you've been anything less than truthful and candid, you will instantly lose all credibility you've built up. It happens. Just ask the agent from the Northwest who told a paperback house that someone had bid on a project when he hadn't. Don't let it happen to you.

You are in this business for the long haul. Your credibility is everything. So don't get so involved in a negotiation that you lose perspective. Keep your head, keep your calm, and keep your credibility.

The fact is, many smaller publishers have had huge sales and marketing successes by being creative and by attacking the wide variety of markets that are available. If you try, you too can be successful.

CHAPTER 11

Direct Response Marketing

Because of the difficulty of obtaining good trade distribution or in an effort to expand markets or target those markets more precisely, many small to midsize publishers turn to direct response marketing.

Direct response marketing is that marketing which encompasses sales directly to the consumer, whether individuals or businesses. It can include a number of sales and marketing techniques under its banner, including

- Direct mail
- Telemarketing
- Catalog sales
- Online efforts
- TV ads and infomercials
- Radio
- And more

The essence of direct response marketing is the sale of a product directly from the source of the product to the end user, eliminating the need for middlemen along the sales path. When done properly, direct response marketing can be a highly effective medium for creating, developing, and growing a market.

The key tenets of direct marketing are

1. Results must always be quantifiable.
2. Results must be constantly tested and refined against a control.

The steps to a successful direct marketing approach are to

1. Develop a list of targeted prospects.
2. Approach that list, whether by mail, phone, e-mail, radio. or another medium.
3. Take the order.
4. Fulfill the order to the customer's satisfaction.
5. Collect the money for the order.
6. Retain the customer's name and order information and add it to your database (house file) for future use.

Develop a List of Targeted Prospects

List selection is probably the most important aspect of any direct response approach. Yet the key word in the phrase I used is *targeted*. Tens of thousands of mailing lists are available on the market, from those as large as the phone book to those as small as a few hundred names. Access to a lot of names, however, does not necessarily net the best results—and often nets the worst results. If, for instance, you want to sell a book on piano tuning, it doesn't make sense to do a mailing to all musicians or all those who play the piano. It definitely does make sense to mail to members of the National Piano Tuners Guild.

Before you can begin your direct response effort, you first have to determine and define who your target market is. This demands rigorous research, analysis, and thought on your part or on the part of your marketing team.

When thinking about mailing lists, you must go back to the earlier question of your book's marketing and sales handle: What is your book about? Who is your primary audience? Are there some segments of this market that will be more interested in your book than others? For instance, if you have a gardening book on annuals, those who buy and plant these flowers are better targets than those who are interested in general gardening.

Once you've identified those people you feel would be interested in purchasing your book, you then have to find lists of people who match your profile. Fortunately, there are many such firms—called *list brokers*—who are retained by list owners to market and rent those lists. Many such brokers are listed in *Literary Market Place*, or *Direct Magazine*, the *Publishers Weekly* of the direct marketing industry. For others, contact the Direct Marketing Association in New York City (see Appendix for address). DMA is the trade organization for the direct marketing industry.

When looking at the available mailing lists on the market, try to test lists that have a large number of names on them. In direct response parlance, you want to find lists with a large "universe" of names. The reason is simple. If you start with small mailings and they work, you want to be able to expand your mailing to similar names. If you begin with a list of 500 names and your mailing works, you have nowhere to go but to start your testing over. If you have a list with a universe of 5,000 names and you test 500, then you have 4,500 additional names for follow-up.

By the way, I mentioned that lists are rented. In the normal course of events, you rent lists of appropriate prospects for a fee per thousand names. The fee is usually stated as $/M. As a rule of thumb, you can ballpark $50/M for more general compiled lists and $75 to $80 plus for more targeted specialty lists or segmented lists of buyers or "hot-line names." In all cases, this is for *one-time use* of that list. If you want "selects"—that is, names selected by sex, age, income, zip code, or other such variables, the cost is added on to the base rate. Similarly, if you want the names on pressure-sensitive labels, in specific computer format, or some way other than what the list broker considers normal, that too will cost extra.

The **Mailing List Data Card** (see page 262) shows these breakdowns clearly. Data cards are available for each list handled by a list broker or manager. There is no charge for the information, which is critical to making educated and sound list decisions.

Once you receive an order or response based upon that rented list, you are entitled to capture and add that responder's name to your own database. It's in this way that you build your own list of respondents with the names of those who are specifically interested in your products. This is why the medium is a targeted one.

Using list brokers to sift through a wide variety of lists on the

Mailing List Data Card
from American List Counsel

 Bookspan NY - Homestyle Bookclub
(Formerly Country Home & Garden
Bookclub)

Specialty book club members who order from a vast
selection of the latest titles in decorating, gardening,
collectibles, and entertaining including books
published by Better Homes and Gardens.

150,600	Universe / Base Rate	$95.00 /M
950	Quarterly Trials	$80.00 /M
1,300	Quarterly Premiums	+ $11.00 /M
42,000	Quarterly Paid Hotlines	+ $16.00 /M
37,000	12 Month Expires	$60.00 /M
	Fundraising Rate ($5/M select cap on non-enhanced selects)	$75.00 /M

The Country Homes & Gardens® members recent book offerings
include *Martha Stewart's Menus, Glorious Country, Laura Ashley Color,*
and *Rose Gardening.*

- Average Age 46
- 79% Married
- 33% College Graduates
- 81% Have Children
- Average Income $42,000
- 49% Employed Full Time
- $25 Unit of Sale
- 64% Internet Access
- 75% Access Computer at Home/Work

A consumer direct marketer's "must test." These readers spend lots
of time decorating their homes and continually purchase household
items that make their lives easier and their homes more beautiful
and comfortable.
Mailers have already discovered their passion for gardening,
decorating, healthy living, and crafts. They also love to give gifts,
shop for clothes, subscribe to magazines, and join charitable
causes.

LIST TYPE
Consumer

SOURCE
65% DMS, 35% 3rd Party, Print,
Internet

GEOGRAPHY
Domestic (US)

LIST OWNER
Bookspan NY

LIST MAINTENANCE

Counts through	07/31/2005
Last update	09/20/2005
Update frequency	MONTHLY

UNIT OF SALE INFORMATION

Average:	$25.00

GENDER PROFILE

Male:	7%
Female:	74%

INCOME

Average:	$42,000.00

SELECTION CHARGES

$100+ BUYERS	$17.00 /M
$25+ BUYERS	$6.00 /M
$50+ BUYERS	$12.00 /M
3 MONTH HOTLINE	$16.00 /M
6 MONTH HOTLINE	$11.00 /M
AGE	$11.00 /M
GENDER/SEX	$8.00 /M
GOOD CREDIT STANDING	$11.00 /M
INCOME SELECT	$11.00 /M
MONTHLY HOTLINE	$21.00 /M
SCF	$8.00 /M
STATE	$8.00 /M
ZIP	$8.00 /M

ADDRESSING

CARTRIDGE	$30.00 /F
CHESHIRE LABELS	No charge
DISKETTE	$30.00 /F
EMAIL	$55.00 /F

Mailing List Data Card
from American List Counsel *continued*

ADDITIONAL SELECTIONS

Crafts:

    53,000 Decorating
    38,000 Gardening
    36,000 Home & Gen. Sewing
    15,000 Stenciling
    36,000 Christmas Crafts

Cookbooks:

    12,000 Baking/Desserts
    18,000 Specialty

Decorating:

    89,000 Inspirational
    109,500 Practical

Terms and Conditions

Sample mail piece required. 3-5 working days required to process order. Payment due 30 days from mail date. Any order received at ALC will be subject to a flat cancellation fee. 20% commission to authorized brokers on base rate.

Publishing Usage

- American Masters Publications
- August Home Publishing
- Country Sampler
- Hachette Filipacchi
- Int'l Masters Publishing
- Merdith Corp.
- Oxmoor House
- Primedia
- Time Inc.

MAG TAPE	$30.00 /F
MAG TAPE SET UP CHARGE	$25.00 /F
P/S LABELS	$8.00 /M

KEY CODING

Key Coding is available
Charges: $2.00 /M

MINIMUM ORDER

Quantity: 8,000
Dollar: $0.00

REUSE

Reuse is allowed
Min Qty: 1,000
Charges: $95.00 /F

TELEMARKETING

Telemarketing is not allowed

CANCELLATION

Charges: $75.00 /F

COMMISSIONS

Broker: 20%

NET NAME ARRANGEMENTS

Net Name is allowed.
Net: 85%
Min Qty: 50,000
Run Charges: $8.50 /M

EXCHANGES

Exchange is allowed.

ADDITIONAL NOTES

Orders canceled are subject to run charges of $15/M.

market and to suggest a number that seem to match the profile you provide and meet your budget needs makes a good deal of sense. Brokers are familiar with the various lists on the market, are set up to identify those lists and to procure the lists for you. In essence, using a broker is a simple way to have expertise at your fingertips— at no cost other than the cost of the name. And if you don't like their selection, you're under no obligation to buy from that firm. In the final analysis, you determine what names you want or don't want. How do you do this? By focusing on

- Affinity
- Recency
- Frequency

What do these words mean?

Affinity

Affinity refers to the *kind* of product being sold. If someone has purchased a book in the past, you know immediately that, for whatever reason, that person is familiar with the type of product you're selling and has taken the initiative to purchase such a product. The closer the purchased product is to your product, the greater the affinity and the likelihood that this buyer will understand your product and not need to be educated as to what it is. The closer the affinity, the better the targeted prospect.

Recalling our garden book buyer, if she's purchased a general book on gardening, that tells us she's interested in the broad subject. If she's bought a book on annuals, we know she has a *specific interest* in that particular aspect of gardening, that she reads about that area, that she's willing to spend money for a book on the subject, and that she is willing to purchase a book by mail. She is, in short, a better target for our annual book than someone who has purchased a shirt from L.L. Bean, and also better than one who has purchased that general gardening book but who may not be at all interested in annuals.

Recency

Recency overlays a *time period* to frequency. It tells you how long ago a buyer made his purchase. *Hot line buyers* are best—they probably purchased within the last month or so. Three-month, six-month, one-year designations of buyers are common. A word of caution: when using names over one year old, be suspicious. As names age, they become less predictive of future behavior and action. And, the accuracy of the addresses diminishes by about 20% per year.

Frequency

Frequency refers to how *often* a person purchases products. Because we tend to be creatures of habit, we tend to repeat actions. This is true of buying patterns in particular. Once we decide to use a particular product brand, for instance, another brand is hard put to get us to switch. Thus, if we can find people who buy a lot of books by direct response, then we're much more likely to sell to these same people than to others who have not previously purchased by this method.

Generally, lists are labeled according to the number of times a buyer has purchased. The most attractive buyers are called *multi-buyers* because they've bought more than once. And the more they buy, the more likely they are to buy again. They've become comfortable with the concept and mechanism of direct response and they willingly buy through this means of marketing. Buyers of book continuities, book club members, and book catalog buyers are examples of such people.

Putting all three of our predictors together, the lists that provide the greatest affinity to your product, with the most frequent buyers, who have purchased most recently, are those lists that will most likely work best for you. As you use these lists and convert the names of prospects to buyers of your own products, you can see how your own house file can quickly become the most targeted and most responsive list of all.

The Package

Before you can mail to your list, you'll be faced with the primary question of *what* to mail. And to a large extent, this will depend upon your budget. The larger the package, the greater the expense of creating it and mailing it. It's certainly less expensive to create and mail a postcard than a six-page letter or a catalog. But economy in direct response marketing isn't always the best approach.

In other words, an inexpensive postcard that generates no response is costly compared to an eight-page letter that generates a 20% response (assuming you've priced your product correctly, but more on that shortly). Conversely, an eight-page letter that doesn't work can be extremely costly compared to a postcard that does.

Herein lies the essence—and beauty—of direct response marketing: the ability to test your mailing piece and all of its elements as part of a coherent direct marketing plan.

Assuming you commit to a plan, your initial mailing piece becomes the *control* against which a new piece can be tested. If your first mailing is a postcard that generates a response of .005 percent (half of one percent), then you can test your next piece to see how the response—and profitability—compare. If you hold other parts of your effort (price, payment terms, etc.) constant, then you can see how dramatically each individual change impacts your results. If the response and profitability is greater than your first effort, your newer effort becomes the new control against which future efforts can be compared.

The essence of direct response marketing is the never-ending pursuit to develop new creative efforts that can become your control piece and that can generate greater response.

There is, therefore, no specific way to suggest what kind of package is best for your individual product. One way to begin your exploration of direct response marketing is to get a feel for what competitors are mailing. Some publishers, like Rodale Press and *Reader's Digest*, two of the biggest direct-response book publishers, mail highly elaborate pieces, from postcards to "magalogs." Most of these larger efforts are in four-color. Other publishers, such as Conde Nast's *Gourmet Cookbook* annual, mail a simple one-color letter in an envelope. Still others use postcards sent individually or as part of a card deck that contains numerous other individual cards. Professional books tend to use four-to-eight-page, one- or two-color brochures.

The point is, by looking at how others market their competitive products, you'll get a feel for what's usual. This doesn't mean you should emulate these efforts, but it will show you what seems to work for some.

Once you've gotten to this point, it's time to run the numbers on your project.

The Economics of Direct Response Marketing

One of the joys of using direct response marketing is that if you sell directly to the consumer, without the need to involve middlemen, you don't have to give away discount to those middlemen. You can sell your book for full price and record all of the proceeds as your revenue. In addition, it's common to recover the costs of postage and to add a bit for "handling." From that standpoint, direct response is very appealing. If your book costs the same whether sold directly to the consumer or to the trade, then your gross margin for direct response sales looks terrific. A comparison clearly shows this:

	Direct Response	%	Trade @ 50% discount	%
Price of Book	$24.95		$24.95	
Price to Buyer	24.95		12.50	
Cost of Goods	4.50		4.50	
Gross Margin	20.45	82%	8.00	32%

Wow! An 82% gross margin. Now that, I think we can all agree, looks pretty spectacular.

But wait a minute. Before you start panting with anticipation, don't forget that the major costs of direct response marketing lie *below* the gross margin line with substantial hits to the marketing and postage lines: creative development, list rental, envelopes, and postage are all elements that trade doesn't have—or at least not to the same degree. These add significant costs to the direct response profit and loss statements in the variable cost areas.

If, for instance, we mail 5,000 pieces, then we have the costs of creating the mailing piece, whether a one-color, 8½" x 11" piece or a 4-color 8-page brochure. Let's assume a one-color, 8½" x 11" mailing piece for the book above costs 50 cents each, which would include the creative copy and the printing. (And that's very cheap. Good creative copy can be very expensive to get.) That's $2,500 for the mailing piece. Then we have list costs. At the bare minimum of $50/M we will pay $250 for the names. Plus postage. If we mail first class, then we'll pay $1,850 (5,000 x .37 = $1,850). If we mail another way it will be somewhat less. Using presorting and precoding will probably save something, but you have to have the facility or software to do this. We'll also need envelopes. That can add $100. And let's not forget the cost of shipping books when we've received the orders. We'll estimate a media mail rate for that of $2.00 per book, or $300. Total of these costs is $5,000.

As you can see, the costs add up fast. In fact, most publishing contracts reduce the royalty paid to authors on direct response sales by a certain percentage to offset the higher costs of doing this type of business.

And the real question is, what kind of response will you get? Most people in direct response feel that a 3% response is excellent and should result in a profitable mailing. However, response is directly related to cost. Three percent may be good, but not if it doesn't cover your costs. You must, therefore, worry about *profit*, not just *response*. Over time, an average has been established by those who mail frequently. And as noted, 3% is considered a good response under normal budgets. Thus, if 3% doesn't cover your costs, you'd better review your plan and your costs.

Making money on direct response mailing is not as easy as it seems. On our 5,000 names, 3% response would generate 150 orders at $24.95, or a grand total revenue of $3,742.50. You can see, if you deduct the costs of the mailing, not to mention the cost of the book itself and the actual shipping cost, that making money on direct response mailing is not as easy as it seems. Now you'll have a bit more sympathy for what book clubs have to do. And generating a 3% response isn't easy.

To summarize:

5,000 pieces @ 3% response	=	150 orders
150 x 24.95	=	$3,742.50 gross dollars received
Less costs of goods		
150 x $4.50	=	(675.00)
Less cost of mailing	=	(5,000.00)
	=	(1,932.50)
Plus shipping recovery	+	300.00
Net profit (loss) on mailing	=	(1,632.50)

Like every other aspect of publishing, you can be successful in direct response, but it's not easy. You must budget constantly and accurately. You can't omit small things that you think aren't important. Every single item is important.

One thing you will find is that it's a bit easier to make a profit on a mailing that contains material promoting more than one item. If, for instance, you send a catalog, your chances of getting orders for more than one book are greater than if you send out a mailing for one or two books. This kind of response

It's a bit easier to make a profit on a mailing that promotes more than one item.

raises your average order to a higher level. And because you're amortizing your mailing costs over more products, each product takes on a bit less of the total cost load. At the same time, your creative and postage costs go up because you're probably mailing a larger, more complex piece and it probably weighs more. And quite often, asking your buyer to make too many choices hinders the decision-making process and can result in a reduced response rate.

There is no easy solution. Every mailing has to be judged on its own merits, and every creative piece is different.

Do your homework carefully and then jump in. But don't jump in over your head. Start slowly and test. Then test again. If your mailing works once with a small number of names, then test more of those names. If those work, roll it out to more and more. That's the beauty of direct response. You get to know what works and why. Which is more than you can say for trade sales, where you know what works, but rarely why.

Tracking Your Sales

Once you've run your numbers, acquired your product, selected your lists, generated your creative package, you put your piece into the mail. The next task is crucial, because it will ultimately tell you if your efforts are successful or not. You must track your sales closely and carefully. You must analyze every aspect of your sales response, shown on the **Direct Response Tracking Form** (page 271) including

- name of the person ordering
- address of that person, including, especially, zip code
- gender of the person
- age of the person, if possible
- media in which you are promoting (if more than one)
- dates your orders come in, from first to last
- number of books sold from each marketing effort
- number of books sold per order
- number of books sold daily
- number of books sold cumulatively to date
- individual dollar amount of each purchase
- cumulative dollars earned from the promotion
- total number of annual purchases per customer
- total annual dollar value of purchases per customer
- cumulative inventory cost
- cumulative net dollars received from each promotion
- length of time your customers have ordered from you

The reason you should track each of these elements is clear: You want to determine, for each promotion source, how much money you make and what the response percentage from that promotion is. If the promotion works, then you want to repeat that promotion. If it doesn't work, then you want to move on to another promotion or change the variables used in mailing to that source. The more accurate your analysis, the better. The higher the response rates and the cumulative net dollars earned, the better your promotion results should be.

By studying your responses, you can, after a fair number of them, begin to develop a response curve and an in-depth database for your products, your promotional sources, and for your customer mailing list. With a response curve in hand, you can begin to project the response that you should get from a similar promotion of that product, or to that source. This then allows you to predict ultimate sales prospects in both units and dollars. With more demographic information about your mailing list and customer file, you can do the same. And the more accurately you can predict, the better you can budget for profitability.

To maintain house files and track sales, many publishers have invested enormous amounts in their databases. And the more invest-

Direct Response Tracking Form

Title	Media	Source Code	Quarterly Mailed	Date Mailed	Date of Order Receipt	# Books sold	Total Books to Date	X Price Received	Gross Sales	Cum. Gross Sales	Inventory Cost per Book	Total Inventory Cost	Cum. Inv. Cost	Less Media Cost	Cum. Net $ Earned
Better Sales, Better Times Test List 1	PW102595	500	10/25/01	11/17/05	5	5	24.95	124.75	124.75	2.50	12.50	12.50	500.00	-387.75
				11/27/05	10	15	24.95	249.50	374.25	2.50	25.00	37.50		-163.25
				12/27/05	250	265	24.95	6,237.50	6,611.75	2.50	625.00	662.50		5,449.25
				12/29/05	100	365	24.95	2,495.00	9,106.75	2.50	250.00	912.50		7,694.25

	# Orders	# Books
Received	4	365
Quantity mailed	500	500
Response rate	0.80%	73.00%

ment, in most cases, the more sophisticated the direct response effort and the analysis of that effort will be. According to a 1998 database survey by *Direct Magazine*, companies with smaller databases (under 100,000 records) using direct response marketing allocate a median 35% of their marketing budgets to this effort. Of these companies, 73% view customer acquisition as their primary marketing strategy. This makes sense, because, as I've said before, once a customer buys from you, that customer is more likely to buy again. The focus, therefore, should be on obtaining the customer in the first place (note the similarity of Amazon's original, and continuing, strategy to this).

There are no easy answers to direct response marketing. Every mailing or promotional effort has to be judged on its own merits, and every creative piece is different. Testing and analysis of that test is the essence of the process. The more you do in a structured, logical manner, the more you'll learn about your customer, your product, your promotional vehicles, your internal systems, and your backend systems of warehousing, fulfillment, and customer service—all of which are critical to a good direct response marketing effort.

Once you start tracking your sales and promotional efforts, you'll become addicted to the numbers. Just because this method of marketing is so calculable and analytical it is a refreshing change from the vagaries and sometimes whimsical nature of trade sales. While direct response marketing isn't easy or simple by any means, it is a method that you should try at some point. You don't have to invest millions in database systems to track your sales. There are some very good direct-response software packages on the market, at relatively low cost, that will help you get started. You can upgrade as you go. You can also use outside services that have highly sophisticated databases to help you.

So investigate your options—and give direct response marketing a try.

CHAPTER 12

Operations, Fulfillment, and Accounting

Operations and fulfillment refer to those business functions that occur once your books leave the bindery. I have also linked accounting to these functions because the flow of orders, shipping, fulfillment, returns, and collections are functions that must be closely integrated if they are to work. The typical flow of these functions is

- receive advance orders from customers
- receive the books into the warehouse
- place the books in warehouse locations
- bill the order
- send the order to the warehouse
- evaluate and prioritize the order
- pick the order
- pack the order
- ship the order
- confirm order was shipped
- post the accounts receivable
- send invoice to customer
- send statement to customer
- receive payments
- post payments to each account
- if uncollectible, send account to collection

As you can see, this is no small function. This is a critical part of your total operation with any number of areas for delay or error. No wonder so many publishers decide to let others handle these jobs.

Operations and fulfillment systems can range from the use of laser scanning and the automation of huge warehouses to handpicking and packing in someone's garage or basement. In the case of most smaller publishers, it tends toward the latter, with many falling somewhere in between. Often, because smaller publishers tend to get into publishing to disseminate information, they don't think about operations and fulfillment at all until it's too late.

Many start to sell their books thinking they will ship out all their orders from their garage or kitchen table. Then they find that their publishing efforts are working and that they are now bogged down in the time it takes to invoice the order, collect the money for it, pick and pack the book, and then ship it. Even worse, they spend more time immersed in the bookkeeping effort when they have to unpack books and credit the account when returns come in.

Operations and fulfillment systems are the bane of most small publishers' lives. In fact, the larger publishers don't relish these functions much either—especially the returns processing. And to be frank, larger publishers don't do much better at shipping than smaller ones do. In fact, because the smaller publisher has fewer titles and fewer distractions, in many cases the smaller publisher can ship faster than the larger.

If you've ever tried to special-order a book from a publisher, you know how slow their processing can be. Bookstores routinely quote four to eight weeks for books that are not carried by wholesalers and that must be ordered from the publisher. Why this is the case I've never understood. In this era of overnight delivery, when L.L. Bean can have a package in your hands within 24 hours, when MacWarehouse and so many other mail-order houses can do the same, why can't publishers? The fact that publishers deal with a vast array of *SKUs* (stock-keeping units, or items, or books) doesn't excuse the slow service. L.L. Bean or Land's End certainly has an equal, or greater, array of inventory and SKUs as most major publishers. Ingram Book Company, the largest wholesaler in the book business, with hundreds of thousands of SKUs, can ship a book overnight to an account. So why can't publishers? The fact is, they haven't committed the resources to it. They have left these processes as an afterthought.

Obviously, smaller publishers have operations and fulfillment problems of their own, which are different in degree, not in kind.

What I will concentrate on here are three issues that are critical to smaller publishers: Electronic Data Interchange, accounts receivable, and returns. I will leave the technical end of warehousing to others.

Electronic Data Interchange

It is axiomatic today that anyone providing publishing fulfillment, whether an in-house function, an outside service, or a distributor, must use electronic data interchange, more commonly called *EDI*. This mechanism imposes standards for transmitting certain information electronically and enables the electronic interchange of orders and of accounting information, directly from the buyer's computer system to the publisher's and vice versa. It allows orders and returns to be processed quickly and efficiently, without the need to generate hard copy orders, chargebacks, and other forms of transaction data that were the norm before computers revolutionized the process.

Imagine what it would be like if Barnes & Noble sent you 800 individual orders with one book on each order. Then imagine how difficult it would be if some of these books were returned for credit in similar fashion: each on an individual chargeback, most without original invoice information. For many publishers, up until only a few years ago, this was the reality—and it was a nightmare. Today, this mass of paperwork and confusion has been significantly reduced through the use of EDI. It is absolutely essential, when working with the major wholesalers and chains as well as with most of the smaller chains and better independents, that you have EDI or are handled by an organization that does.

If you do not conform to the industry standard, it's not the industry that will suffer—you will. As I've discussed with almost every facet of the publishing business, if you want accounts to buy your books, you must make it easy for them to do so. If most accounts send purchase orders and accounting functions electronically, you must have the capacity to respond in kind. If not, accounts will stop working with you. And if that happens, you're obviously in trouble.

EDI is not difficult to set up. It is somewhat expensive. If you're planning to do your own distribution, you should certainly budget for EDI as part of your start-up expenses. If you're currently a going concern that is doing your own fulfillment and not on EDI, then you should put it online immediately. The business world is littered with the remains of those who were slow to change or who refused to change to meet industry demands. When that demand becomes the norm, then you must adapt or die. EDI is now the norm.

Accounts Receivable

The importance of accounts receivable to cash flow is impossible to overstate. Too many smaller publishers who haven't been in the publishing business before think that the accounts that buy their books will pay for them quickly, within 30 days or so. This is a pipe dream. Book publishing is unlike the magazine business, in which subscribers generally pay up front, before they receive their first issues. The average collection period in the book industry is between 90 and 120 days from the time of invoice. That's 90 to 120 days *without cash*. And that's *if* you get paid on time. Many accounts routinely hold payments for 180 days. And to make matters worse, many then return books for credit.

We all know the book business is essentially a *consignment business*, because most publishers sell their books on a fully returnable basis. It is not, however, the publisher's role to be a bank for the bookstores or for others who buy books from the publisher, or who owe the publisher money. Thus, the publisher must maintain the highest priorities on collecting its money from its accounts, and collecting it earlier than 90 to 120 days. You must have a reporting system that ages your accounts receivable so you can focus on those unpaid for long periods of time.

Business affairs are extremely time-consuming, especially when one deals with collecting accounts receivable.

And while most systems provide aging, it's up to you to review the reports and use them day in and day out. This is why I feel a business manager is so important as a core member of your team. Business affairs are extremely time-consuming, especially when one deals with collecting accounts receivable. It's an endless and thankless job that must be done well. Anyone who has ever tried to reconcile a Barnes & Noble account or any other account from a multistore chain understands this implicitly.

The difficulty of collecting accounts receivable is, indeed, one of the primary reasons publishers use distributors and find that relationship fruitful. In this context, the distributor is the one who has to cope with this job of collection, and if it doesn't do it well, then the publisher in theory doesn't suffer because the distributor has taken the accounts-receivable risk and guarantees payment to the publisher no matter what.

That's in theory. In practice, if the distributor doesn't collect enough from its accounts, then no publisher using that distributor will get paid. If the distributor goes bankrupt from lack of funds and cash flow, all of its client publishers suffer. In addition, you must oversee your distributor to ensure the timely payment of that which you are owed.

Monitor your accounts receivable every day.

There is no easy answer. If you decide to invoice accounts, then you must have an excellent accounting software package in place and monitor your accounts receivable *every day*. The closer you watch it, the more you can focus on those accounts who haven't paid in a while. Keep a very close eye on those who are more than 90 days overdue. The faster you get paid, the less you'll have to borrow or fund yourself. You've sold the accounts the books, now it's their turn to pay for them in a timely manner.

There are a few accounting systems that many smaller publishers use, some with enthusiasm, others with less enthusiasm. Some systems work better than others for some phases of the publishing process. Cat's Pajamas, and their recent spin-off MiniCat, is one that has a wide array of publishers who have used the program for many years. Unfortunately, it's not available for Mac systems. Acumen, which has excellent flexibility and is available for both Mac and PC systems, is another. Some publishers simply use QuickBooks or another standard bookkeeping system. Piigs is yet another for smaller system needs. Costs for these systems vary depending upon the modules you want and the number of users. All of them track sales, returns (credits), inventory, royalties, cost of goods, and other basic business functions. (See Appendix for addresses.)

The key is to select a system that works well given your needs. Don't buy too much system, don't buy too little. In many cases, given the intricacies and technological nature of today's operations and fulfillment systems, consultants can be highly useful to you. They can review your needs with you, search for the appropriate software packages, and guide you through the implementation process. As you build your system, remember, you're not just building for today but also for tomorrow when you'll be a larger publisher doing more volume with ever more complex needs. Think ahead and build in extra capacity. You'll need it.

Warehousing and Shipping

As I said previously, even if you have a distributor, it's unwise to store all of your inventory in that distributor's warehouse. If, for some reason, that company goes bankrupt, your entire stock of books will be frozen (locked up) by the bankruptcy court and unavailable to you for some length of time. Therefore, even if you use a distributor, you should also maintain stock in a separate warehouse.

Warehousing books is relatively inexpensive. Warehouses are commonly available and space is usually charged at reasonable rates assuming you're storing your books outside of a major metropolitan area.

What you want to be sure of is that your warehouse is secure, dry, fireproof, and insured against loss to the fullest value possible. Before committing to a warehouse, be sure to inspect the premises personally. Insist on seeing its insurance and inspection papers and check it out with the local fire authorities. Be satisfied and err on the side of caution. It's your books that will be in the warehouse. It's your money.

In most cases, you will want to find a warehouse that can also ship some, if not all, of your books. Even if you use a distributor, you may want to ship review copies from your own warehouse, so you don't incur the distributor's handling fees. You may want to sell different markets yourself and maintain separate inventories for that

Find a shipper that is familiar with books and publishing norms, that is used to dealing with various book accounts that may have different requirements than other customers.

purpose. You may want to ship book clubs, or premium sales to catalogs or nontraditional markets, from a warehouse different from that of your distributor because every time your distributor ships or handles these kinds of sales, they will charge you a surcharge. It's highly likely that if you find a good warehouse that ships books or other items for their clients, they can do the same for you at a fee less than that of the distributor. To be certain, compare.

Many smaller publishers, when looking for a local warehouse or fulfillment house, select one that is not used to shipping books or working with book-industry customers. When working with non-book shippers or warehouses, you should be extremely careful. Although they may be used to handling hard goods, they may not understand or be prepared to deal with more fragile books, which can easily be damaged. As most of us know, it doesn't take much effort to tear a jacket, bend a paperback, and otherwise cause minor damage that renders the book useless to the various book markets. And damaged books mean lost revenue and increased costs to either put them back into good condition, print a new run, or write off the damaged inventory. It also means angry customers. Any way you look at it, it will cost you.

In most cases, I recommend that my clients find a shipper familiar with books and publishing norms, one used to dealing with various book accounts that may have different requirements than others. For instance, some accounts want books packed on skids of a certain size, in cartons of a certain weight, and other such details. If your warehouse is used to these demands, shipping your books will be easy. If it is not, confusion can easily come into play—and this too will cost you money.

Should you ship your books yourself? This question is often asked, because most publishers like to control their efforts from start to finish. The answer is, it depends. If you are very small and don't have the budget to hire someone for this role, then no, you shouldn't maintain your own warehouse and do your own shipping. If you live and work in the middle of a city where extra rent can be very expensive, again, you probably should not do your own fulfillment.

If, on the other hand, you have the budget and don't mind the extra administrative effort to track shipments and deal with freight companies (which can be a real pain in the neck); if you have access to reasonably priced space near your location; and if you have a good supply of low-cost labor, then you might decide to do your own warehousing and fulfillment. And for many publishers, these assets do exist. I know of many very good smaller publishers who do their own warehousing and fulfillment and do it very well.

At the same time, I receive many calls each year from smaller publishers who are completely bogged down in warehousing and shipping issues. These publishers become immersed in dealing with these issues and don't have any time left to do what they most enjoyed about the business—editorial creation and acquisition. As I said earlier, most people get into this business for the joy of creating books and seeing them sold. Few ever thought of themselves as warehouse managers or shipping clerks.

My recommendation is to sit back and decide what it is about your business you like. Once you know that, do that. Structure your business so you can concentrate on what you like doing and delegate the other, less-appealing facets of the business to those who are better skilled, or better motivated, in those areas. This will keep you creative and involved. You can still provide oversight and direction in these areas, but that is quite different than trying to do it all yourself. There are only so many hours in the day; use each of them fully.

> *My recommendation is to sit back and decide what it is about your business you like. Once you know that, do it.*

What is the industry average cost for warehousing and fulfillment? In most cases, it should always come in around 9% of your net sales figure if you are to be successful as a publisher. This is your benchmark. Use it as such. If you find your costs, including allocated space costs, going over this percentage, then you should think seriously about farming out your fulfillment to someone expert in the function. Someone who can do it at your benchmarked cost.

CHAPTER 13

Electronic Publishing and Marketing

The mighty have fallen. Within the recent past the enthusiastic expectations for electronic books, or e-books, has come and mostly gone. During the early years of e-books, around the mid '90s, e-books were hailed by many as the next great technological step for books, a step that would relegate printed books, or p-books, to what Bill Cosby called, in another context, the "appliance graveyard." E-book companies were founded almost daily, supported by optimistic forecasts of audience demand, venture capital money, and print publishers that didn't want to be left behind.

But a funny thing happened on the way to the revolution: people didn't want to buy e-books in any great quantity, and certainly didn't want to spend over $300 for an e-book reading device that would enable them to do so. The technological revolution slammed head on into the business realization that "eyeballs" and "hits" for the most part didn't translate into revenues and that the business models for many e-commerce companies of all kinds, not just e-book publishers, didn't work. With the rapid realization that most e-book and e-commerce companies weren't profitable and weren't going to be profitable for some time, venture capital money dried up, and strapped for cash, many of these businesses folded forever.

Mighty Words, Contentville, Reciprocal, and numerous other e-content aggregators, resellers (that is, distribution companies), digital rights management companies, and e-book publishing divisions such as Bertlesmann's AtRandom, have closed. Yet others remain, notably Simon and Schuster's e-book division, Barnes & Noble's e-book division, many academic publishers' divisions, and many scientific-technical-medical publishers' e-divisions (both book and, especially, journal divisions). In short, e-books and e-publishing are somewhat wounded, but far from dead. In addition, one particular segment of the e-book business, Print-on-Demand, has already proven its worth. Unlike e-books, Print-on-Demand does have a current market and provides to many publishers a cash flow benefit that in itself makes this method of printing and publishing worthwhile for publishers of all sizes that wish to conserve cash and print limited quantities of specific titles.

The size of the e-book market is extremely difficult to pin down. Because some define it as strictly e-books, others define it more inclusively as e-books, Print-on-Demand, and online business, the estimated figures are widely divergent. In 1998 Dick Brass, Vice President of Microsoft, said that by 2003 e-books alone would be a $5 billion industry. In actuality, from all indications, current e-book sales of the United States book publishing industry as of 2003 are somewhere around $10 million according to press releases from the Open eBook Forum, an industry research organization. Approximately 1.3 million ebooks were sold in that year.

While the gloss is off e-book publishing, it's an improving part of the market. Let's look at this area of publishing in a business context and see how it can be applied profitably to your publishing program.

E-Books

What is it about e-books that appeals to publishers? There are basically four primary benefits:

1) New products, new markets, new sales
2) Portability
3) Minimal added cost of goods
4) Elimination of returns

Let's look at each of these benefits.

New products, new markets, new sales

E-books may best be viewed in the context of a new format, or product, that creates new, incremental sales by building on an investment you are already making in the core market format, the print edition. The results of this new format are new opportunities for sales through new markets.

The true benefits to publishers of this new format are twofold:

1. You can create it at little extra development expense, and
2. The new format can be sold through current and new distribution channels and can therefore expand sales.

Given a new format, it is relatively easy to create an internal structure in which all revenues, cost of goods, and expenses of the e-book are held against the appropriate division or profit center and judged according to whether or not they result in profits. Note that we've said nothing about hits, eyeballs, or any other measure of website "visibility" here. These terms are a result of marketing efforts and are inconsequential in a sales context, though one would hope the former would lead to the latter. In other words, a publisher needs to get people to the sites from which its e-books are sold, but *just getting hits or eyeballs doesn't guarantee sales.* That false paradigm was probably the major cause of the huge fallout in the e-commerce and e-book business in the first place, so you certainly don't want to replicate it.

What's important for publishers is to market their books in e-book format just as they do the books in p-book format. Marketing methods may differ somewhat, specifically being more reliant on links and e-marketing techniques, but the overall goal of the marketing is the same: generate sales within budget.

It is important, therefore, to view e-books from a standard profit perspective. We can see the relatively small difference between p-books and e-books easily:

Core Product (P-Book)	Incremental Product (E-Book)
Revenues	Revenues
– Development costs	– *Conversion expense*
– Paper, printing, binding	– Manufacturing
– Royalty	– Royalty
= Gross margin	= Gross margin

Note that allocating all of the development costs to the core p-book, and leaving few for the e-book, is similar to the way many publishers, when printing simultaneous hardcover and paperback editions, allocate all of the development costs to the hardcover edition, leaving few development costs allocated to the paperback edition.

Converting p-books to e-books basically means reformatting the digital file. This can be expensive or relatively inexpensive depending upon the original formatting and when the reformatting is done. In addition, the "manufacturing" costs of e-books are basically zero, since they are delivered online, which is what makes this format so appealing.

Putting some numbers to the above example, let's say the p-book and the e-book both retail for $20.00, each sells to the "retailer" for a 50% discount, royalty of 10% of retail for the p-book and 50% of revenue for the e-book, and that we've allocated the main development costs to the p-book; the conversion expense to the e-book. Then, the model above might look like:

	Core Product (P-Book)	Incremental Product (E-Book)
Retail price	$20.00	$20.00
Revenue:	$10.00	$10.00
Development/Conversion	$ 1.50	$ .10
PPB/Manufacturing	$ 1.50	$ ——
Royalty	$ 2.00	$ 5.00
Gross Margin	$ 5.00	$ 4.90

Note that the e-book brings in just ten cents less than the p-book (assuming a much higher royalty payment) but that the costs of creating this new product are very low, and the continuing costs of "manufacturing" new editions is virtually zero. In addition, keep clearly in mind that *any revenue generated by this new product is new, found revenue—that is, it's incremental revenue* that you wouldn't have had if this new product hadn't been developed.

As we said, any new electronic product must still be viewed in a business context and must still earn profits if it is to successfully contribute to the health of the company. Thus, the expenses for e-books must be directly proportional to the sales revenue generated in order to have a positive contribution to profit.

What is the current status of e-book sales? As noted, e-books are currently a $10 million part of the U.S. book business. The top five categories account for approximately 60% of total sales, led by:

Category	Price Total	Average Price/Book
Sociology, Economics	$230,404	$31.66
History	$144,831	$30.79
Science	$ 94,100	$33.28
Philosophy	$ 70,522	$32.07
Language	$ 68,183	$41.27
Total:	$608,040	
Percent of total:	59%	

Source: R. R. Bowker Bookwire

As you can see, the top five categories are heavily weighted to the social sciences, where price points have greater elasticity because up-to-date information is important and people are willing to pay for it. Compare the prices above, for instance, with the average price point for fiction, at $6.78, or poetry and drama, at $5.83. In these categories, price is a major factor and it will be difficult for publishers to carve out profitable businesses unless demand is substantial.

E-books, therefore, should be treated no differently than any other product line, category, or division of the company. Profit is the goal, nothing more or less. If you can't generate profits, then either rethink the business or get out of the business. But don't squander good money on a losing proposition.

Portability
The primary benefit of e-books that most people think of is portability. The digitization of a book allows the reader to take not just one book, but multiple books, anywhere and read them at any time assuming the screen, the lighting, and the format of the books are conducive to that task. Reduction in size and weight are paramount if the technology is to gain widespread acceptance. Yet portability is still one of the major hindrances to the overall acceptance of the e-book among the general public.

As the reading devices evolved, they have become smaller, lighter, and have better light sources and type design. Microsoft introduced ClearType and Adobe introduced CoolType in an effort to make the e-book reading experience better and more enjoyable to those who were willing to invest in a device or read e-books from their computer screens. Today, the reader continues to evolve and become more multifunctional. Currently, the devices are the size of a Blackberry and can handle a variety of tasks in addition to being readers, such as making phone calls, checking e-mails, serving as calendars, and more.

As this evolution towards portability continues, it will make reading e-books and other information in e-formats more appealing and popular. If the prices on the devices can come down further, there should be a demand for them. When this happens, e-book sales will pick up. I expect this to happen within the next five years. These devices and e-books won't replace p-books, but they will provide a viable alternative for those who prefer electronic formats. The size of that market remains to be seen, but one fact is certain: younger generations are more attuned to receiving information electronically. They will certainly be more willing than the current generations to read books in this electronic format.

Reduced Cost of Goods
The more publishers can sell e-books, the more their cost of goods will be reduced. Why? Because publishers can consolidate their formatting, which in essence is the "make ready," or electronic component of the development costs, for all product variations including p-books, e-books, CD Roms, and the world wide web when they edit the book in the first place. By coding the work with metatags up front, time and significant money can be saved later—which means on each "reprint" of the work.

Currently, in most cases, the author creates a book using a word processing software (Microsoft Word or such) and then gives it to the publisher, whose designers import that word processing file into a design software, typically QuarkXpress, Adobe Pagemaker or InDesign. Once designed, the digital file is then sent to the printer.

Quark or Pagemaker, however, isn't particularly conducive to e-book design. Instead, electronic products require a different format, typically HTML (HyperText Mark-up Language), PDF (Portable Document Files), or the more recently created XML

(Xtensible Mark-up Language). Currently, most publishers go through a two step process: first creating the p-book files as above, then going backward and creating the e-book files. In this process, not much time or money is saved creating e-books, although certainly the primary editorial development costs can be allocated to the p-book, freeing the e-book from these costs.

If, however, publishers can combine the production procedure and consolidate two steps into one by coding or metatagging the word processing file prior to its final design and formatting, then significant savings can result. Rather than going from a word processing file to Quark to p-book and then reformatting if a different final format is needed, the publisher can metatag the original word processing document, as the first step, with codes that work in all formats. Thus, it's metatagged once and is then available for all end products, whether printed books, electronic books, CD-ROMs, or another. This saves time, effort, and additional cost in the long run. Publishers can either do this metatagging in-house, or can contract it to companies such as Texterity, which specialize in this kind of work. Additionally, newer versions of Quark enable XML formatting as a "save as" choice.

While current e-book publishers are certainly saving money on some of the costs of producing e-books, it is the potential for significantly reduced cost of goods on future products that is tantalizing to all.

In addition, as Eugene Schwartz, a consultant with significant print background, makes clear, quality control becomes an issue. The more conversions that can be done at the same time, the less "revisiting" needs to be done later. And usually, the more "revisiting" that is done, the more chance for errors to be introduced.

Additionally, as we've seen in the example above, e-books have virtually no manufacturing cost associated with them (unless they are put on CD-ROMs). Thus, the more e-books can be sold in digital form over the World Wide Web, the more the publisher saves.

Finally, the royalty component of cost of goods is always negotiable. If you can pay less than 50% of net dollars received, you can increase your gross margin significantly.

All told, e-books lend themselves to profitability if they can find a market of buyers.

Elimination of Returns

One of the real boons of e-books is their elimination of returns from the sales equation. E-books are purchased on a nonreturnable basis, so publishers and authors don't have to worry about reserves for returns or what their net sales will ultimately be. As is seen in chapter 14, Returns, eliminating returns means instant dollars that go right to the publishers' bottom lines.

In addition, eliminating returns can substantially reduce warehousing and fulfillment costs, since large quantities of inventory don't have to be carried. Production and fulfillment, through digital delivery and controlled by digital rights management software, is extremely efficient. In many ways, the paradigm of print and deliver is changed radically to deliver and print. Thus people can buy e-books when they want to and access them from almost any point in the world instantaneously. This immediate access at reasonable prices is a huge benefit over p-book technology.

Print-on-Demand

While e-books are still trying to catch on, one facet of e-publishing has arrived already. Print-on-Demand is being used successfully by many publishers to

- create bound galleys
- keep out-of-print books in print
- maintain backlist
- produce academic books and course materials that sell in limited quantities

What is Print-on-Demand? It is, in essence, what its name says it is: a printing technology that allows publishers and printers to print and bind books and other materials in one operation in very short runs—from one copy upward. Compare this to normal short-run presses, which only start to become cost effective at around 500 copies due to the high make-ready costs of preparing the press to run.

What differentiates Print-on-Demand (POD) technology from other short-run printing presses is that the POD machines are more closely related to copy machines than they are to large presses. (It's no surprise that Xerox, a leader in copying technology, is also one of the leading providers of POD equipment.) In fact, POD machines use toner, like regular copying machines. Because of this, there is little or no spoilage and waste, as opposed to commercial presses that use ink and that need to run to get the colors properly adjusted. Commercial printers, therefore, generate spoilage in the make-ready process but gain significantly in efficiency and productivity once the press is running smoothly.

POD technology is best suited to standard sized books, such as 6" x 9" or 8½" x 11", and those books with limited illustrations (line illustrations work best; halftones are improving quickly). The technology, however, is changing quickly and good color printing is not far off. POD can be used with paperback and hardcover binding.

Paperback covers can now be printed quite nicely. In early POD versions, four-color covers had a raised type effect that immediately set them apart from commercially printed covers. Today, this "raised effect" has been eliminated and for the most part the general public would not be able to tell if a book was printed as a POD product or not.

The cost effectiveness of POD depends a good deal on the flexibility, or elasticity, of pricing that your book has. If, for instance, the book is a very small product, or is in a highly price sensitive category where competitive pricing will force and keep your price down, POD may not meet your needs. But if you are publishing books in less price sensitive categories, such as history or psychology, in which pricing can go to $30.00 and up, you may be able to make POD pricing work for you. In academic areas, where price sensitivity is even less of a factor, and where professors often need to take chapters from many texts and combine them to make a coursepack specifically for their course and their students, POD is the perfect vehicle to accomplish the task.

The other key benefit of POD, which publishers of all sizes enjoy, is that of cash savings. While unit costs of POD books are currently higher than those of commercially printed books, the ability to print just the number of copies one needs, when one needs them, is extremely appealing from a cash-flow standpoint. Why print 1,500 copies of a book and pay for the total print run if you only have a current need for 500 copies? Since most publishers always need cash, it may well behoove publishers to print fewer copies at somewhat higher prices, but put the cash saved from printing a limited quantity to good use elsewhere. A comparison will help show how this can work to your benefit:

	POD	**Commercial Press**
1,500 copies @ $2.00 per unit:		$3,000.00
500 copies @ $4.00/ unit	$2,000.00	
Cash savings:	$1,000	

For smaller and midsized publishers especially, this cash saving is important. It can make the difference between success and failure since it can be applied to paying rent or salaries. More important, assuming you have price flexibility as just noted, your profit per unit may not change.

Print-on-Demand Models

At the moment, there are basically two business models that POD printers offer to publishers:

1. Short run digital
2. Print and distribute

Let's look at the way each of these works.

Short run digital printers function much the way regular commercial presses function. Short run digital printers basically print for the inventory needs you, the publisher, have. They quote you a price on printing a number of copies, and that price usually declines as the number of copies printed increases. Unit costs, therefore, vary with quantity. Some vendors have high break points, so that you may pay the same per unit for one copy as you do for 500. Each printer is different, and each has its own scale. There may or may not be minimum quantities required. Finished books are sent to the purchasing publisher's warehouse and that publisher does its own fulfillment. This method works well for bound galleys and for books that have a modest demand. Publishers of course must have some warehouse space available to store the books. The short run printer usually retains a digital archive of the book for future reprint use.

The print and distribute model is a bit different. In this case, the printer truly prints on demand. When an order for a book comes in from either the publisher or a third party-customer, the printer will print the book to order and ship it directly to the customer. The POD publisher will then send the original publisher a check for the agreed upon percentage of the transaction, less the cost of goods incurred by the POD printer. In most cases, the original publisher establishes the discount and price that the POD publisher extends to the customer. This method is excellent for backlist books that aren't selling quickly, for books that may otherwise go out-of-print but that may have residual value over time, and for those books with high price flexibility. Again, the print and distribute printer retains a copy of the digital archive for future use.

In both of the above cases the printer can "drop ship" directly to the ultimate customer. If there is a third-party involved, such as a retailer that orders from a wholesaler, which in turn orders from the POD printer, the discounts to the publisher are a bit higher than in the other two procedures. The largest POD printer today is Lightning Source, a division of Ingram Book Services. They claim to have 100,000 titles in their database. There are many other POD printers as well.

POD Comparison with Commercial Printing

Let's look at three books, one as priced and manufactured by a regular commercial printer; one printed as a POD product but with little price flexibility (that is, with price constraints) and one with favorable price flexibility that allows us to price the book up to a level that makes margin sense for us as publishers. We'll estimate that each is 256 pages; 6" x 9". We'll also estimate a print run of 5,000 for the commercially printed book with 30% returns; 500 copies of the POD books with 5% returns (we'll have fewer returns because we're printing more to order—that is, more to immediate demand). We'll also assume a 50% discount and paper, printing, and binding costs of $1.75 per unit for the commercial press and $4.85 per unit for the POD press. (We can estimate the unit cost for the POD version by multiplying the number of pages by 1.5 cents per page and adding about $1.00 per book as a base fee. Thus 256 pages x 1.5 = $3.84 + $1.00 = $4.84.) For simplicity's sake, we'll figure royalty at 10% of retail.

Note the results of this comparison. While net sales are obviously much less for the Print-on-Demand product because we're selling fewer copies, our cost of goods are also significantly less. We're actually saving $10,847 in out-of-pocket cash in the first instance and

$10,135 in the second (less cash is saved in the POD book with the higher price because we have to pay higher royalties on those sales).

	Commercial Press	POD–Price Constrained	POD–Price Unconstrained
Quantity	5,000	500	500
Retail Price	$14.95	$14.95	$29.95
Sales (50% disc't)	$37,375.	$3,738.	$7,488.
Returns (30%/ 5%)	$11,213.	$187.	$374.
Net Sales	$26,163.	$3,551.	$7,113.
PPB (1.75/4.85/ unit)	$8,750.	$2,425.	$2,425.
Royalty (10%)	$5,233.	$710.	$1,423.
Total COGS	$13,983.	$3,135.	$3,848.
Gross Margin	$12,180.	$416.	$3,266.
GM%	47%	12%	46%
Cash Saved	$—.	$10,847.	$10,135.

Look, too, at the gross margin percentage. In the case of the price constrained POD book, our gross margin clearly suffers. But in the case of the unconstrained POD version, our gross margin is virtually equal to that of the commercially printed book. Yet we've been able to maintain a lower inventory, which saves some warehouse cost; reduce returns, again saving warehouse and fulfillment cost; and directly save a good amount of cash in the manufacturing process, cash that we can apply elsewhere in our business!

One can make an equally strong argument that even though the constrained version's gross margin is only 12% it still makes sense to print this way. Why? Because if you only print one book at a time, and only print that book when you have a firm order for it, you've eliminated risk from the transaction. In other words, you have no cash tied up in inventory and an order in hand. Every penny of gross margin will cover some part of your fixed overheads. Why wouldn't you print the book under these circumstances? You also reap another benefit: you keep the book in print when it might otherwise go out of print. The more books you have in print, the greater the chance that you can sell more, and the greater the chance that something could happen in the external environment to dramatically change the level of demand for the book.

In short, there are valid, cogent reasons and benefits to using Print-on-Demand technology to produce books when the demand is short and limited and when we have upside pricing flexibility.

The other factor that comes into play in relation to print on demand is digital formatting. Print-on-Demand vendors will frequently convert your current QuarkXpress or Pagemaker files into XML or PDF files. While this may not seem like a benefit, the fact is that such conversion allows you to subsequently put your book into numerous other digital sales venues, such as CD-ROM, web enabled, etc. It's a benefit that you can bank since this saves you the cost of converting your own material.

While I certainly don't recommend that all publishers print every book they have as a POD book, many publishers, especially smaller publishers, should seriously investigate the possibility of using POD technology. The benefits are sometimes too good to pass up.

For information about e-publishing and ISBNs, refer to chapter 7, The Editorial Process, page 148.

Internet Sales Methods

Remember what I said about the differences between marketing and sales (see chapters 9 and 11 in particular). In essence, marketing focuses on identifying the needs and wants of your target market and positioning your products within and to that market. Once that's done, it's up to the sales team to get those products into the market and to ensure that they sell through to the ultimate buying consumer.

Sales takes an outward focus. It is concerned with the "push" function of getting books into the various markets that can sell our books and other products best. This means that sales has two options when it comes to internet selling:

- Using its own website from which to sell
- Using other, externally based, websites from which to sell

The best way to sell is, of course, to use both of these options at the same time. This will allow the company to generate sales from as many sources as possible at the same time.

Selling from Your Own Website

For most new publishers, setting up and selling from your own website is exciting. It's where your ideas about who you are as a publisher take shape in content, form, and image. A new website gives you an immediate identity you may not have had before—a professional identity that tells the world, literally, that you are a professional publisher.

I can personally vouch for this: the very first client who came to Cross River Publishing Consultants after our website (www.pubcon sultants.com) was set up was a journal publisher from Dusseldorff, Germany. How did that publisher find us? Through the internet search engines that identified our website as a member of a worldwide community of vendors offering our services to companies throughout the world, not just a U.S. vendor selling to the U.S. market. That is the elegance of the internet!

You need to keep this in mind: a good website is your sales tool—and image—to the world, not just to the U.S. market. And like all of your products, your website has to look and feel professional. Just as you can't skimp with book design, you can't skimp with website design. A website, like a book, has to be attractive but highly functional. You don't want your customer trying to figure out how to buy your products. The sequence has to be easy to use and navigate, customer friendly, and visually easy to look at. It needs to be seamless. Good website design facilitates the transaction and allows for

A good website is your sales tool—and image—to the world.

up-selling, that is, the purchase of other products from your site that may be more expensive, and cross-selling, that is, the purchase of other related products from your site.

The first key to selling, then, is to make your website attractive, highly functional, and reflect the professional image you wish to convey to your buyers. You also need to have e-commerce capability in place. See Chapter 4 for the details of how to do this.

With your website up and running you can focus on the key questions that impact your sales:

- How can you get customers to your site?
- How can you get your products known to your customers?
- How can you get the customers to buy from your site?

Once you know your target market, you need to sell to that market. Don't waste your time trying to sell to people who will not be interested in your market. Focus 95% of your energy on those people who have a vested interest in your products. They are by far the easiest to sell and by far the most likely to actually spend their discretionary dollars on your products. Let's look at the key ways you can let your customers know about your products and get the customers to your site.

1. Tie your website to all of your current branding efforts. Many publishers don't think of their stationery and products as brand identifiers. Yet everything related to your publishing efforts must be thought of in that way. Your letterhead and envelopes—and the signatures on your e-mail—convey your corporate image and identity; your book covers and logo on the spine do the same. We mentioned a moment ago that your website needs to do the same. In order to maximize the overall effectiveness of your branding, you should interweave all of the branding efforts as much as possible. Simply putting your website URL on all of your products is the first step to getting people to your website; it's the first step to selling your products online. When current buyers see the website URL on your hard copy letters, your e-mail, and your products, it gives these buyers another place to go to find out more about you and your products. And from a sales standpoint, that's exactly what you want them to do.

2. Add fresh content to your website and continually update it. Content is king in more ways than one. New content is not just of interest to your target buyers, but content is picked up by search engines and helps keep your site higher on the engines' rankings than competitors' sites with little or no new content. You need to spend time on your site and keep it interesting and vital. Doing this will not just work to your brand's advantage, it will truly help sell books from your site.

3. Generate publicity. Your publicity efforts overall should support your website sales. Every press release, every radio or television effort, every postcard that goes out from your publicity department needs to note the company's website URL and needs to alert those receiving the publicity that your website is available 24/7 to accept orders from them. A constant stream of publicity to a targeted group of interested people has a cumulative effect. Over time, if those people don't buy from you they will buy from another site that offers your books. But at least they'll buy.

In his excellent and comprehensive book *Complete Guide to Internet Publicity: Creating and Launching Successful Online Campaigns* (John Wiley & Sons, © 2002), Steve O'Keefe, a veteran internet publicist, provides insights into the many and varied ways to use the internet's publicity reach to both promote and sell your books. Among the ways you can get publicity and drive people to your site, according to O'Keefe, are:

- E-mail news releases
- Online news rooms
- Discussion group postings
- Newsletters and direct marketing
- Chat tours
- Online seminars and workshops
- Contests and other fancy promotions
- Syndicating your promotions

Obviously, these are just some of the many ways to draw attention to your books and your website. When it comes to publicity, your imagination is your only limitation.

4. Fully use your authors. Closely related to publicity is the need to use your authors fully. Your authors are your best promotional tools. They know the subject matter intimately, they know the resources related to it and their book better than you do, and it's to your author's best interest to constantly promote his or her book to the target market. You need to tie your promotional efforts into those being done by your author and vice versa. If your author is speaking somewhere, be sure to support him or her by either providing books on site, or providing a flyer or postcard that lists your website on it. Provide a special "attendee" discount to those attending the author's lecture or presentation. When the author is on a television or radio show, be sure he or she gives out your website address frequently. Tell your authors they need to help drive buyers to your site. They'll understand and help out.

5. Be sure you are listed in the key online databases. One of the great advantages of selling on the internet is that buyers can find you just as readily as they can find Bertlesmann or Penguin or Harper-Collins. The internet levels the playing field in terms of obtaining shelf space and in terms of getting face-out placement of your books. The smallest publisher can and does get treated as equally as the large.

Unlike most sales outlets that make it difficult for small and independent publishers to sell their books, the internet booksellers actually make it fairly easy. And they make it no more expensive than typical book wholesalers do. Amazon.com, for instance, has its Advantage Program, which allows publishers to sell their book, video, and music products through Amazon, with Amazon providing customer service and fulfillment. At the same time, the price

The smallest publisher can and does get treated as equally as the large.

for being able to do this is an annual fee of $29.95 per year, a 55% discount off of the retail price of your product, and payment of freight costs to Amazon.

Check each of the individual retail websites to see what their requirements are and be sure to submit all of the information requested when it's due. Make sure that you comply fully with the formatting requirements each site needs.

In order to get a basic listing on the widest range of book sites, you need to get your title listed in the various key databases from which the e-retailers get their title information. This means you need to list your books in at least the following databases:

- Books in Print (R.R. Bowker)
- Ingram Book Company (wholesale title database)
- Baker & Taylor Company (wholesale title database)
- Amazon.com
- bn.com

While it gets more difficult for smaller and independent publishers to access Ingram Book Company and Barnes & Noble directly, it is simple and essential to get your titles into the Books in Print database, from which both companies draw their database information. Baker & Taylor Company, as well, welcomes this information.

In order to list your books in Books in Print, the easiest way is to go to www.BowkerLink.com. From there you can enter title information quickly and edit it as necessary.

If you work through a Master Distributor that sells and fulfills your books, you have a step up on the competition. Many of the major Master Distributors, such as National Book Network, Independent Publishers Group, Publishers Group West also provide data feeds of their titles to all of the major online databases, including Ingram, Baker & Taylor, Amazon.com, bn.com, and many others. According to Curt Matthews, CEO of Independent Publishers Group, IPG feeds its publishers' information to a minimum of 45 key e-commerce databases and sites through a contract company whom IPG uses.

6. Link often, but link wisely. One of the benefits of doing the focused marketing research we spoke of in Chapter 3 is that it forces you to identify those publishers who have similar products to yours, and those organizations and consumer outlets that will be interested in your books and products. This means you have identified places that have an affinity to your products and that your products have some affinity to the products of those other organizations. This being the case, then it makes sense for each of you to have a symbiotic relationship with each other: each can send the other those who share the affinity for the products you both have and offer. The net result of this shared effort is the potential of added sales for each organization.

The internet makes such symbiotic relationships easy to set up. Through the process of links and linking one organization can quickly promote itself and its partners. In most cases, it offers the same opportunities in exchange. The technical process of linking is quite simple and we'll leave it to your IT consultants to show you how to do it. The key for you, though, is to understand that the more you link your site to those of other related organizations or companies offering related products or services the more people will click on those links and be transferred to your site. This gives you more opportunity to sell your products to those customers, and gain new sales. It has been proven that the more links you have, the more your site will benefit.

An added benefit is that the more quality links related to your own areas of interest you have, the greater the search engines will key in on your keywords and therefore the higher the position on the engine you'll get. This definitely helps you compete against other companies who offer products similar to yours. Keep in mind that linking just for the sake of linking won't provide you with maximum benefit. In her excellent article in the March 2005 PMA Newsletter, Shawn Campbell, cofounder and chief search engine optimizer at Red Carpet Web Promotion points out that linking for visibility is not as easy as it once was. Current search engines use a complicated algorithm that involves:

- number of links to your site
- the words in those links
- who is linking to each site that links to yours
- what key phrases appear in those links
- the quality of each site that links to yours
- how many other links each of those sties has
- how many links out your site has, and to what sites
- and more

In other words, search engines now look very carefully and critically at who is linking to you, and what it is that they are saying about you. A link from a leader in your industry carries a lot of weight and means that your site is important. Two links from your industry's leaders means your site is even more important. On the other hand, 100 links from random websites related to industries that have nothing to do with you means almost nothing. Thus getting links is only the start; the important thing is getting good links from quality sites.

7. Use associate marketing. Associate Marketing is to some extent similar to linking. You build a network of organizations that support your products and are willing to sell them for you. This can be done in two ways: either they can sell your products directly from their sites (see Selling From External Websites below) or they can send customers to your site through linking. The difference between Associate Marketing and linking per se is that Associate Marketing usually entails paying the associate a commission percentage on sales.

Linking is usually done free of charge. What kind of percentage do people give to Associates? That's negotiable, but it's generally in the 5%–7% range based on the net price the seller receives.

Like linking, the more Associates you have in cyberspace referring potential customers to you, the better. If you publish gardening books, for instance, and you can set up associate marketing relationships with garden supply sites, or the National Gardening Association, or organic growers, or with any other gardening-related organization, you can see how your potential reach can extend exponentially. If it costs you 5%–7% for the sale, it's probably a bargain since normal sales efforts usually cost 7%–10% of net sales anyway, and adding marketing costs to this takes your normal marketing to the 13% range.

8. Use adwords and advertising judiciously. It's easy to spend money on advertising, but often very hard to spend it wisely. A fairly recent innovation for those using the web allows advertisers to purchase adwords or phrases on the major search engines. When a person keys in this word or phrase to their search on the search engine, a link and or short advertisement for their product comes up at the same time. This association of product or website link to the search phrase is an excellent example of target marketing because you're focusing your ads to those interested in the subject of your product.

Costs for this type of advertising vary, but are usually reasonable and can usually be limited to fit your budget requirements. At the same time, every time someone clicks on your link, it costs you money. There is a move afoot in the advertising world to change the model so advertisers only pay for sales, not clicks. Time will tell if this shift will take hold.

From an advertising and marketing standpoint, purchasing adwords makes sense. But keep in mind that every advertising and marketing expense must be budgeted and must fit within that budget. Don't spend money just for the sake of visibility. Analyze your expenditures and be sure you're getting sales for your dollars. That's the ultimate test of successful selling.

9. Use carefully targeted e-mail marketing. One of the wonders of the internet is that you can get targeted mailing lists of those who fit the demographic profile of your optimal buyers. These lists are

fairly inexpensive and can be bought from a wide varie
list brokers (start with the members of the Direct Marke
tion, whom you can find online at www.the-dma.org). \
lists, you can send a targeted promotion with your wet
embedded. This simple strategy makes it easy for those with a
interest in your books to find your site. One world of caution.. don't
send spam—don't send people continuous e-mails that they don't
want. This is why you must target your lists carefully to those who
have an interest in your products. The last thing you want to do is create a negative image of your company, your products, and your authors
in the mind of the consuming public.

Getting Customers to Buy From Your Site

Once customers learn about your products and get to your site, then
how can you get them to buy from your site?

1. Make your site sticky. Stickiness refers to the ability of your site
to retain potential customers. The best sites keep browsers sticking
to the site by creating offers and features that appeal to the browser.
The longer you can keep that potential customer on your site, reading your marketing copy, and going from page to page, product to
product, the more likely you are to make a sale. According to the
ClickZ Stats article "Merchants Need Some Timely Improvements"
(February 2, 2004), an e-tailing group, inc., survey that examined the
average response and fulfillment times of online merchants in 15 consumer categories showed that the average shopping time per site was
3.67 minutes.

To make your site sticky you need to make it interesting. This is
one reason you need to have a professional website designer working
on your site. The fonts you use, the layout you have, the buttons and
tabs you create, and the links taking the buyer from page to page all
help to create an atmosphere that reflects your image and conveys the
information you want to give your customers so they'll buy your products. One sometimes overlooked page is a "contact us" page with specific address, phone number, and personal information for those who
want more traditional customer service help. Customer service is critical in an electronic age and sometimes the old fashioned way of talking to a real human being is the best approach.

One of the best methods of making your website sticky is to put as much about your book and the author as possible on your site. Creating separate, distinct pages or sites for each book is a strategy that makes sense because the more potential buyers know about your book the better informed their buying decision can be and the more satisfied your customer will be with that purchase. This, in turn, means fewer returns and customer complaints.

To make your site sticky you need to make it interesting.

Thus, creating "look inside the book" sections with the table of contents, interior illustrations and chapters, index, and more help to sell the customer. As a visual medium, it is imperative to put your book jacket or book cover up on your website. And again, one of the benefits of the internet is that it levels the playing field of large and small publishers. In this context, you, the smaller and independent publisher get to show your book on your own "shelf" with your jacket or cover *face out, thus ensuring that your book will be highly visible*.

Other ways to make your site sticky is to infuse it with interactive quizzes, contests, or both that get your visitors involved with the site. Offer a newsletter that they can opt into and sign up for. This allows you to capture vital demographic information that you can use to refine your marketing and sales pitches. Put up your authors' calendar of speaking engagements and let people sign up for them online. Another way to keep people on the site is to have an excellent search tool, so visitors can find what they want quickly.

In sum, make your site work for you. Keep it vital and fresh by adding new features to it on a regular basis and by adding new content and new offers frequently. The more time your customers spend at your site, the more likely they are to buy from it.

2. Create appealing offers. In today's bookselling world, the 100 pound gorilla that everyone competes against is Amazon.com. But it's absolutely not just this one vendor you need to be concerned about. It's every other e-tailer and bricks-and-mortar retailer as well. Thus, you need to ask yourself how you can best work with these customers to sell your books. At the same time, if you're trying to sell books from your own website, you also need to ask how you can best compete against these vendors.

Many publishers take the approach that they want to support their key customers by not competing against them from a price standpoint. This approach leads the publishers to the strategy of selling their books on their own website at full retail price. By doing this, they feel, they are supporting their customers and positioning themselves on an even keel with others vendors selling their products. At the same time, it begs the point that the publisher is still positioning itself against the customer as a competitive seller.

The fallacy of the strategy can also be seen by going to bizrate.com or any other price-comparison internet shopping site. As noted before, when plugging in my own book's title, I came up with a wide range of pricing running from $14.95 to $24.95. If I am selling my book on our site at $24.95, the chances of selling very many is slim to none given the competitive pricing. What's a publisher to do?

There are two approaches. First, create offers with added value. Offer the book at full price, but offer another product at a significantly reduced price or free with every purchase. This effectively gives the customer something extra while maintaining your retail price. The extra product can be a book, some other product you create or sell, an e-chapter that you give away for free, a poster, "bonus dollars" the customer can spend later on a product of his or her choice, or something else. The offer is only limited by your creativity.

The second approach is to take a more aggressive position. This strategy posits that as a vendor, you need to meet the competition just like any other vendor does. Using this approach, you'll price your products either at the low end of the competitive pricing, or somewhere in the middle. You can state, as many of the airlines do now, that "we guarantee our website pricing to be the lowest available." Like publishers, airlines have to compete against the many travel sites offering rock-bottom pricing. If they want customers to book on their sites, they have to offer competitive pricing.

There is no easy answer to the question of which of these strategies is best. As more and more publishers, large and small, take the stance that they need to use their websites as competitive sales tools in order to compete against the large chains and e-tailers that are taking market share and demanding added discount, it makes more and more sense for these publishers to offer discounted pricing on their own sites. A price comparison site won't pick up an "added value" offer. It keys in on the selling price. As more and more buyers become increasingly web savvy and books become more and more subject to commodity pricing, we think more and more publishers will turn to discounted pricing as the answer.

Will this impact the relationship of publishers to their retail customers? It probably will. At the same time, everyone has to remember that the more books that are sold, the more reading that is encouraged, the better for the industry as a whole. Right now unit sales in the trade area are flat. Whatever the industry can do to get people reading is good for everyone in the business.

3. Accept credit cards or use PayPal. If you want to get customers to buy from your website, you need to provide them with a mechanism to do so. This means you need to accept credit cards or use a payment service such as PayPal to facilitate the transactions. While some customers may want to send you cash, those will be a very small percentage of your total customer base.

Accepting credit cards, or establishing a PayPal account is easy. See chapter 4 for an in-depth discussion of this topic.

4. Focus on fulfillment. If you are going to sell books from your site, you had better provide overnight fulfillment. To the credit of the giant e-tailers, they have set the standard for fulfillment—a standard that publishers just didn't meet. When a retail bookstore tells a customer that it will take four–five weeks to get a special order book, which was not unusual before Amazon.com came to town, that bookstore was effectively turning away sales. And yet the bookstore was really only reacting to the time frame set up by the publishers and wholesalers.

Amazon.com and bn.com took up the challenge and won. Today, as every publisher knows, you can get the great majority of books from any of the big e-tailers virtually overnight. In fact, as this report is being written, Amazon.com has just announced "Amazon Prime," which it describes as "our first ever membership program, which provides 'all-you-can-eat' express (two-day) shipping . . . for a flat annual membership fee . . . of $79 per year, which includes sharing the benefits with up to four family members in your household."

According to the e-tailing group, inc., survey mentioned above, the average delivery time for the 15 merchants reporting in the survey was 4.4 days with an average of 4.6 clicks needed to actually complete an order.

Because the bar has been set so high now, you have to match this kind of service if you want to sell books from your site. Whether you fulfill orders yourself or have it done by an outside vendor, you need to have a fast, seamless flow from taking the order to fulfillment of that order. If you don't, you simply won't get repeat customers.

5. Provide excellent customer service. Nothing is more frustrating than having a problem with a product and being unable to get answers. Publishers have historically been very good about taking back defective books and providing attentive customer service. In today's world of instant gratification, this becomes even more important. You need to answer this challenge and maintain not just high standards for resolving customer questions and complaints, but the highest standards. That means you need to answer your customer's questions and complaints within twenty-four hours and make sure you convey the answers and responses to your customers within that period. Publishers should keep in mind that one of the weaker aspects of the large e-tailers is their customer service areas. Here's a challenge: go to Amazon.com and try to find out how to return a book. . . .

What you'll have a hard time finding out is how to return a book (and you only have 30 days in which to do it) and an even harder time getting a phone number of a customer service rep to talk to about it.

Again, make it simple to work with your company. It's not hard to do, it just takes your attention to detail and your time. The better your customer service, the more likely customers will return to do business with you again.

6. Keep your costs proportional to your revenues. One of the keys to website selling is that's it pretty low cost in and of itself. Once your site is up and running it doesn't cost much to maintain it. Still, you need to have a good handle on your editorial costs, cost of goods (royalties, paper-printing-binding, development costs, freight in to your warehouse), and on your sales, marketing, warehousing, and fulfillment costs. You never want to sell at a loss, so you need to be sure that your costs are in line with your revenues, and that the net result of any sale is a profit.

Publishers should also estimate website sales very conservatively.

As consultants, we are constantly seeing publishers not just overestimating the sales they think will come from their websites, but vastly overestimating the numbers! The internet contains literally hundreds of millions of websites. The chances of any one person getting to yours is very small. Keep in mind that in traditional direct marketing, a good response is usually thought to be about 3% of the quantity mailed. Thus, if you mail 100 pieces directly to customers, a good response would be 3 sales. When it comes to the internet, unless your target market is extremely well refined, your response is likely to be much less than 3%. In fact, it's more likely to be less than one-half of one-half a percent, or about .0025. Thus, on an e-mail campaign or mailing, if you mail 1,000 names, you'll probably get about 2–3 orders. You can see that you'll need a lot of names to generate a lot of orders. This is why you need to target the list and use the multitiered sales efforts noted above.

Estimate website sales very conservatively.

Selling on other e-tailing websites

The second method of extending your reach and your sales takes advantage of the fact that there are literally hundreds, if not thousands, of websites that sell books. Each of these sites is a potential sales venue for your books.

In order to sell from these sites, just as with a regular retail bookseller, you need to know what the terms of sale are and accept them. If you don't accept them, for the most part these vendors won't do business with you. If you already do business with the bricks and mortar book retailer who runs the website, you won't have to do more than you do now: get material to the buyers seasonally, well in advance of publication, and get them all of the key information they want, including

- Cover or jacket
- Title
- Author
- ISBN
- Price
- Publication date

- Special offers
- Author biography and information
- Blurbs or early reviews from reputable reviewers
- Table of Contents
- Sample chapters/illustrations
- Other key marketing information

The more information you can provide, the better the books can be displayed on the websites and the better they can be sold to the ultimate consumer or buyer.

Some e-tailors have special terms for smaller publishers. While the terms may call for steep discounts, at least the sites are, for the most part, open to legitimate publishers. Amazon.com's Advantage Program is tailored for small publishers. For a $29.95 annual fee, 55% discount off the retail price, and inbound freight paid by the publisher, Amazon.com will take 5 copies of your book on consignment and put the books on their website with the notation "this book ships in 24 hours." Publishers should keep in mind that Amazon.com provides the marketing venue and does fulfill the orders.

One of the better ways to sell your book is to take advantage of the bestsellers that are already in the market. The internet allows you to do this by teaming up your book with the bestseller. Amazon.com calls this method "BXGY", for "Buy X, Get Y." What this means is that you can pay for placement, if Amazon.com's buyers accept your matchup. If you have a pregnancy book, for instance, you might want to pair it up with the perennial bestseller *What to Expect When You're Expecting*. Since web buyers interested in pregnancy books will more than likely go to the *What to Expect* page, if your book is paired with it, your title will be much more visible. If it's of interest to those interested in *What to Expect*, those buyers will then click on your book, get more information about it, and buy it if interested. In short, by using BXGY you are creating a direct marketing link between your two books.

Of course there are many other ways to help online e-tailers sell your book. Again, using your authors to drive traffic to general websites helps the ultimate sale of their book. You can try to influence positioning on the various sites by having authors or companies buy copies of their books on specific websites in bulk quantities. While these bulk sales are reported as such, they frequently drive up the book on the site's "bestseller" lists. This, in turn, can help gain more visibility for the particular book. Some publishers feel that this is more important to them than getting a greater percentage of the revenue for themselves, as they would if the books were sold off their own site. Trading bestseller status for dollars can be thought of as another form of spending marketing dollars—which is fine as long as you factor it into your title P&L.

Setting Up Your E-Commerce Capability

When you've got your basic site up and running, in order to sell products on it you'll need to set up the capability to order from your site and accept payment. This part of the process is called e-commerce capability.

There are two basic elements you'll need to put in place in order to handle the payment side of standard e-commerce:

1) a merchant account and
2) a payment processor (also called a gateway).

Behind the scenes of every credit card transaction there is a wide variety of financial institutions, service providers, agents, and rather complex technology involved. Fortunately, it's *not* a complex process for a publisher to establish the payment processing capability to sell its books online. The main steps are simply to select and coordinate compatible merchant account and gateway providers. Be sure to allow time to research your options because you'll have a lot of choices among merchant account and gateway providers. This is due to the growth and proliferation in the internet retailing and credit card processing industries. The best fit for you and your business will take a bit of investigation and a little analysis.

While it's possible to operate an online business without a merchant account, your options are limited. However, if you can't get a merchant account, the options presented are *definitely* preferable to trying to survive in e-commerce without any ability to accept credit cards. Besides discouraging tangible impulse sales, not offering credit card payment options may also have an intangible, negative impact on your image if you are selling directly to the consumer market.

Setting up the order module can be done on your own, using packaged software or through your own IT programming. There are many vendors and website hosts who offer this service. Many coordinate this service with merchant account and payment processing service as well. If you're looking for low pricing on both hosting and payment processing you might start at Costco.com. For those with business membership at Costco, the company offers both website hosting and merchant account services at very competitive rates. Publishers Marketing Association also offers merchant accounts at low rates to its members. Many others offer these services at competitive rates. Look around, compare, and find the services you need from vendors with whom you're comfortable working.

Before describing what's involved with setting up your merchant account and payment processor, let's look at how credit card processing works.

A Day in the Life of a credit card transaction

In order to understand credit cards, let's see what happens when you use one of your own credit cards, regardless of whether your card is swiped at your local big box retailer or self-keyed online. Let's say you are browsing on Amazon.com and end up putting three books in your shopping cart. What happens after you enter your Visa card information and check out?

- An authorization request is sent to Amazon's clearing, or acquiring, bank
- The acquiring bank routes the request to Visa
- Visa forwards the authorization request to the financial institution that issued your card (the "issuer" or "issuer bank")
- The issuer send its response (approve or decline) back to Visa
- Visa forwards the authorization approval or denial to the acquiring bank.
- The acquiring bank forwards the response to Amazon, and if approved the purchase is completed and sent to the processing/shipping queue.
- The final purchase amount ($) is sent to the acquiring bank

- This amount is then sent by the acquiring bank to Visa for settlement.
- Visa debits the issuer bank and credits the acquiring bank
- The acquiring bank credits Amazon's deposit account
- The issuing bank or institution adds the purchase amount to your next Visa bill.

For a more in-depth look at the authorization and settlement process, as well as risk management guidelines geared toward e-commerce start-ups, please see *Visa E-Commerce Merchants' Guide to Risk Management* (© 2002, Visa U.S.A. Inc.).

An excellent place to go for a very good introduction to e-commerce, including definitions of services and guides to getting started, can be found at www.usa.visa.com/business/. Another excellent starting point is Mal's E-commerce site, on the web at www.mals-e.com. This site helps you establish a free gateway to e-commerce for your site, providing configurations and technical mechanics for your shopping cart and much more. It also has relationships with merchant banks to get lower cost credit card processing (keep in mind that PMA also offers excellent credit card relationships as well).

Step 1: Set Up a Merchant Account

What exactly is a Merchant Account? In order to process credit card orders (either in real time, one at a time, or batch processed—that is, a group of orders processed all at once), a merchant account is needed. A merchant account is a specific account set up with a credit card clearing bank, also called an acquiring bank. This account is not associated with your other business bank accounts, but is set up to allow you to deposit the net credit card sales into your business account.

The Merchant Account agreement. Because the card owner is not physically present during an online transaction you cannot verify the person's signature or other identifying details. Thus, in order to compensate for a higher level of risk to the card companies, the rates paid by internet merchants are higher relative to other types of retailers. The range of rates varies from 2%–6% for Mastercard and Visa, with premiums for other card brands. In addition, set up and other fees can vary dramatically so you need to do some analysis in order to determine the total cost of each proposal you receive. An acquiring bank can charge a bevy of different fees, some of which may be buried in the small print of its agreement. Make certain that the agreement itself matches what was quoted to you, and don't hesitate to ask questions about any of the clauses. Also, look into the length of term and the cost to end your agreement early. Going forward, you'll want to keep your eye on other options available to you as the card processing industry evolves and the competitive landscape changes. Your business needs might change dramatically as well over the course of a three year agreement period.

Be prepared to describe your business and its history, as well as to forecast the amount of your credit card sales. For instance, you'll need to estimate anticipated credit card sales in terms of average ticket size or transaction price per unit sold, monthly sales volume, and maximum ticket size. The agreement itself will detail your responsibilities as a merchant.

PayPal and Similar Accounts.

If you don't have, or can't get, a merchant account, another option for low volume merchants is to utilize PayPal or one of its competitors. Using this kind of a system, the credit card, debit card, or bank account payment flows through a PayPal account on both the buy and sell side of the transaction. As the seller, you transfer the funds yourself into your bank account from your PayPal account. Because of PayPal's association with eBay, PayPal is probably the most well known of these kinds of merchant account alternatives, but there are other options such as 2checkout.com. While more cumbersome from the buyer's and the seller's perspective, this kind of payment system has some advantages over a merchant account. The advantages include cost and simplicity (e.g., no set up fees; approximately 3% commission taken plus a per transaction fee), as well as no long-term commitment or exit fees. Bottom line, if you can't get a merchant account, there are viable options to get you in the game.

Cost Structure Example

Discount Rates:

Visa & Mastercard

Qualified Rate	2.75% (taken off of the gross sale)
Non-Qualified transaction	
Rate premium (+1.5%)*	3.25% (taken off of the gross sale)

Merchant Account Fees:

Monthly Minimum Fee	$20.00
Chargeback Fee	$10.00 per item
Monthly Statement Fee	$7.50
Initial Setup Fee	$100.00
Annual Membership Fee (staring year 2)	$125.00
1-800 voice (i.e., phone in) authorization fee	$1.00
AVS authorization (fraud control)	included

A Brief Look at Fraud Control. A non-qualified premium (the additional 1.5% in the above example) is typically charged for transactions involving international cards or when other risk management strategies are not used.

In addition to your card number, Address Verification Service (AVS) is a standard fraud reduction process that MOTO—mail order and telephone order—and internet retailers should use. Using AVS, your clients' stated billing address is verified to match the cardholder of record. Card Verification Value 2 (CVV2) is a more recently introduced risk management tactic. With this option, you request that your client inputs the last three numbers of a sequence of numbers found in the signature panel on the back of his or her credit card. This code is submitted with the authorization request and if it doesn't match, you'll be in a good position to hold the order as potentially fraudulent. A separate charge may or may not be levied for these services in the merchant account fees, but again their use keeps fraud and disputes in check, and helps minimize the discount rates you pay.

For new internet retailers, a very efficient way to research merchant account options is by researching payment gateways, since the two work hand-in-hand as described in the next section.

Step 2: Select Your Payment Gateway

In order to process credit cards in real time (when entered by your customer on your website), you need to integrate your shopping cart with a payment processor. Using a gateway allows you to collect your funds faster, is less labor intense, and eliminates the need to have a credit card swipe terminal or software. Of course, there is also less chance of data entry error as well, since the data is manually entered only once by the consumer.

Some considerations to keep in mind when shopping for an e-commerce service provider include: integration, data security, uptime, and payment processing time.

Integration. The shopping cart you use must support use of the payment gateway. Similarly, the acquiring bank for your merchant account and payment gateway need to have a relationship. For this reason, you may see package deals where the three (shopping cart services, merchant account, and payment gateway) are marketed together for a packaged price. This probably won't simplify any of the paperwork, and you'll need to ensure that each of the three separate agreements reflect the package pricing terms. Keep an eye out for extraneous fees and charges in each case.

Security. Fortunately, Visa has created a stringent industry compliance program to safeguard cardholder data. The Cardholder Information Security Program (CISP) ensures data integrity throughout the network of card issuers and across the entire spectrum of processing agents and sales channels. It is important for you and your clients to ensure that your payment processor is reputable and has a current CISP compliance validation. Ask your vendor and verify current certification status at www.usa.visa.com. Once at the Visa site, you'll see the list of CISP compliant providers under the Service Providers section. Merchants are also expected to share the burden of data security, but at this point if your e-commerce credit card transaction volume is less than 20,000 transactions per year, a formal compliance certification is not required. Visa outlines some suggested steps for merchants in this category.

Uptime and payment processing time. In short, if the gateway's systems are down (or not functioning) your clients' orders could get hung up, and the customer may lose the urge to buy off your website. Look for 100% uptime reliability to avoid unnecessary lost sales. After all the work you did to drive business to your website, it would be more than frustrating to lose customers due to your gateway's failure behind the scenes. Payment processing speed simply reflects how much elapsed time it takes to complete the authorization and capture process. In today's marketplace the expectation is for "instantaneous" transaction speed.

Proposal Example

In order to analyze two different proposals for a merchant account and payment gateway packages, we need to make some assumptions about the credit card sales of your publishing business. Given a forecast of 15 orders per month with the average sales price of $20, we can compare the two proposals. Proposal A is a processor that collaborates with the acquiring bank. Proposal B has a higher discount rate, but the fee structure is quite different.

Assumptions: 15 orders per month; average sales price of $20.00; total of $300.00 per month in sales (15 x $20).

	Proposal A	Proposal B
Discount Rates:		
Visa & Mastercard Qualified Rate	2.75%	5.5%
Non-Qualified transaction Rate		
premium (+1.5%)	3.25%	7.0%
Merchant Account Fees:		
Monthly Minimum Fee	$ 20.00	n/a
Chargeback Fee	$ 10.00/item	$10.00
each		
Monthly Statement Fee	$ 7.50	$ 5.00
Initial Setup Fee	$100.00	$49.00
Annual Membership Fee		
(starting year 2)	$125.00	$85.00
1-800 voice (i.e., phone in)		
authorization fee	$ 1.00	$ .50

	Proposal A	Proposal B
AVS authorization (fraud control)	included	included

Gateway Fees

	Proposal A	Proposal B
Transaction Fee	$ .40/tran	$ .35/tran
Pre & Post Authorization	$ .10/tran	included
AVS/CVV2 (fraud controls)	included	$ .10/tran
Monthly Gateway Fee	$20.00	$15.00
Setup Fee	$50.00	$75.00

Analysis of Proposal A versus Proposal B

Let's assume everyone is using MasterCard or Visa each month and there are no disputed charges (chargebacks). Thus the qualified rates would apply, and you'd pay A discount fees of $8.25 and B discount fees of $16.50 on your $300 in book sales. Ignoring membership/start-up fees for a moment, you'd also pay combined merchant account/gateway fees (for monthly statements, all per transaction fees, and monthly gateway fees) of $35.00 per month for A and $26.75 for package B.

Here's the breakdown of how the combined merchant account/gateway fees were calculated, given our baseline assumption of 15 orders per month:

	Proposal A	Proposal B
Monthly Statement Fee$	$ 7.50	$ 5.00

All Per Transaction Fees (including fraud control)

	Proposal A	Proposal B
	$.50 x 15 orders = $7.50	$.45 x 15 orders = $6.75
Monthly Gateway Fee	$20.00	$15.00
Total Monthly Fees	**$35.00**	**$26.75**

So, the total outlay—the discount rate charges plus the monthly fees above—equates to $43.25 for A and coincidentally $43.25 for B, right? Actually, no, because proposal A is a package designed for higher volume merchants—so on top of the discount rate charges of

$8.25 you'd pay the remaining $11.75 of your $20.00 monthly minimum merchant account fee—or a grand total of $55.00 per month. In terms of your top line, $55.00 represents 18% of the $300 in sales, while the $43.25 is closer to 14%. A significant difference in terms of your profit margin.

In terms of the bottom line on Proposal A versus Proposal B, your decision relies initially upon the confidence you have in your sales forecast. If you're uncertain about the volume of your future sales, it might be better to start with a package geared to low volume. When assessing the relative start-up and annual fixed costs, you'll want to calculate the time to break even given the difference in monthly profits for each scenario. In our example, the start-up costs are $150 for A and $124 for B, which incorporates set-up charges from both the merchant account and gateway providers. Ongoing fixed fees for the second year and beyond are the annual membership fees.

To summarize, as part of your final selection process take into account your needs for compatibility with your shopping cart, your need for technical support, as well as the vendor's reputation and quality of service.

Analyze Your Sales and Site Results

Many publishers get so enmeshed in the daily activity of trying to create, market, and sell their books that they forget an equally important component of sales and promotion: analyzing the results of your efforts. If you don't do this on a regular basis, you won't be able to tell accurately and knowledgeably if your efforts are resulting in profitable sales.

Almost all website hosts have the ability to provide you with "metrics," that is, statistics about the traffic you are receiving, how those coming to your site use your site, the sales you're generating, the number of hits vs. the number of sales, the patterns of page use on your site, and much more. If your website host can't or won't provide you with the statistics you need to run your site effectively, then find another host.

When you begin to analyze your sales, there are a number of key line items you should focus your attention on. They are similar to those we always want to look at when it comes to sales figures.

Total sales dollars

Are the total sales dollars you actually generate equal to or greater than the sales dollars you need to cover your costs? Do they meet or exceed the sales dollars you budgeted when you did your initial analysis and budget forecasts?

If you don't meet your key revenue targets, you need to rethink your sales and marketing strategies. It may well be—especially when you just begin to sell from your website—that you have overestimated the potential of the site. You may, therefore, have to reforecast based upon your actual results. At the same time, you want to continue to set your budgets as targets, so don't underestimate either. Select revenue targets you feel comfortably achieving, and then begin to push and stretch those targets for future projections.

Total Units

At the same time you analyze total sales dollars, also analyze total units sold. How many books overall are you selling from your site? Again, does it meet, exceed, or fall short of your expectations and budgets? Just as with the sales dollars, you may have to adjust your budgets initially and then expand them as you grow.

Individual title sales and units

Once you have an overall understanding of total sales and units, dig into the key question of what books are selling the most, both in dollar and unit terms. Are there certain books that continually outperform others? Rank your titles from best to worst in terms of dollar sales and unit sales. Do you see any patterns that emerge in terms of subjects that continue to do better than others? Are there certain authors that continually sell better than others?

From a strategic standpoint, you want to do more of what works, less of what doesn't. *Don't just analyze your sales, use the results to infuse your choice of new titles.*

Gross Margin of each title

One of the keys to publishing success is to make sure your revenues exceed your costs of producing your products, and then the costs of selling them, and then the costs of maintaining your business. A gross margin analysis helps to answer the first tier of this financial pyramid.

You can do a gross margin analysis by looking at the net revenue you bring in for the overall line of books, or for each individual book. In fact, you look at both. When you know your net revenues (gross revenues minus returns), then simply subtract the cost of manufacturing the book (your paper, printing, and binding costs), the costs of creating the book (editing, permissions, illustrations, etc), any royalties that must be paid relative to the books, and any freight that gets the books from your place of manufacturing to your warehouse. Once you subtract these costs from your revenue, you're left with a number: your gross margin dollars. If these dollars are 50% or less of your revenue, then you are at the benchmark gross margin percentage for trade publishers. As an example:

Retail price:	$20.00	
Dollars received after sales to customer:	$10.00	
Cost of Goods:		
Paper, printing, binding:	$ 3.00	
Royalty	$ 1.00	
Development costs	$ .80	
Freight-in	$ .20	
Total Cost of Goods	$ 5.00	
Gross Margin	$ 5.00	50% (of $10.00)

If you know your costs are in line with your revenues, then you know that all other costs of doing business must be less than 50% of your net revenue (in the example, $10.00) if you are to make a profit in your business.

When you do the gross margin analysis on each title, rank those titles in terms of those having the highest gross margin (the most profitable titles for you to publish) to the least (the least profitable titles for you to publish). When you rank your titles like this, again, you want to do more of those that work best, and less of those that don't do as well.

Your customer demographics and metrics

As we mentioned at the beginning of this report, one of the key benefits of selling from your own website is getting information about your customers. At the end of the day, the more you know about who is buying your books, the better you can find more of them and sell more of your books over time.

Look at your customer demographics carefully. Among the questions you should ask are:

- Are you selling more to women than men? If so, what is the percentage breakdown for each?
- Geographically, where are your orders coming from? Are there regions of the country that are stronger for you than others? Are you doing promotions in certain areas of the country, and is this having an effect on your direct sales? Knowing this can help you target your marketing and advertising to those regions.
- Can you get any information on the age of your customers? On their other interests?
- Have your current customers bought from you before? Are you capturing their ordering history? Your current buyers are your best buyers. After them, past purchasers are better bets to buy again than new purchasers—and they're easier to reach.
- How recently have customers purchased previously? Can you create a loyalty program that rewards frequent buyers?
- How frequently does your customer buy? Those who have purchased most recently are your best targets to sell for future books. Be sure to keep track of them and go back to them with new books and new offers.
- How are your customers finding out about your books and website? Track the places your customers are coming from, whether from large search-engine referrals or directly from their own websites (your metrics will allow you to see this). Build bridges to these sites through links, keywords, ad-words, and other methods that will help keep your site visible to visitors to those sites.
- How do buyers use your site? What page do they go to first? What next? How many pages in total do they visit before either buying or leaving your website? Using these statistics you can try to strengthen each page so it retains the customer or leads them more clearly or dynamically to the next page and to ordering your books.

Look at your customer demographics carefully.

The amount of statistical data that you can work with to analyze your website marketing and sales is virtually unlimited. The key, however, is to use that which you feel will give you the best insights into your customers and the books they are buying or want to buy. With those insights in mind, continue to refine and update your website to implement the impact of those analyses on your marketing strategy.

Clicks don't count

One of the great mistakes of websites in the early 90s is that they became enamored of counting clicks, at the expense of counting actual dollar sales and looking at profits. The theory was that if there were enough clicks to your website, enough traffic coming to it, then surely sales would follow and all would be right with the world.

Guess what? The theory was as flawed as any ever put forth. First, website owners spent inordinately on setting up elaborate websites; then on marketing those sites; and then on trying to get those who did come to visit to buy the products. The faulty proposition, though, was thinking that just because someone visits, they will buy. The fact that so many web businesses went bankrupt is a testament to the fact that visiting doesn't guarantee buying or profitability.

Keep in mind at all times that you need to convert visitors into buyers. If your marketing doesn't do that, you need to rethink the marketing and restructure your website to make it more user friendly and buyer supportive. Don't count clicks—count sales and buyers and make sure that your sales are profitable ones. Analyzing your customer base and your sales will allow you to make your website a profit center and a database at the same time. And that's the best kind of website to own.

Selling from your website or any other website is not a hit or miss proposition. Like any other form of marketing and selling, it is one that is refined over time. Websites exist in a very fluid medium with competitive publishers and competitive books aggressively seeking your space and your customers. You need to actively market and sell your products using aggressive, continually updated marketing and sales strategies. The goal should not be to get visitors. The goal must be to get buyers and to sell your books.

Websites should form one component of a successful publishing plan. Whether it becomes the major percentage of your sales program depends on your company and its long-term marketing and sales strategy, whether you have access to alternative markets, the profitability of generating sales off your site versus the profitability of generating sales in other ways, whether you can continue to refine your knowledge of your customers so you can continue to expand the average order size of each, and how well you can bring new cus-

Keep in mind at all times that you need to convert visitors into buyers.

tomers to your website and convert them into buyers of your products.

Understanding the internet, creating an attractive and highly functional website, instilling excellent customer service and fulfillment mechanisms, creating excellent marketing and sales plans, and analyzing the results will help you increase your sales in a consistent way. Take nothing for granted, and continue to upgrade and renew your content. In the world of the internet, one thing is certain: whatever happens today will change quickly tomorrow. Be sure to capitalize on that certainty to sell books better from your own website and from the sites of others.

CHAPTER 14

Returns

It is only fitting to speak of returns at the end of this book, for it's the last topic publishers want to see or discuss. I have already mentioned returns in relation to sales. Returns, however, are one of the most difficult aspects of the publishing business, and the subject deserves a fuller discussion. In fact, it deserves a chapter to itself.

Returns have been a part of the publishing industry since the mid 1940s. Only recently, however, have return rates for hardcover and paperback trade books jumped to the 25%–30% mark and, in 2001, rates over 35%–40% have been noted. The seven year average of returns in major categories, from 1992 to 1998, are:

Category	Average
Adult Trade Hardcover	31.3
Adult Trade Paperback	22.7
Juvenile Trade Hardcover	18.0
Juvenile Trade Paperback	19.0
Technical, Scientific, & Business	15.0
University Press, Hardcover	17.4
University Press, Paperback	20.5
College	22.7

Source: CRPC adaptation of AAP figures

The good news for smaller and independent publishers is that their return rates are significantly lower than those of the larger publishers. The 2004 Huenefeld-PubWest Survey shows return rates at 11%. A study done by Cross River Publishing Consultants for the Publishers Marketing Association ("Book Industry Returns: An Analysis of the Problem; Opportunities for Improvement; With a Focus on Independent Publishers," © 2001 by PMA) showed that smaller publishers' rates run closer to 13%, on average. Obviously there are reasons these rates are lower, including the primary one of not being able to access the marketplace well enough to get larger numbers of books into the accounts. Nevertheless, in most cases, lower return rates are usually better.

When books are "'sold" and do not sell, current publishing norms mandate that these books are fully returnable to the publisher, almost always for full credit to the original "purchaser." This process benefits no one other than the shipping companies and the contract warehouses or distributors that charge for returns—and it really doesn't do much for them either.

From the publisher's perspective, processing returns does many things—all of them negative from a business standpoint. Chief among them, returns

- distract the publisher from its primary business—selling books
- reduce sales and accounts receivable, and therefore cash flow
- increase inventory levels and reduce inventory turnover
- add more cost to the publishing process, especially to the warehousing and fulfillment costs

The fact is, returns are an expensive nuisance to everyone involved in the book publishing process including the wholesaler, distributor, retail bookstore, sales representatives, and publisher. And because so many are involved in every stage of return processing, the costs associated with these activities are high.

How high? According to the PMA returns report, it is a $5.2 billion problem based on return rates established by the Association of American Publishers and the Book Industry Study Group. But this doesn't include returns from smaller and independent publishers. Those publishers account for another $1.95 billion in returns based on a PMA-sponsored survey of member publishers' return rates and sales estimates published in the PMA/BISG study "The Rest of Us." The total return rate, therefore, is over $7.1 billion—or one dollar in returns for every four dollars in industry sales; or one dollar of returns for *every dollar* of trade sales—an astounding rate that doesn't include the cost of processing returns, only the actual sales dollars lost. Factoring in the "reverse logistics" to get the books back into the warehouse and restocked, at an average of 7% of net sales, adds another $.5 billion, bringing the publishers' total cost to $7.6 billion!

From the retailer's standpoint, returns are no less of a problem. A Book Industry Study Group report on returns projected the cost to the retailer at $2.74 *per unit* for picking, packing, storage, transportation, and administration of the return. If a chain distribution center is involved, according to one of the chains, it adds an additional twenty-five to thirty cents, raising the total to $2.99–$3.04 *per unit*! Based on that analysis, the total cost of returns to the retailer is $1.7 billion.

Yet this is just part of the cost incurred by the industry. It doesn't include the cost to the sales reps in wasted time selling and lost commissions; it doesn't include the "problem" returns, those that come back damaged or in which the return counts don't match those on the packing slip, those that may need to be returned again to the bookstore or wholesaler, and those in which corre-

It is incumbent upon everyone in the industry to attempt to figure out how to reduce returns.

spondence may be involved. For each step that must be repeated or for new work that results from returns, costs continue to accrue to those involved. None of this is reflected in the current figures.

It is incumbent upon everyone in the industry to attempt to figure out how to reduce returns. The reason is simple: if returns can be reduced or eliminated (believe it or not there was a time when returns were not allowed in publishing), the savings will go directly to every publisher's bottom line. These are savings in direct expense and savings in time as well. Despite all of the new short-run printing technology that has been installed and used in the last few years, and despite the recognition on all sides that returns must be controlled, the problem remains, with some larger publishers reportedly experiencing 40%–50% return rates in 2001!

Reasons for Returns

There are many reasons for high return rates. Let's review some of them.

Publisher's expectations are too high

Publishers are, by nature, optimists (especially editors). False expectations about what a new title should realistically sell leads publishers to overpay advances and therefore print too many books. This, in turn, leads to unsold books and heavy returns, particularly on bestsellers and frontlist.

Large advances

As noted, this factor is usually a function of high expectations and competitive bidding for big books from big authors. In almost every case, at one point in every bestselling author's career, or that of a well-known personality who gets paid a large advance to write a book, a book will be a flop. When large advances are paid for lesser-known authors, there's more of a chance for failure. These large advances necessitate printing and selling a lot of books in order to make them economically feasible and viable. In many cases, too many books are printed and sold; too many come back as returns.

Overprinting

Overprinting is a direct cause of false title expectations and large advances that require a large number of books to be printed. This is not just a cause for returns, but for negative cash flow as well.

Overpricing

As Len Riggio, President of Barnes & Noble, will gladly point out, most books sell better at lower prices. In a press release following the 2001 holiday season, in which Barnes & Noble posted gains that were superior to many other retailers, the nation's largest book retailer gave independent publishers everywhere renewed hope and deserved praise. The company said that sales increases among publishers ranked 21–100 of those they do business with, "tended to double those of the majors (ranked 1–5)." In explaining why he thought this was so, Riggio stated that these independents "are clearly more conscious about pricing" than are publishers that are margin driven and part of conglomerates. As the release put it, "Smaller publishers tend to be run by people who own them and they price accordingly."

Such praise for independents is rare indeed, but it must also be put into perspective. From the publisher's standpoint the question remains: is the lower-priced product that is good for Barnes & Noble good for the publisher? Whether small, medium, or large, publishers also need to make profits to stay in business. If publishers can price a product lower and still achieve real dollar profitability while selling more units, the gross margin dollars can add up quickly. And while a lower gross margin percentage may result, the dollars can more than make up for it. Tom McCormick, former President of St. Martins' Press, was a great proponent of just this kind of publishing and was extremely successful.

Dropping prices, however, may not provide either the gross margin contribution dollars or the gross margin percentage necessary to be profitable. In this case, selling more of an unprofitable product won't lead to business health, just larger losses. If publishers link pricing to the margin they need for profitability (and there is a direct relation), it may well result in pricing books higher than the current market condition dictates. When this is the case, those books may not sell well—and result in returns.

Lack of promotional and marketing support

Too many books are published that don't get the proper support. Because so many books are published each year and publishers need to support the major books on their lists, many of the midlist titles on a publisher's list don't get much, if any, marketing or promotion. These books are simply printed, sold into the stores, and are expected to sell on their own, hopefully after getting a few reviews in newspapers or magazines. Because increased visibility helps to sell books, and many, especially bestsellers, get this visibility, those that don't often get returned.

Poor market research

Publishers usually publish under the "throw it against the wall" policy. Because it's more expensive to do proper market research than to actually publish a book, most publishers don't do adequate market research on their products. The result of this is the publication of a lot of books for which there may be no demand or marketing support that is misplaced. Again, the result is returns.

Poor coordination of sales and marketing information

When book expectations are high but publishers don't coordinate their plans well, it leads to returns. Retailers and wholesalers, in order to purchase accurately, need to know what books publishers will be promoting and where they will promote them, whether nationally, regionally, or locally. They need to know how much money the publisher will spend supporting the book, and how that money will be spent. Without this knowledge, retail and wholesale buyers can't accurately allocate their own buying funds or promotional dollars— to the detriment of all.

Publishers need to convey this information to their accounts in a coordinated way. The fact is, larger publishers are pretty good at this. They have systems in place to alert the accounts about initial plans and changes that occur along the way. Smaller and independent publishers are frequently not as consistently organized and don't convey the information in time or don't alert the accounts to changes that occur. This is compounded if a publisher uses a distributor, because the publisher must then convey the information to the distributor, who then must convey it to the accounts. There is, in short, more room for slipups to happen—and they do. Again, the result is more returns.

Publishers oversell—accounts overbuy

Editors are optimists; sales management and reps are often paid on the amount they sell. This is a recipe for returns. There is a fine line between selling too few, selling just enough, and selling too many copies of any book. Because publishers, especially large public companies, need to show increased sales and profits each quarter, not to mention each year, they often oversell in pursuit of this goal. Smaller and independent publishers try to do the same in order to generate enough accounts receivable and cash to survive.

The wholesalers and retailers try to contain this onslaught with such devices as

1) "Open to buy" budgeting, whereby the accounts allocate only a certain amount of money to purchase books in any given month

(based on publishers' stated promotional plans and publication dates).

2) "Just in time" inventory management, which leads them to order only that amount of inventory from publishers that can be sold by the account within a very short period of time, usually a few weeks or so.

3) Point-of-purchase inventory control systems. By knowing what's selling, when it's selling, and where it's selling, accounts can control their buying better. They can order more of what's selling and direct it to those locations that are selling it best; conversely, they can order less, or not reorder at all, those titles that are not selling as expected.

To a large extent, wholesalers and retailers have used these tools very successfully. Unfortunately, market conditions and publishers' inability to control other factors as noted has led to today's greater return levels.

The last point noted, point-of-purchase inventory control systems, holds a good deal of promise and deserves a bit more discussion.

In the past, only national wholesalers and retailers, primarily Ingram and Baker & Taylor, Barnes & Noble, and Borders had computer inventory sales systems that would allow them to monitor sales of books on a national level. The wholesalers, though, could only monitor sales through their own national warehouses, which provided valuable but limited information. Only the two major retail chains, Barnes & Noble and Borders Group, have had the capability of knowing what books are selling through their nationally based bookstores (900 and 1,200 respectively as of 2002, including Dalton and Walden stores). For obvious reasons, the chains did not want to share that information with each other, nor openly with the publishing community. Yet as we've just noted, without this information, publishers can't do their jobs properly.

Within the past few years, one company has made major inroads into the bookselling community to try to ameliorate the problem and offer a service to any publisher that can afford it. BookScan, a division of the A.C. Neilson Company, which specializes in the collection and sale of point-of-purchase information, offers retailers and pu¹ system that can and does provide this critical information.

BookScan is the sibling of SoundScan, which revolutionized the recording industry's information systems about a decade ago. At that time, the recording industry's return rate was about 28%, not much different from that of today's trade hardcover rate. Over the subsequent seven years, after the introduction of SoundScan to the industry, returns fell to 5%, according Judy Stoffman, in an article in the *Toronto Star* ("Scanner to Spell End of 'Skewed' Bestseller Lists," March 30, 1999). What is most interesting in relation to the phase-in of SoundScan to the recording industry is that it's introduction in 1991 "completely changed the landscape of the industry.... Soundscan crowned new superstars who were previously deemed unimportant by uninformed executives; embarrassed established acts when they suddenly disappeared from the new Top 10; focused attention on completely unexpected trends; and rerouted concert tours from over-worn paths." It played such an important role in confirming country music's boom and Garth Brooks's overall dominance of the charts that Brooks sent a framed platinum record for display at the SoundScan offices. ("Sound Figures: SoundScan has Taken the Hype Out of Reporting How Many Albums are Sold," David Bauder, Associated Press, May 27, 1996.)

As a result of SoundScan's implementation throughout the industry, record marketing executives were able to target their budgets to where the sales were coming from and to those recordings that were beginning to sell—especially to those artists whose work was previously not noted but that sold significantly, in different music genres, such as country, rap, alternative rock. The numbers also influenced radio and video channel DJs and executives to increase the video/play rotation of these newly discovered artists, and add their records to the play lists. Thus, SoundScan provided a stimulus to the retailer, the recording company, and the recording artist, to the benefit of all.

BookScan is now having such an impact on the publishing industry. Barnes & Noble, Borders and key independent stores as well as Amazon.com and others have made a commitment to use BookScan's technology and allow the company to access and report their sales figures to those publishers that want to buy it. At the moment, fees for purchase are high. But this may well come down in the near future. And if publishers can reduce returns, the money for purchase of BookScan's information can come directly from internal savings. In addition, there is no reason BookScan's impact can't result in the "discovery" of previously ignored authors and books that merit more promotion and publicity allocation than they currently receive. As Rhalee Hughes, publicity manager at Penguin Putnam Books for Young Readers, points out, if BookScan helped reduce return rates by 1 or 2%, it would mean a savings to trade book publishers alone in the range of $50–$90 million. A lot more than paying for the cost of subscribing to BookScan data!

BookScan is only one company providing sales information to publishers and retailers. Whether it is this company that ultimately prevails or another, the important aspect is that the effort to overcome the informational deficiency is well under way. The hope is that it will continue and be available to publishers of all sizes at a fee all can afford.

Paying with returns

Wholesalers and retailers are supposed to pay publishers for books they purchase within the terms specified by publishers for that payment. Net 30, or payment within thirty days of the end of the month in which a book is shipped, is the norm that most publishers stipulate as their terms. In the book industry, though, most accounts actually pay in 90–120 days.

Given just-in-time inventory methods and better computerized point of sale information, many accounts can determine within this 90–120-day period whether there is a reasonable chance a book will sell during that time, or whether to carry the book for a period despite its inability to sell within that time. If the determination is made that the book won't sell, it is possible that the wholesale or retail account may return the book to the publisher for full credit before paying the publisher for the original invoice. If this is the case, and it is getting to be more and more so, then the publisher is basically functioning as the short-term bank for the wholesaler and retailer. Books coming back in this context find themselves in the worst possible light: sold but never paid for, incurring the distinct possibility of damage and perhaps write off. In short, books become consignment items, never "sold" items.

While publishers need to closely monitor their sales to ensure that this does not happen too frequently, wholesalers and retailers should also pay their invoices on time. It's not just publishers who make this business a true business; it's the wholesalers and retailers as well. They too must take responsibility for their side of the return issue in order to keep it to a minimum.

Reprinting too soon and too many
Because publishers, until recently, haven't had the precise tools to know which of their books have been selling in specific quantities in which locations, and, for the most part, smaller and independent publishers still don't have these tools because of the cost, publishers are often forced to base reprint decisions on educated guesses rather than hard data. The last thing a publisher wants to do is interfere with, or curtail, the success of a book that seems to be working. This often leads to reprinting too many books at the wrong time. Books that may well be at the apex of their life-cycle may be reprinted under the false assumption that the current trajectory will continue, when in fact it will probably decline.

It is for this reason, as well, that publishers find wholesalers and retailers placing new orders for books that are then almost immediately returned to the publisher (often leading to higher levels of damaged books) or ordering books for one location while at the same time returning them from another. Wholesalers and retailers properly follow the information coming from their own computers, which alert them to those books that are selling well and/or those that are in a low-stock condition. When this happens, many of the systems generate automatic reorders to the publisher. This causes the publisher to react in the manner described above. If both publisher and retailer/wholesaler don't review the data they have, or if one is more optimistic in expectation than it should be, too many books will be printed and placed into the various accounts. And more returns will result.

Poor analysis of sales and returns data
Most of the time, larger publishers analyze and scour their sales and returns data for information that will help them publish books more accurately. Sales management is often incentivized not just on how high their sales are, but on minimizing return levels (though frankly, more attention should be focused on this part of the incentive structure).

Smaller and independent publishers, unfortunately, often don't analyze their sales and returns enough; they are too frequently involved in running the day-to-day operations of their business. Without such analysis, good publishing decisions can't be made accurately, and high returns are the result.

Print-on-Demand and e-books
One method already showing promise of minimizing print runs and .containing cash flow is Print-on-Demand and electronic books. See chapter 13 for an in-depth discussion of this new technology and its impact on returns.

Other Return Issues

Damaged Returns
One of the major complaints publishers have against booksellers and wholesalers is the fact that many returns come back damaged. The publisher feels that once the book leaves its warehouse, it is the retailer's or wholesaler's responsibility and that the book should either be returned in saleable condition, or the retailer/wholesaler should pay for the damaged book.

While this is good in theory, it doesn't usually work well in practice. Why? Because the retailer can blame the wholesaler or publisher's shipping department; the wholesaler can blame the retailer, and the publisher can blame both. Who's to say who's right in this triangle of incrimination? The result is that the books end up in the publishers' warehouses and both wholesaler and retailer take the credits anyway. If publishers don't make the credits, the entire accounts receivable ledger gets thrown off and enormous amounts of time are spent trying to reconcile these accounts.

There is no easy answer to this problem. If publishers want to keep working with wholesalers and retailers, and they do since it's usually the primary market for their books, then ultimately there must be some reconciliation of the accounts or the publisher must accept the chargeback and cost. If the publisher doesn't do this, it risks the very real probability that the accounts will simply stop buying its books. Especially so for smaller and independent publishers.

Damaged goods write-offs account for about 3% of a publisher's profit and loss statement. For smaller publishers, it can be significantly higher. Most publishers should resolve the issue of damaged books if it is a consistent and significant problem. Just alerting the other parties to the fact that you're checking and on top of the matter will help make them pay more attention to the problem you're having. You may also come to an accommodation with the other parties that will result in your getting reimbursed for some cost. At the same time, if the problem is intermittent, it's probably easier and less costly in the long run to simply take the loss and write it off.

How to Reduce Returns

While it's easy to say returns are an inevitable part of the book business and do nothing about the problem, if publishers want a sustainable, healthy business they must address this critical issue and attempt to minimize its impact industry-wide and at the company-specific level. There is a common industry hypothesis that 80% of a publisher's books fail and only 20% are successful. If that's the case (I, for one, don't think it is) then publishers must reevaluate their current procedures. How can this be done? Let's look at some of the ways returns might be reduced.

Have realistic expectations

Unrealistically optimistic expectations drive up advances and print runs. It's one thing to pay millions of dollars for a Stephen King or a Bill Clinton. It's another to routinely overpay advances to those whose names are not well-known and whose book concepts aren't overly stimulating. Agents and authors thrive on competitive bidding for manuscripts, but publishers often end up overpaying.

By paying less for books of quality, publishers won't be forced to print excessive quantities of those books in order to make them profitable. With fewer books printed, fewer will be put into the marketplace, and fewer will be returned. This method is supported today by just-in-time inventory demands, which minimizes the number of books accounts buy at any one time. It's also supported by access to historical sales data, especially that of an author who has published more than one book in the same genre.

Pay smaller advances

As noted above, smaller advances are directly tied in to unrealistic expectations. If publishers pay smaller advances, or more realistic advances, the pressure to print and sell unrealistically large quantities of books is reduced—as are returns.

Don't overprint

Again, this is tied directly into having realistic expectations and managing print runs. The fewer books printed, the fewer put into the market and the fewer returned. In today's world of efficient short-run printing, publishers are far better off, for most books, to print smaller quantities and go back to press if demand supports that decision. This strategy saves cash and reduces the chance for returns at the same time.

Price competitively to your needs

The need to maintain profitability must be balanced against the need to price books at a level at which they'll sell. It does no one any good to price too high or too low. While publishers are usually forced to price low by competitive pressure (externally from the accounts but internally as well from the sales staff), a commonsense approach must prevail. If pricing to margin routinely results in comparatively high pricing, publishers must reevaluate those margin requirements. If pricing to meet the competition results in prices that don't support profitability, that strategy too must be reviewed. There is no easy answer to this issue except to say that publishers should price books at the lowest price that will sustain profitability. What price that is depends on the book itself, the author's reputation, the category, the season, and many other variables.

One way around the dilemma of what constitutes appropriate pricing is for the industry to switch to a method of pricing used by many other industries: net pricing.

Using this method, the publisher would not place any "suggested retail price" on its books or in its catalogs. The publisher would simply sell the books at prices that are appropriate and profitable for it as the publisher. The customer, whether wholesaler or retailer, would then mark up the books, adding whatever profitability margin they needed to the publisher's price. Each vendor, in turn, would do the same until the book achieved a de facto retail price. Each vendor, in short, would be responsible for determining its own needs. Those with high overheads would price higher; those with low overheads lower. If those with lower overheads wanted greater profits, they could charge a higher price.

The net pricing method takes the guesswork out of pricing from the publisher's perspective. The publisher has no idea of what the wholesaler's or retailer's overheads are. A retailer in Des Moines, Iowa, for instance, probably has lower rent costs than one in San Francisco. Yet by setting a "suggested retail price" the publisher essentially equates the two. Net pricing allows the vendor in Des Moines to price lower if it chooses. Or, it allows more efficient vendors of all sizes to price lower and take advantage of their efficiency.

In effect, discounts do the same thing. When a bookstore discounts, it's saying that it can sell books cheaper because it is more efficient than other stores, or it's willing to take less of a profit and sell more books. Even in such cases, though, the suggested retail price caps the amount of upside potential, since no vendor will ever sell a book for more than the suggested retail price.

The argument against net pricing is threefold:

- Agents want the retail price because it is an objective standard against which to base royalty calculations.
- Booksellers want a retail price so customers know the store is competitive with other bookstores selling the same book.
- It takes a lot of work on the part of the supply chain vendors to determine what their margins are and to apply them to each book in order to price them appropriately.

None of these arguments makes much sense in light of current bookselling procedures:

First, most publishers outside of New York use net pricing for royalty payments (and large ones in New York, for instance John Wiley & Sons, do so too). Most in academic and professional publishing base royalties on net. It can be, and is, done frequently.

Second, by discounting, booksellers eliminate the suggested retail price benchmark of competitiveness. In effect, they use it to their advantage anyway by undercutting it and telling consumers that their lower price is more competitive than the competition—which is exactly what net pricing would enable them to do.

Third, every bookseller should know its costs. And given today's computerization and inventory control mechanisms, pricing by ISBN is no more difficult than logging the book into the store's inventory and applying a multiple to it. This price can then be scanned at the checkout counter and the transaction completed.

In short, net pricing could help keep prices down and help ameliorate returns. It's a strategy that I recommend be implemented throughout the industry.

Support your books

Books are like all other commodities: they can't sell on their own without some kind of support from the publisher to make them visible. Given 50,000 new books each year, any single book stands a very poor chance of standing out from the crowd. You must provide each one of your books with a marketing plan. If you don't have much money, then publicity should lead the way. If you have a modest budget for your book, then perhaps ads in the library magazines or retail specialty catalogs will work for you. If you have a lot of money, then perhaps a satellite tour, an end-cap at the retail level, an internet promotion, or some other promotion will work. The key is to do something—almost anything—to get visibility for your book or your line of books. It's not enough to get your books into the wholesalers or even the retailers; you have to focus your efforts on getting your books off the shelf and into the hands of the ultimate consumer or enduser. While it's no guarantee of success, marketing support is essential for "moving the merchandise" and reducing returns.

Coordinate sales and marketing information

When you know how you'll market your books, make sure you share and coordinate this information with others in your own company (the sales, marketing, sub-rights departments especially) and with those key people at your distributor; the wholesalers; and the key retailers. Only when everyone is on the same page, with the same information, can you expect everyone to be efficient and order properly. The result of being late, or of not providing the proper information, will be fewer sales and greater returns; the result of coordinating properly is greater sales and fewer returns.

Conduct market research

As we have said before, most publishers don't do enough market research. In order to reduce returns you must know what attributes your book needs to stand out on the shelf. You must do your homework and understand the category you're selling into; the competition; the price points; the buyer's preferences; and more. Spend some time on market research. The result will be fewer returns.

Don't oversell; don't allow accounts to overbuy

It's alluring to try to push buyers into buying more copies than they really need. It's a sign of your success, of your power. Or is it? When you oversell, all you do is spend money needlessly. You end up printing more books than you need and spending more than you have to on fulfillment and postage. Accounts won't appreciate it if you sell them too many books that they then have to pack up and return. Do this too frequently and you'll see all of their purchases severely cut back, because your credibility will be shot. Sell only the number of books that makes sense for everyone. In today's world of quick reorders, as long as you have your books listed in the databases of the wholesalers and retailers, as long as they know where to get your books, and as long as you have inventory, it's no problem getting books out to buyers. Of course you want the accounts to have them immediately, preferably to have at least a few on their shelves, but that's a few, not a lot. There's a fine line between enough and too many. Each book is different and the line changes for each. The key is to understand that conservatism is ultimately going to reduce your returns, and that's better for everyone's business.

Don't accept payment by returns

There's a significant difference between accepting and crediting returns in the normal course of your business and letting accounts get away with returning inventory in lieu of paying you for the purchases. Accounts must pay you for the books they buy; they must do so in cold cash; and they must do so on terms that are acceptable to both of you. That's their responsibility as vendors. There will always be reasons why accounts can't pay, or pay on time, but it's your responsibility to ensure that they do pay. If you see accounts that constantly return your books without paying for them on the terms you've agreed upon, then you must seriously consider cutting off that account, or discussing other terms with it. You are not in the banking or credit business. You are in the publishing business, which means you must sell books and collect for them if you are to survive. Merely exchanging inventory for a short period of time won't help you or your accounts and it will cost both of you money. Keep control of your accounts receivable. Don't accept payment by returns. It will help your cash flow and help you control your inventory, especially your returns.

Analyze Returns to Control Returns

One way to review returns is to establish a "returns index" that focuses attention on those subject categories that are most responsible for high return rates. The way to do this is:

1) Calculate the average return rate for your entire line of books (or any individual category). This is then your benchmark average, and is delineated as 100.
2) Review each category against the average, by dividing the category returns percentage by the total returns percentage (in the chart below, for instance, you would divide any category return percentage by 21%, the average for the whole line) to get an "index" score.
3) Review the results. If the category average is less than 100, then returns are better than average; if, on the other hand, the category average is over 100, then returns for that category are higher than average and should be reviewed further.

Category	Sales $	Return $	Return %	Index
A	$225,000	$60,000	27%	130
B	$375,000	$50,000	13%	65
C	$130,000	$20,000	15%	75
D	$25,000	$12,000	48%	233
E	$68,000	$20,000	29%	143
F	$55,000	$20,000	36%	177
G	$12,000	$1,000	8%	41
TOTAL	$890,000	$183,000	21%	100

As can be clearly seen, categories B, C, and G have indexes significantly below the average. This publisher should clearly think about publishing more of these books, especially those in categories B and C, because the dollar sales within the categories are high. At the same time, categories D, E, and F are not doing well. Dollar sales are lower in each category, and returns significantly higher than the norm.

It is this kind of simple review, both at the category level, and following that, at the individual book level within the category, that will help publishers increase their commitment to better categories and reduce their commitment to poorer performing categories.

Control what you can

From a publisher's perspective, you can only control those events for which you have responsibility. This means, in particular, selecting the right books to publish, those with quality that will sell over the long-term; making sure that the number of books on your list and the number of books printed of each individual title you publish makes sense and is conservative. It means using your money and your efforts to market the books you publish to maximize the sell-through; it means working with the wholesaler and bookstore to find creative ways to limit their exposure and help them sell your books. Returns can do more than anything else to wreak havoc on your business. It's your responsibility as a publisher to contain returns, preferably to far below the 31% average in 2004 for hardcover trade books.

Conclusion

Some years ago I wrote an article entitled *A Matter of Degree, Not of Kind*. The thrust of that article was that smaller publishers have the same concerns and the same problems as larger publishers. After many years, I am more convinced than ever that this is true.

There is nothing in this book that can't apply as equally to large publishers as to small. Just the degree is different, whether it's the 000s following the net sale amount or the number of names mailed in a direct response mailing.

Smaller publishers today have an opportunity that's both tougher and more opportunistic than ever before. Tougher because the market has changed so dramatically and is now increasingly dominated by the chains and superstores as well as by fewer and fewer major wholesalers and major publishers.

At the same time, smaller publishers have an advantage that their predecessors didn't. The technological breakthroughs of the past 20 years have resulted in the ability of every small publisher to have affordable computers and desktop publishing systems in-house that can quickly streamline the editorial and design process, if not the actual printing process itself.

In addition, smaller publishers today have a mechanism for breaking into the chains and major wholesalers that barely existed 25 years ago: distributors. While there are good distributors and bad, these organizations have filled a need for both publishers and buyers. They give the publisher access to major accounts in a simple, straightforward way; they also provide the major accounts' buyers a way to access a vast number of books from a multitude of publishers in an expedient, cost-effective way. It works for everyone.

Distributors give the publisher access to major accounts.

Publishers also have equal access to the large—and increasingly influential—e-tailers. Here, small publishers can have equal "face out" space to the large company's space; they can position their books next to the bestsellers by using "BXGY" ads; they can get readers "inside their books," just as the large companies can. In short the Internet levels the playing field between small and large publishers. My prediction is that the publishing world will continue to change and evolve. In my crystal ball I see a future in which

- Online ordering will become more and more popular.
- Printing on demand will become much more feasible and accessible, which will certainly benefit the publishers.
- For a period of time, the superstores will continue to take market share from the independents.
- Those same superstores will, in 15 year's time, be forced to change their own strategies. They will find that stocking a wide array of inventory that doesn't sell doesn't make sense and will ultimately be unprofitable. If the buyers at these superstores follow what their inventory systems tell them, then they will cut back on the breadth of inventory and focus on that which already sells. And if they do this, they won't be able to support the 50,000-square-foot store that is currently the norm. I think—and I am probably alone in this thought—that the superstore theory will revert to the strategy of the mall chain stores. That is, somewhat smaller stores selling primarily high-volume, high-turn bestsellers.
- If the superstores revert to the mall theory, then the independents will ultimately return. These stores will be highly specialized and focused in specific book categories, whether mysteries, how-to, travel, etc.
- Going from disk to plate will become the norm.
- Going from disk to finished book will supplant the need for plates.

- It will become common for books to be downloaded from a publisher's website or from a bookstore's website.
- The book industry itself will see declining sales of books over the next 25 years as television, the internet, and other digital forms of entertainment compete for the time of today's readers.
- Sub-rights sales will become more important as digital convergence creates new avenues for content on TV, the internet, and yet-to-be-developed future technologies.

What all of this means for the publisher is that it must target more, plan more carefully, and budget better than ever before. The advent and expansion of the internet and the technological revolution means that there is more opportunity for publishers to reach broadened markets more effectively and less expensively. The publisher, however, must know how to use these technologies within the profit-and-loss structures these technologies impose. Publishers must understand what profitability is and how to achieve it within the current publishing environment so they have the foundation to knowledgeably address the evolving structure and environment.

The one sure thing is that the current norms will change.

The one sure thing is that the current norms will change. By understanding the fundamentals of the industry and your business, by becoming completely familiar with the process of strategically planning and managing your company for your environment—both the present and the future, by putting in place the proper templates and management structures so your staff understands what you want and how you want it, then you will have done your job. Then, no matter what the future brings, your company will succeed.

Appendix

1. Accounting packages and vendors

Acumen, Inc.
1596 Pacheco Suite 203
Santa Fe, NM 87505
505-983-6463 Phone
505-988-2580 Fax
e-mail: linda@cyberwolfinc.com

The Cat's Pajamas; MiniCat™
1253 Highway 20
Anacortes, WA 98221
360-293-8372 Phone
800-827-2287 Phone
360-293-7372 Fax
e-mail: cpj@sos.net

Piigs™
Upper Access Inc.
PO Box 457
Hinesburg, VT 05461
800-310-8716 Phone
800-242-0036 Fax
e-mail: UpperAcces@aol.com

2. Associations

American Booksellers Association
200 White Plains Road
Tarrytown, NY 10591
914-591-2665 Phone
800-637-0037 Phone
914-591-2720 Fax
e-mail: vlahos@ambook.org

American Library Association
50 E. Huron Street
Chicago, IL 60611
312-944-6780 Phone
800-545-2433 Phone
312-440-9374 Fax
website: www.ala.org

Association of American Publishers
71 Fifth Avenue
New York, NY 10003
212-255-0200 Phone
212-255-7007 Fax

Direct Marketing Association
1120 Avenue of the Americas
New York, NY 10036
212-768-7277 Phone
212-302-6714 Fax
website: www.the-dma.org

Book Industry Study Group
19 West 21st Street, Suite 905
New York, NY 10010
646-336-7141 Phone
646-336-62142 Fax
website: www.bisg.org

Publishers Marketing Association
627 Aviation Way
Manhattan Beach, CA 90266
310-372-2732 Phone
310-374-3342 Fax
e-mail: info@pma-online.org
website: www.pma-online.org

3. Books about Publishing

Book Publishing: A Basic Introduction. John Dessauer. (Continuum Publishing Company, 13th Edition, 2002). Paperback. $19.95. Dessauer is one of the deans of the publishing industry. Anything he has to say is well worth reading—this book in particular.

The Book Publishing Industry. Albert N. Greco. (Allyn and Bacon, 1997). Paperback. $24.95. A lot of excellent statistical information and in-depth publishing procedures. A bit on the textbook side in terms of design and presentation.

The Complete Guide to Self-Publishing: Everything You Need to Know to Write, Publish, Promote and Sell Your Own Book. Tom and Marilyn Ross. (F&W Publications, Third Edition, 1989). Paperback. $18.99. The title overstates it a bit, but a good basic start-to-finish guide.

How To Get Happily Published: A Complete and Candid Guide. Judith Appelbaum. (HarperCollins, Fourth Edition, 1996). Paperback. $13.00. A wonderful book that every writer should read. Provides in-depth advice on how writers should prepare and submit their work (and to whom), as well as excellent insight into the realities of today's market.

The Huenefeld Guide to Book Publishing. John Huenefeld. (The Huenefeld Company, Inc., Revised Sixth Edition, 2001). Paperback. $35.00. An excellent book that focuses on the business aspects of publishing. Its discussion of pre-press development and management issues alone is well worth the price. Huenefeld's statistical surveys, used to provide detail in this book and in his other analyses, provide an invaluable service to the smaller publishing industry. Books are available directly from the Huenefeld Company for $35 plus $3 postage and handling.

Kirsch's Handbook of Publishing Law. Jonathan Kirsch. (Acrobat Books, 1995). Paperback. $21.95. Quite simply the best non-technical legal reference between two covers for publishers of all sizes.

A Manual on Bookselling: How to Open and Run a Bookstore. Edited by Robert D. Hale with Allen Marshall and Ginger Curwen. (American Booksellers Association, Fifth Edition, 1996). Paperback. $24.95. If you're going to be a publisher, you should understand the intricacies of the bookseller's business. There's no better place to start than with this book, which should be essential reading for every publisher—and which few publishers ever read.

1001 Ways to Market Your Books. John Kremer. (Open Horizons Publishing Company, Fifth Edition, 1998). Paperback. $27.95. The one book to have when it comes to marketing ideas. It's particularly good on non-traditional ways to market. Covers the whole gamut of markets, including bookstores, distributors, libraries and more.

The Self-Publishing Manual: How to Write, Print and Sell Your Own Book. Dan Poynter (Para Publishing, 10th Edition, 1997). Paperback. $19.95. The bible for smaller and self-publishers. Chock full of essential information from start to finish. This should be on the bookshelf of everyone interested in publishing. Focuses on the practical as opposed to the more managerial or theoretical.

4. Publishing Magazines

ALA Booklist
American Library Association
50 E. Huron Street
Chicago, IL 60611
312-944-6780 Phone
312-337-6787 Fax

Direct: The Magazine of Direct Marketing Management
11 River Bend Drive South
Box 4949
Stamford, CT 06907
203-358-9900 Phone
203-358-5831 Fax
website: www.mediacentral.com

ForeWord
129-1/2 E. Front Street
Traverse city, MI 49684
231-933-3699 Phone
231-933-3899 Fax
www.forewordmagazine.com

Independent Publisher Magazine
(formerly *Small Press Magazine*)
121 E. Front Street
Traverse City, MI 49684
800-706-4636 Phone
616-933-0448 Fax
e-mail: jgbp@northlink.net

Library Journal
360 Park Avenue South
New York, NY 10010
646-746-6800 Phone
website: www.libraryjournal.com

Publishers Weekly
360 Park Avenue South
New York, NY 10010
646-746-6758 Phone
646-746-6631 Fax
website: www.bookwire.com/pw

5. Publishing Newsletter

PMA Newsletter
Publishers Marketing Association
627 Aviation Way
Manhattan Beach, CA 90266
310-372-2732 Phone
310-374-3342 Fax
Website: www.pma-online.org
An excellent newsletter covering a wide
range of issues for smaller publishers. Free
with membership in PMA (see above).

6. Publishing Statistics, Sources

American Bookseller's Association
200 White Plains Road
Tarrytown, NY 10591
914-591-2665 Phone
800-637-0037 Phone
914-591-2720 Fax
The primary source for statistics relating
to bookstores and bookselling.

Association of American Publishers
71 Fifth Avenue
New York, NY 10003
212-255-0200 Phone
212-255-7007 Fax
Industry statistics focusing primarily on
larger companies.

Book Industry Study Group
19 West. 21st Street, Suite 905
New York, NY 10010
646-336-7141 Phone
646-336-62142 Fax
website: www.bisg.org
Industry-wide studies, trends and statistics.
Well worth the price of membership.

The Huenefeld-PubWest Publishing
   Survey of Financial Operations
PO Box 3759
Boulder, CO 80307
Email: pubwest@aol.com
Publishers that wish to participate in this
survey and receive a free copy of the
results in exchange should send a
stamped, self-addressed envelope to the
above address, to the attention of Survey
Questionnaire. Because AAP's operating
statistics have become sporadic, I highly
recommend publishers participate in this
survey.

Publishers Communications Industry Forecast
Veronis, Suhler & Associates Inc.
350 Park Avenue
New York, NY 10022-6022
212-935-4990 Phone
212-935-0877 Fax
Independent statistics from a highly
regarded media investment banking firm.

7. Websites and Internet Resources

A. U.S. Government Websites of Interest to Publishers

Main listing of 60 federal agencies. Website is run by Villanova University.
www.law.vill.edu/Fed-Agency/fedwebloc.html

Internal Revenue Service: www.irs.ustreas.gov
A very good site for downloading tax forms and getting information. Easy to use.

Library of Congress: www.lcweb.loc.gov (search for books)
www.lcweb.loc.gov/copyright/forms.html (for forms)
www.dawi@loc.gov (for CIP electronically)

Securities and Exchange Commission: www.fedworld.gov or www.sec.gov
If you want financial information on your publicly traded competitors, this is the
place to go.

Small Business Administration: www.sbaonline.sba.gov

U.S. Postal Service: www.usps.gov/busctr/busctr.html.

B. Publishing-Related Websites — On-Line Central Sources.

An excellent starting place for you to begin your search for any product or
service related to publishing:
www.bookwire.com

C. Publishing Sources

Amazon.com: www.amazon.com
Great for checking the competition.

Bar Code Basics: www.barcodehq.com/primer.html
Everything you wanted to know about bar codes and more.

Barnes & Noble: www.barnesandnoble.com
Another great place for checking the competition.

Book Industry Study Group: www.bisg.org

Copyright Clearance Center: www.copyright.com

Ingram Book Company: www.ingrambook.com
Terrific for getting the top titles per week in various categories.

Library Journal: www.LJdigital.com

Publisher's Marketing Association: www.pma-online.org

Pubnet Online: www.pubnet.org

Index

*Page numbers in **bold** refer to a chart or a form.*

trends
  effect upon sales, 187
  electronic publishing, 281–82
  researching, 26–28

U, V, W
unsolicited manuscripts (slush pile), 112
U.S. Copyright Office, 91
Vanguard Press, 92–93, 143
warehouse clubs, 10
websites
  advertising on, 300, 302–4
  authors and, 296–97
  branding, 295
  co-op advertising, 307

websites *(continued)*
  counting visitors, 320–21
  customer service, 303, 305
  e-commerce, 301–21
  linking, 298–300
  pricing books for sale on, 303–4
  publicity, 295–96
  sales analysis, 305–6, 316–321
  sales transactions on, 304
  search engine indexing of, 299, 300
  stickiness, 301–2
  updating, importance of, 295
wholesalers, 9–10, 56, 183–84
working capital, 67–68, 79
work-made-for-hire 112–13